LARSON'S BOOK OF FAMILY ISSUES

LARSON'S BOOK OF FAMILY ISSUES

Bob Larson

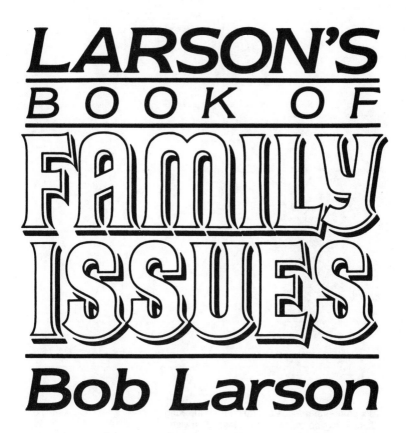

Tyndale House Publishers, Inc., Wheaton, Illinois

Scriptures references are taken from the King
James Version of the Bible unless otherwise
indicated. Quotations marked NIV are from *The
Holy Bible, New International Version*. Copyright©
1978 by New York International Bible Society.
Used by permission of Zondervan Bible
Publishers. Quotations marked TLB are from *The
Living Bible*. Copyright© 1971 by Tyndale House
Publishers.

First printing, November 1986

Library of Congress Catalog Card Number 86-50655
ISBN 0-8423-2459-3
Copyright© 1986 by Bob Larson
Printed in the United States of America

Contents

Introduction

Pessimists repeatedly predict the demise of the family. This collapse is unlikely to occur soon. While dire predictions fill editorial columns and magazines, people continue to marry, have children, and love their families. Our nation and Western civilization as a whole have wandered far from the Christian ethic, but the way is not completely obscured. In spite of adultery, premarital sex, single-parent households, and surrogate parenting, most people are motivated to create stable homes in which to provide emotionally healthy environments for loving children. Thus the family as an institution is likely to endure, although threatened by malignant forces.

If every family were a model of Christian love, this book would be unnecessary. Regrettably, men and women divorce, commit adultery, abuse their children and spouses, experience sexual problems, face the agony of infertility, cope with rebellious and suicidal youth, and commit incest. Some even abuse their bodies through gluttony or starvation, partake of such unwholesome entertainment as soap operas and X-rated films, and worry about a future in which genetic engineering may indeed render the traditional family dinosauric.

If American public schools affirmed Christian morality and if children could grow without fear of divorce and parental abuse, this book would probably gather dust on closet shelves. But critical problems do beset the contemporary family, and Christians are not exempt from human frailties. They divorce and suffer depression. They become prey to workaholism, beat their wives, use pornography, and are susceptible to the dozens of aberrations covered in this book.

These problems are constantly discussed in magazines and daily newspapers, on TV and radio, and in the work place. Occasionally they are discussed in reference to the Bible and Christian morality. Christian magazines, books, and radio do address these issues, but seldom comprehensively. The purpose of this book is to explore contemporary issues affecting the family and discern solutions in a biblical context. This is a family guide for the parent, spouse, pastor, or anyone interested in the family's future.

My coverage of topics is not intended to be exhaustive. No single volume could cover everything affecting the Christian family. Using current sources, I have focused on the most crucial issues. Readers can find guidance in this book to help understand Christian and secular thought on timely topics like home schooling, working women, and teenage suicide. I fervently plead that readers pray for the future of the family. Its survival cannot be assured without diligent effort and beseeching God's blessing.

The sixty-six chapters of this book are divided into six sections. Each chapter treats a specific topic, such as child abuse, spanking, or dieting. Most chapters include a bibliography of recent books with further information on that chapter's subject. In many cases, I included the names, addresses, and phone numbers of agencies and organizations that can provide additional assistance. Not all of these references are biblically based, but they can provide valuable resource materials and advice. Local chapters of particular organizations can be contacted through phone number listings.

As we face the waning years of the twentieth century, Christians must be well-informed about the family and how to preserve it. Let us pray for the willingness to dream great dreams for the family—and for the faith and moral stamina to activate those vital aspirations.

DATING, MARRIAGE, AND AND STARTING A FAMILY

1

Singles

Ruth Guillou had had her share of bad blind dates. Then one day Ruth noticed she was encountering intriguing men. Unfortunately, the apparently eligible singles were speeding past her on the freeway at sixty miles per hour. So, Ruth created a new way for singles to meet: an automobile dating service.

For thirty-five dollars, a member of her Freeway Singles organization gets an addressed decal to paste on the rear windshield. Each decal has a number. While making a pass (in the navigational sense of the term), prospective partners write down the address of Freeway Singles and the decal number and send a letter with an accompanying photo. The letter and photo are forwarded to the person whose automobile the seeking single happened to encounter.

Chance meetings on a freeway are not the only imprudent encounters sought by some singles. Many eligible men and women venture bold introductions at singles bars or look for an inviting glance across a crowded room at parties. Plenty of people are looking as the result of widespread divorce.

Fifty-six million Americans are single, one-third of all adults in the U.S.[1] Many are staying single until their early thirties, and there are signs an increasing number may never marry. Between 1970 and 1982, the population of never-married men grew by 84 percent.[2] Today, 12 percent of women and 17 percent of men ages thirty to thirty-four have never entered into matrimony.[3]

In her book *Singles: The New Americans,* author Jacqueline Simenaeur surveys the state of never-married men and finds that 10 percent say they have had more than a hundred sexual partners, and a significant portion believe marriage entails too much responsibility and commitment.[4]

The plight of many singles is piteous. If singles want to date, where do they look? One out of three meet potential lovers at a singles bar. In keeping with new social mores, half of all singles say it is OK for a woman to ask a man out. The same percentage say it's all right for a woman to pay on the date. Eighty percent say they don't mind if a woman initiates sex, and 16 percent say they expect sex on the first date.[5]

How does the Christian single differ from his or her unconverted counterpart? Only the most naive person would think Christian singles are paragons of innocence who never entertain thoughts of sex and passion. Single Christians face the same sexual pressures as their non-churched peers. They must also deal with loneliness and snide accusations that they are gay or unable to establish close relationships. Whether never-married or divorced, they face the public image of a single person: carefree, emotionally maladjusted, and shamelessly promiscuous.

Can singleness be blessedness? In 1 Corinthians 7, the Apostle Paul addressed this issue in the context of persecution facing the church at Corinth. He elevated celibacy to a spiritual virtue by suggesting, "I wish that all men were as I am" (v. 7, NIV). He permitted those unable to control their passions to marry, however, rather than burn with lust.

How does Paul's advice apply to our age? In the early

church, some became literal eunuchs for the sake of Christ. No one suggests today that emasculation should be practiced as a way to further one's spiritual calling. But some singles may wish to commit their remaining unmarried lives to spreading the gospel. This decision should be admired rather than ridiculed. Jokes about old-maid missionaries and spinster Sunday school teachers are unkind cuts made at the expense of dedicated servants of the Lord.

The increasing number of singles allows the church an excellent opportunity to provide appropriate social settings where the unmarried can meet. Evangelicals should view the single state as a virtue, providing advantages for evangelism not accorded the married man or woman. Singles who struggle with sexual longing and self-esteem should not be intimidated by innuendos that they are unable to find a husband or a wife. The church should provide opportunities for singles to meet and form relationships. But there should be no overt or covert pressure to "find a mate before it's too late." Indeed, the church, working as a family unit in itself, can affirm a person's worth, build up his self-esteem, and remove some of the pressure to marry.

The advantages of being single should be stressed: pursuing an education or a career, traveling abroad, developing a broader perspective on life before settling down with home and children, and, above all, having time to serve God through various ministries. It may not be good for man to live alone (Gen. 2:18), but it is also not good to rush into matrimony because of sexual longing or because our society—and, also, the church—is so couple-oriented.

RECOMMENDED READING BIBLIOGRAPHY

Pearson, Bud and Kathy. *Single Again.* Ventura, Calif.: Regal Books, 1985.

Towns, Jim, ed. *Solo Flight: Twelve Perspectives on the Single Life.* Wheaton, Ill.: Tyndale, 1980.

COUNSELING/INFORMATION SOURCES

National Association of Christian Singles
915 W. Wisconsin Avenue
Milwaukee, WI 53233
(414) 271-6400

Spirit Magazine
P. O. Box 1231
Sisters, OR 97759

2

Live-ins

An early Beatles hit declared, "Money can't buy me love." Neil Sheldon didn't agree, so he started a matchmaking service for the wealthy and forlorn. For a $100,000 fee, Sheldon guarantees an arranged date with the possibility of long-term love. Sheldon claims he has satisfied his clients with a formula that measures attraction. According to his criteria, sex appeal and personality are the initial lures, but integrity, morality, and religion keep a relationship going.

Whether or not a person has $100,000 to spare, falling in love, or at least falling into bed, is getting easier. The most recent Louis Harris poll indicates that 63 percent of the public think it's all right for adults planning to marry to live together and have sex. The U.S. Census Bureau calls such persons "persons of the opposite sex sharing living quarters without benefit of wedlock." In journalistic parlance they're called "live-ins," and their numbers have quadrupled since 1970. Fifty-five percent of live-in partners have never been married, and 32 percent are divorced.[1]

Cohabitation has become a substitute for marriage for

some and an introductory step to matrimony for others. Its participants include college students, divorcees, young adults, and even elderly pensioners who don't want to lose their combined Social Security benefits. "Living in" is another indication that marriage isn't working for millions of Americans. (There are other indications as well. Only 37 percent think it's important for a bride to be virgin. Ironically, when these same poll respondents were asked if fidelity in marriage is important, 96 percent said yes. Louis Harris also found that 79 percent of young men and 70 percent of young women see nothing wrong with premarital sex.[2])

The idea of living together—and the overall idea that sex outside marriage is not immoral—has changed our language. One-night stands are now "brief encounters," perversion is "sexual variation," promiscuous means "multi-friended," and wife-swapping is "expanding the circle of love." An affair is a "relationship," homosexuals are "gay," and dirty books are euphemistically sanitized into "erotica." Concerned to maintain propriety in a changing culture, Emily Post suggests that people living together be called "covivants." But whether they are referred to as lovers, roommates, paramours, or apartmates, the intent is to condone the conduct by avoiding morally harsh language.

Warning of sexual sin, 2 Timothy 2:22 says, "Flee also youthful lusts...follow righteousness...with them that call on the Lord out of a pure heart." The Bible also commands in 1 Corinthians 7:2, "to avoid fornication, let every man have his own wife, and let every woman have her own husband."

In our post-biblical age, we have departed far from this foundational morality. In about half the states it is legal for two consenting adults of the opposite sex to live together without being married. Many live-ins write marriage contracts much like employer-employee agreements. Such contracts are legally recognized by the Internal Revenue Service. Prenuptial legal arrangements designed to formalize the relationship may include allowances for either party to engage in affairs not limited to their cohabitant. Such contracts generally can be terminated on thirty days' notice. Those who enter this kind of relationship see themselves as practical cohabitants, not sinners. But even secular sociologists wonder if the live-in trend indicates that personal commitment to another human being has lost its meaning.

Live-ins raise unique questions about traditional morality, forcing Christians to face delicate dilemmas. What if a wayward son or daughter brings a live-in home for the weekend and wants the two of them to sleep in the same bedroom? How should we view elderly widows and widowers for whom the Social Security system created a no-win situation? If they marry, their pensions and Social Security benefits may be decreased significantly. If they don't, their common-law arrangement violates God's moral law. We can sympathize with their plight, yet we cannot condone a live-in arrangement, even for the elderly.

Regrettably, those outside the church aren't the only ones pursuing the live-in option. An increasing number of divorced Christian singles are considering live-in arrangements. They don't want to "burn," but they don't want to risk another bad marriage. So, they reason, it is better to experiment with love instead of risking failure in marriage again.

Those who have lived together and are truthful acknowledge the drawbacks of such arrangements. Though some live-ins say their eventual marriage commitment was strengthened, those who lived together and split up say they experienced the same emotional pain as with divorce. Little was gained by lack of a license. Instead of live-ins being less likely to take each other for granted, the opposite generally occurs. The argument, "If you really loved me, you'd marry me" is true. Practical experience confirms that living-in is still living in sin.

3

Dating

"A social engagement between two members of the opposite sex that comprises awkward greetings, contrived conversation, feeble attempts at levity, a groping through mutual interests, adolescent endeavors at intimacy, and clumsy goodbyes."[1]

That's the way one writer described America's dating game. Others think of it as a burger and fries, a movie or concert, a slightly hesitant goodnight kiss, and nagging questions about whether it's the beginning or end of an affair. The mention of dating (also called "going out with" or "seeing") inspires goose bumps on a teenage boy or girl. In the mid-twenties, it causes anxious apprehension. For divorced men and women, or those still single in their thirties and forties, dating may be a traumatic experience warily approached with hope and anticipated rejection.

Finding a mate wasn't always easy in biblical times, either. It wasn't easy for Jacob. When he saw Rachel at the well, he wasted no time. Jacob kissed her, and wept. Whether the smooch was erotic or merely a typical oriental greeting didn't matter. He labored seven years before their love was consummated.

It was only slightly simpler for Isaac. His father Abraham sent the servant Eliezer to his home country to find a woman willing to accept Isaac's hand in matrimony. The servant journeyed with ten camels to Mesopotamia in search of a fair young virgin who would meet Abraham's requirements. The venture succeeded because Rebekah offered water for the camels to drink.

What relevance do these stories have for those dating today? Should a seeking single drive his Mustang to the filling station and wait for a female attendant to rush out and fill up his tank? The analogy may seem humorous, but there is nothing funny about the prospect of finding a Christian dating partner in this permissive age. Twenty-five million Christian singles in America confront the dilemma of nurturing biblical love through Christian dating, pursuing a potential mate while honoring Christ in the midst of sexual frustrations and fears about marriage.

The dating issue is complicated by new game rules in our sexually aggressive society. Traditionally, man pursues while the woman waits coyly, inviting advances. A recent survey, however, shows two-thirds of men and three-fourths of women think it's acceptable for a woman to initiate dating.[2]

Today women even introduce intimate encounters. Since women are unaccustomed to instigating that first step, they risk the possibility of devastating rejection if the man says he won't go to bed. Conversely, women face the problem of so-called "date rapes," dream dates that turn into nightmares when the gracious gentleman at the door becomes violently abusive and won't leave until paid what he thinks is due him for the evening.

Such situations have become almost stereotyped for singles. Christian singles are familiar with these—and a few others. Ecclesiastes 3:1 says, "To every thing there is a season, and a time to every purpose under the heaven ... a time to love." That time for many Christians is during the years at a Christian college. Almost every young woman at such institutions must cope with knowing looks of those who presume she's there to find a Christian husband. The proof seems to be in the pudding, since many young ladies in this situation lose academic interest shortly after romance progresses to matrimony.

Another familiar Christian stereotype is the young, single person who goes from church to church on the pretext of seeking a suitable pastor. In fact, the quest's motive is to determine how many eligible members of the opposite sex sit in the pews. And some of them must be successful; a typical evangelical gathering reveals that the majority of married couples met at revivals, conferences, camps, and other places where Christians congregate.

How should the Christian single person go about finding a mate? Should he or she wait for God to bring the right one through the front door, or overcome geographic inconveniences by "reaching out to touch someone," checking out the prospects from the local Promised Land to distant Mesopotamia?

The price of pursuing might make one think something can be said for arranged marriages. With divorce statistics reaching tragic proportions, our philosophy of meeting a mate by the social interchange of dating relationships doesn't seem very successful. And, after fending off intimate advances of Christian dating partners, born-again women ask, "Are there any good men left out there who love Jesus and love me for more than my anatomy?"

A recent study of women revealed that 29 percent said they had been physically or psychologically coerced into sexual intercourse. Even 12 percent of men said they had been compromised by aggressive women.[3] Consequently, any dating Christian single should be wary of those who, under the guise of Christian faith, are immorally motivated. Some may even justify indecent liberties by arguing, "After all, we both love the Lord, and we love each other."

A recent television report supports many women who believe that men often want their bodies more than their brains. NBC studied the situation of singles and concluded that women are increasingly concerned about the lack of emotional satisfaction in dating relationships. Not only do women worry about men seeking sex rather than emotional commitment, they also rebel against the lack of etiquette men exhibit while dating. Many men have lost their sense of shame in this promiscuous age, and also their gentlemanliness. Regrettably, many women have followed suit. Too many females have forgotten the meaning of the word *demure*.

Knowing that this situation exists, should a Christian single accept a blind date? There is certainly reason for hesitation, unless the individuals arranging the blind date are committed Christians concerned about bringing together those of like faith to avoid unequally yoking together a believer and unbeliever (see 2 Cor. 6:14). Even then, the Christian should be aware that the person they have been temporarily paired with may not have a strong dedication to biblical morality.

A Christian single encounters other serious questions in today's treacherous moral climate. For example, if one is dating a recent convert, it may be necessary to discuss whether the potential mate contracted any sexually transmittable diseases in the past. Before things get too serious, both partners should openly and honestly talk about the possibility of herpes or pelvic-inflammatory disease affecting a marital relationship. Genuine love involves honesty, particularly in this delicate area. Prolonged involvement with a person suffering from an incurable sexually transmitted illness might lead to a marriage that could damage both partners and any children born of the union.

So many factors have to be kept in mind, but one stands out above all others: The dating Christian should seek someone to live with until death parts the relationship. Though no serious social thinker with a Christian ethic would recommend returning to the dating techniques of Jacob and Isaac, their pattern of pursuance did have one important element: God's blessing was sought for the proposed union. And while a person cannot breathlessly approach each date as a This-will-make-me-or-break-me situation, he can look upon each date as an opportunity to begin a relationship that could lead to a meaningful friendship—or to a marriage—rooted in mutual respect and love for God.

COUNSELING/INFORMATION SOURCES
Christian Dating Service International
P. O. Box 678
South Orange, NY 07079
1-800-523-2445

4

Mate Selection

"The man who finds a wife finds a good thing; she is a blessing to him from the Lord" (TLB). The words of Proverbs 18:22 speak highly of the wedded state. Earlier in that same chapter there is another bit of advice not directly related to marriage but equally important when it comes to selecting a mate: "How stupid to decide before knowing the facts" (Prov. 18:13, TLB). In the arena of romance, this wisdom suggests it is better not to answer the question "Will you marry me?" until you hear the entire proposition.

The purpose of the dating process is to find a mate, one of life's most important decisions. A wrong turn at that junction can mean a lifetime of marital misery and possibly the loss of faith if one's partner does not walk equally with the Lord.

What is the best way to find someone with whom you will be compatible for life? Some marriage experts say the best time to select a mate is *before* you fall in love. Once the glands are pumping and your perception becomes misty, you can lose sight of the importance of commitment to marriage.

Lovesickness isn't all it's cracked up to be. Nor is it even universal. Dr. Dorothy Tennov, a professor and psychologist at the University of Bridgeport in Connecticut, analyzed the love relationships of one thousand Americans over a seventeen-year period. She found that romantic love is experienced by only 25 percent of the married population.[1]

Dr. Tennov also discovered lovesickness lasts approximately three years, after which married partners tend to reestablish a new basis of compatibility—or they divorce. Tennov says the symptoms of love are universal—ecstacy when together, despair when apart, and agony when love isn't returned. She concludes, "Certain cases of lovesickness border on mental illness." Dr. Tennov has determined, "Love is not a bad place to start a marriage, but it is not going to keep one going. Love burns out."[2]

One might take these findings a step further and warn those seeking a mate that marriage isn't the greatest thing in the world. It's not at all like the libidinous fantasies portrayed on soap operas and in romance novels. Marriage can be fun, but it's mostly hard work. It can last if there is intellectual compatibility, mutually shared intimacy, reasonably commensurate social backgrounds, and a common faith in Christ.

The problem is how to determine if these factors are present *before* saying "I do." "Being in love" is not enough. Choosing spiritual values and social skills in the person with whom you will spend your life is the crux of today's Christian dating dilemma. The dating period, the period of "being in love," is only temporary. But many marriages break apart because one partner expects too much emotional support, having predicated his or her satisfaction in marriage on the amount of love shown during the dating period. One could say that love is easy enough to find, but true compatibility requires an arduous search and the ability to continue the relationship after the starry-eyed romantic period has ended.

The secular response to the dating dilemma has been codified by Columbia University psychology professor

Richard Sauber, who coined three euphemisms to describe today's means of mate selection.

Lockage is a commitment in which a couple lives together in an exclusive, permanent relationship though unmarried. *Linking* is a steady relationship (involving sex) in which the man and woman don't live together. *Amourant* is a sexual relationship in which physical needs are the essential ingredient.[3]

Christians with a biblical worldview must reject such immoral arrangements. Bible-believers view the dating period as a time to establish the basis for marriage. Instead of perceiving the mate selection process as a starry-eyed romantic adventure, they should consider it a prelude to matrimony when all its potential problems are thoroughly analyzed. The advice and consent of both sets of parents should be sought. Ample opportunity ought to be prayerfully provided for God to alter any plans the couple may have set.

If you are a single Christian seeking a mate, don't assume that because you and your potential marriage partner are believers marriage will work automatically. Your zealousness for the Lord will not overshadow potential physical and emotional incompatibilities. Common faith cannot make a marriage work if unstable human factors adversely affect the relationship daily.

Beware the danger of provoking a premature plunge into the marriage bed after engagement. Don't believe the lie that sexual compatibility can be discovered by experimentation. Joy may evaporate from the sexual segment of the marriage bond if you base the dating relationship on carnal appetite. Sexual dysfunction and boredom can cause one of the partners to seek greener pastures. Using sex as the glue to bind your potential marriage relationship may make you or your partner look elsewhere for titillation when periods of mutual satisfaction wane. Remember that erotic disenchantment is not biblical grounds for divorce.

With all the talk about sex pertaining to mating and dating, counselors say the primary marriage problem— money—is often overlooked. Before buying the marriage license, Christian couples should carefully analyze their financial expectations. It is advantageous if both come from similar backgrounds so that one doesn't harbor economic considerations the other is incapable of providing. The decision to tithe and make Christ Lord over one's finances should be made before any vows are uttered.

RECOMMENDED READING BIBLIOGRAPHY

Hocking, David and Carole. *Good Marriages Take Time.* Eugene, Ore.: Harvest House, 1984.

5

Marital Sex

In the 1950s, an era of unprecedented prosperity and peace, sex was still fairly private. One can imagine what a Christian couple from that decade must think today browsing in a Christian bookstore, thumbing through pages of *The Act of Marriage, Celebration in the Bedroom,* and *Intended for Pleasure* (evangelical manuals on the spiritual delights of physical pleasures).

For those more attuned to audio than print, a Grand Rapids, Michigan, company produces a supplement for the dinner-by-candlelight routine. "Intimate Encounters" produces sixty-minute subliminal romance tapes for $14.95 each. The listener hears harp and flute music, while the subconscious mind is bombarded with subliminal sexual messages. During one hour, there are nine-thousand solicitations of sex.[1]

Does it work? Producers of the tape don't really know, since they haven't followed their recordings into the bedroom for documentation. If they were to look behind closed doors, however, they could gather interesting information about today's sexual attitudes.

In a book entitled *Sex and the Married Woman,* the

author claims that 52 percent of women surveyed are unsatisfied with their sex lives.[2] Other attitudes about marital sex were revealed in a *Psychology Today* poll of twelve-thousand people: the majority said love and companionship are more important to a happy sex life than physical compatibility.[3] A study by the Population Center of the University of North Carolina found that lovemaking was affected more by the time of the day and the day of the week than by phases of the moon.[4] A book entitled *The Intimate Male* concludes that men emphasize emotional commitment more than physical aspects of lovemaking.[5] Research goes on, and information about sex abounds. Married people clearly want to know all they can about sex.

An earlier generation saw sex as partially recreational but mainly functional (it produced children and thus perpetuated families). Current couples ponder issues of masturbation, pornographic aids, sexual devices, fantasizing, and mutual orgasms. They also want to know about tenderness, romance, and intimacy in marital relationships. Christian spouses a few years ago were intent on reproducing another generation. Their offspring ask questions about the intent of making love, whether the love-making produces offspring or not.

Sexual interest within the marriage bond is certainly not sinful—not according to the Bible. "Let her be as the loving hind and pleasant roe; let her breasts satisfy thee at all times; and be thou ravished always with her love." Proverbs 5:19 bluntly addresses the sensual dimension of love for love's sake. The Song of Solomon is full of beautiful, sensuous imagery. Unfortunately, somewhere between Solomon and our present age, the church got off course.

"Anyone who is too passionate a lover with his own wife is himself an adulterer." Those are words from Jerome in the Middle Ages.[6] Jerome and his contemporary, Augustine, were godly men who enriched theology and biblical study. But they, and many other well-meaning Christian thinkers, began to exalt the ideal of celibacy. Marriage was seen as legitimate, but sexual relations in marriage were considered concessions to weakness of the flesh and categorized as venial sin. (Jerome and Augustine should not be judged too harshly. Both lived in the declining days of the Roman Empire, a time when sexual sin was rampant. No wonder Christians, rightly concerned for purity, sometimes went overboard.)

Throughout the Middle Ages the life of celibacy—life as lived by priests, monks, and nuns—was seen as holier than married life. It was believed that singleness was always preferable to marriage, though most people did continue to marry, produce children, and (no doubt) enjoy sex. The church, however, did not encourage this pleasure. Into this milieu walked Martin Luther, the Reformer. He taught that husband and wife should live together in pleasure as well as peace. (Luther was a former monk, by the way, and he married a former nun.) He recommended that couples marry young so they could produce more children. Luther saw marriage as a sanctifier, making good what was otherwise evil.

Luther's attitude was a healthy corrective to the almost antisexual teaching of the medieval church. Traditionally, Protestants affirm marriage and encourage the begetting of children, though occasionally there has continued to be a tradition that frequent contact between husband and wife is unnecessary and even unhealthy. If there has been any benefit at all from the so-called sexual revolution, it is that most Christians today feel no qualms about enjoying marital sex without reservation. Having lived through the sexual revolution, today's evangelical parents probe both the quantity and quality of their lovemaking.

Fortunately, most Christian couples aren't as obsessed with sex as their non-evangelical contemporaries. Supposed liberation from Puritanical morality spawned a Sexaholics Anonymous organization, which seeks to cure those obsessed with trips to prostitutes, extramarital affairs, pornographic films, and strip-tease bars. Jettisoning Victorian ideals created what psychologists call an addictive personality that finds sex so compulsive it mimics the bondage of alcoholism. (Regrettably, some Christians do let themselves become sexually obsessed.)

With all this concern for sex, some people are blasé about the issue. Psychiatrist Harold Lief, a sexologist in private practice, estimates that 20 percent of the population is bored by sex. They suffer from what's called "inhibited sexual desire."[7] Still others think sex is virtually a big pain. Dr. Marian Bartusis, psychiatry professor at the Medical College of Pennsylvania in Philadelphia, says the most common cause of headaches and backaches today is anxiety about one's sex life.[8]

Considering this, one might wonder if this generation will bother to produce another. But, in spite of dysfunction and dissatisfaction, sex remains an important part of most marriages. And Christians do well to remember that sex is a good gift from God, something to be used lovingly and rightly—that is, used only within marriage and only as an expression of intimacy. It is not, contrary to what the secular world may lead us to believe, the supreme pleasure of life, nor an addiction, nor the central focus of our thoughts.

RECOMMENDED READING BIBLIOGRAPHY

Alcorn, Randy. *Christians in the Wake of the Sexual Revolution.* Portland, Oreg.: Multnomah, 1985.

LaHaye, Tim and Beverly. *The Act of Marriage.* Grand Rapids: Zondervan, 1976.

Wheat, Ed and Gaye. *Intended for Pleasure.* Old Tappan, N.J.: Revell, 1980.

35

6

Birth Control

Contraception isn't new. According to ancient manuscripts, it was used as far back as 1900 B.C. John Calvin commented on the practice of coitus interruptus. Martin Luther prohibited contraception. Instead, he encouraged his followers to "beget children, to nourish them, and to bring them up to the glory of God."[1]

Nineteenth-century Protestant churches universally opposed contraception. When Margaret Sanger and Planned Parenthood came on the scene, things changed. (Mrs. Sanger, incidentally, practiced adultery, and, according to one published pamphlet, encouraged premarital intercourse.) Those who bear her legacy champion birth control pills as a way for sexually active teens to avoid unwanted babies. Sanger once wrote that a future civilization would "depend upon a simple, cheap, safe contraceptive to be used in poverty-stricken slums ...among the most ignorant people."[2]

Some say birth control will solve the problems of unwanted pregnancies, overpopulation, and famine, creating a better quality of life. Feminist Betty Friedan even credits the pill with the growth of women's lib. She says the pill gave women "new ability to control their reproductive lives."[3] The pill is a fact of life, twenty-five years after it first appeared on the market. It is the world's most widely used prescription medicine, chosen by almost 10 million American women.[4] (Yet, while birth control methods are readily available, more than half of approximately 6 million pregnancies each year in the United States are unintentional.[5] Half of these conceptions are terminated by abortion.)

Opinions about birth control differ around the world. The Chinese, faced with chronic overpopulation, use coercion to encourage single-child families and use many forms of birth control to hinder population growth. In Ireland, the Senate approved legislation permitting anyone over eighteen to purchase condoms, a previously forbidden act.[6] Conversely, large families are encouraged in Romania, and abortion is allowed only if a woman is over forty and has four children.[7] Americans, it seems, have an ongoing love affair with artificial birth control, especially the pill. But the pill has its detractors.

Critics of the birth control pill cite an array of diseases connected to its use, such as heart attacks, brain hemorrhages, liver tumors, and strokes. Studies published by the British medical journal *Lancet* show a strong association between the pill and increased risk of breast and cervical cancer.[8] A Center for Disease Control study indicated women who took the pill had two to three times the risk of becoming infertile compared to non-pill users.[9] Each year five hundred women die unnecessarily from the pill; many of these deaths could be avoided through the use of other contraceptive methods, such as the diaphragm or condom.[10]

Supporters of the pill say its dangers have been exaggerated. For every 100,000 women taking the pill each year, there are about five pill-related deaths, compared with about ten deaths per 100,000 women who give birth.[11] Studies conducted in the late 1970s suggest that the pill protects against infertility caused by sexually transmitted infections. Other research shows it prevents cancer of the uterus lining, ovarian cancer, and benign ovarian cysts. The pill also apparently reduces menstrual cramps and the possibility of breast cysts.

Proponents of the pill say it prevents multiple pregnancies and protects the general health of women for whom childbirth is dangerous. It also allows people to plan their families, creating fewer financial burdens. Thus, children are wanted and not neglected.

The pill is not the only widely used method of birth control. The number of couples using sterilization methods as birth control measures has tripled since 1965. These methods, like the pill, cause problems. Critics say vasectomies have long-term effects on the immunological system. Evidence indicates that tubal ligations lead to hysterectomies because of severe menstrual problems. Four deaths occur for every 100,000 sterilization procedures.

These are the facts concerning vasectomies: (1) The cost ranges from $500 to $1,100; (2) it becomes effective six to ten weeks after surgery; (3) the current vasectomy failure rate is 16 per 10,000 men; and (4) reversibility is 70 percent to 90 percent successful in producing viable sperm, but with only a 50 percent to 60 percent chance of achieving pregnancy. The cost of reversing a vasectomy is $3,000 to $5,000.[12]

Those considering female sterilization should know that: (1) the cost ranges from $1,500 to $2,000 when done in the hospital; (2) the current sterilization failure rate for women is 28 per 10,000; (3) reversibility is difficult, though there is a 60 percent to 70 percent success rate in reattaching tubes, and 30 percent to 40 percent are successful in achieving pregnancy.[13]

Because of increased use of sterilization, courts have granted permission for persons to sue for medical expenses and anguish in the case of a failed vasectomy or tubal ligation. So far, judges have refused lawsuits for costs of rearing the offspring, since a healthy child cannot be considered an injury.[14]

Other forms of birth control produce varying hazards. Diaphragm users are two times more likely to be infected with bacteria, according to one medical report.[18] Problems with IUDs and the Dalkon shield have been widely reported. Women using IUDs are two to three times more likely to become infertile compared with those who do not.[16]

Because of questionable safety of many birth control methods, the sale of condoms is up. Five hundred million will be sold this year.[17] Part of that increase stems from a 1977 U.S. Supreme Court decision making it legal to advertise them, an offensive practice to many. Other birth control methods include the vaginal sponge, injections (such as the injectable contraceptive Depo-Provera), and implant contraceptives. Doctors are experimenting with new ways to block pregnancies, such as vaginal suppositories, subdermal implants, and disposable diaphragms.

Since Christians believe their bodies are temples of the Holy Spirit, they question what kinds of contraceptive implants and pills should be used. They wisely avoid contraceptives that cause bodily harm. Some find the pill a blessing; others consider it a curse that causes permissiveness among the unmarried and too much concern about frequent sex among married couples. Some Christians fear that selfishness has replaced sexual continence in many marriages, for use of contraceptives means couples can engage in intercourse whenever they like, with no fear of unintended pregnancies. But because of the health hazards associated with artificial birth control, natural family planning (using the rhythm method) is once again on the rise. Proponents say it is the only non-sexist form of birth control and contend it improves a married couple's love life by emphasizing non-genital forms of communication. If, as in the pre-pill era, couples must abstain from intercourse during certain periods, they are forced to communicate via touch, speech, and other ways. This is to be encouraged.

A more restrictive Christian viewpoint teaches that the reproductive process as established by God should not be interfered with under any circumstances, lest man profane a sacred act. Those who hold this position believe God deliberately joined the pleasure of the marriage act with the responsibility of having children. They feel that contraceptives work against the natural laws of the body, interrupting biological functions God intended to function normally. Some opponents of all birth control claim that references to sorcery in the Book of Revelation (actually a reference to drugs) prophesy the use of birth control chemicals.

Roman Catholics steadfastly oppose birth control. Pope John Paul II recently told pilgrims to Rome that contraception is "harmful to man's interior and spiritual culture," and that good Catholics must express "mature availability to fatherhood and motherhood." But 91 percent of Catholic women between the ages of fifteen and forty-four who have had sexual intercourse say they have used artificial birth control methods.[18]

First Corinthians 7:3 says, "The husband should fulfill his marital duty to his wife..." (NIV). Some feel that this conjugal duty rules out vasectomy, though that stretches the biblical context of the verse. Certain conservative Christians even argue that man must never deliberately interfere with the sacred procreative process. They point out that when Onan spilled his seed on the ground (see Gen. 38), he incurred God's displeasure for violating divine moral law by using the contraceptive method of withdrawal (coitus interruptus).

The author holds a differing exegetical conclusion. Genesis 38:8-10 tells us that Onan was an enemy to his brother Er. He wanted his brother's name blotted out and wouldn't allow the first-born child to carry on the dead man's name instead of his, as was the custom. God's condemnation of what occurred was directed toward his spiritual disobedience, not the specific act of coitus interruptus.

Some Christians who practice birth control argue that Matthew 19:12, referring to those who made themselves "eunuchs for the kingdom of heaven's sake," gives responsible Christian couples the choice to practice birth control and free themselves for special service to God.

Even Christians who condone artificial birth control recognize its dangers. No wonder, since 53 percent of America's 8 million never-married women in their twenties are sexually active.[19] Birth control unquestionably increases the potential for promiscuity. Other Christians are concerned that certain forms of birth control, such as the IUD and some strong oral contraceptives, actually abort a fertilized egg. Others see artificial birth control as a means for selfish couples to preserve their freedom by avoiding the responsibilities of raising a family. Such persons can be seen as deliberately refusing to receive the biblical blessing God pronounced on childbearing (Ps. 127:3).

There is no Christian consensus on the issue of birth control. Suffice it to say that God wants us to avoid abusing our bodies (which means we must use methods that are potentially harmful with great caution) and to avoid selfishness. There is nothing wrong with family planning. There is a great deal wrong with using artificial birth control strictly as a means of indefinitely postponing family responsibilities or letting genital sex become an obsession.

COUNSELING/INFORMATION SOURCES

Couple to Couple League
P. O. Box 111184
Cincinnati, OH 45211
1-513-661-7396
Organization in favor of natural family planning.

7

Infertility

We live in a world full of options. We can, through the use of birth control, engage in intercourse yet choose to avoid bearing children. Some couples wait until their late thirties, after attaining financial security, to decide whether or not to start a family. Unfortunately, many discover the decision has already been made for them.

According to a study based on the National Survey of Family Growth, fecundity has reached an all-time low. Only about half of couples of childbearing age are physically able to have children.[1] The most frequent reason for infertility in women is a blockage or abnormality of the fallopian tubes. Fertilization occurs in these thin, flexible structures, which convey the egg from the ovaries to the uterus. If they become blocked, damaged, or frozen in place by scar tissue, the egg cannot complete its journey.

Many of today's Christian couples survived the sexual excesses of the sixties and converted to Christianity. Though their sins are forgiven, many evangelical women bear the burden of infertility because of past promiscuity. A major cause of fallopian tube blockage is pelvic-inflammatory-disease (PID). Each year, one million women are afflicted by this sexually transmitted disease and 15 percent or more become infertile. In the *Journal of the American Medical Association*, researchers cite two reasons for increased infertility due to PID: sexual activity at an early age and intercourse with multiple partners.[2]

Of course, not all infertility is due to promiscuity. But whatever the physiological reason, the effect is devastating. Counselors who conduct workshops for infertile couples claim that infertility tears at the very core of couples' relationships, since it affects sexuality, self-image, and self-esteem. It devastates finances and harms relationships with family and friends.

Christian couples look to biblical stories of barren women for hope and comfort—Sarah and Rachel in Genesis, Manoah's wife in Judges, Hannah in 1 Samuel and Elizabeth in the Gospel of Luke. They wonder at the words of Psalm 113:9: "He gives children to the childless wife, so that she becomes a happy mother" (TLB). Should they accept this Scripture only in a metaphorical context and believe that God will give them spiritual children? Should they bombard heaven with intercessory prayer, pleading for the womb to be opened?

On a human level, several options are available. Microsurgery allows doctors to successfully reverse up to 70 percent of vasectomies and tubal ligations.[3] Clomid, a synthetic drug used for infertility, has a success rate of 30 percent to 50 percent.[4] And doctors are now able to pinpoint as many as 90 percent of infertility problems.[5] But the arduous task of isolating the physiological deficiency can strain a relationship. Fertility workshops require constant monitoring of body temperature and menstrual cycles to maximize chances of conception. Some couples complain that sex turns from a joyous, spontaneous expression of love into a tedious fertility ritual governed by the calendar.

Who in this busy world wants to bother with monthly pelvic and genital examinations? It is hardly romantic to receive a call from your wife saying, "Quick, come home! The doctor says today is the day if we're ever going to do it. My temperature is right, and the cycle is perfect."

Infertility testing can strain a healthy marriage. Frustration and depression may cause either partner to be irritable, as intimate moments become test-tube encounters with the deficiencies of their bodies. Tensions develop in the home. As with Rachel and Jacob in Genesis 30, the wife may feel like dying, and the husband may declare, "Am I in the place of God, who has kept you from having children?" (NIV). (To paraphrase, "Is it my fault you can't have a kid?") Patience is imperative when amorous moments become clinical encounters, but the search for the cause must go on.

Researchers find that roughly 40 percent of infertility is attributable to men, 40 percent to women, and another 20 percent can't be pegged specifically to either spouse.[6] When infertility's cause cannot be pinpointed, frustration can result. Couples may be exasperated when told they, according to tests, both are fertile. There is also a severe strain when one spouse is found to be infertile. The strain is so great that some couples contemplate divorce so the fertile spouse can marry someone else and have children. Psychic pain can be so severe that some who are infertile say they suffered a grieving process for children they never had.

Meanwhile, as each month passes and the wife's period arrives on schedule, the reminder of failure ticks off days and years on the biological time clock. Percentages in favor of conception diminish. At this time, the Christian whose infertility is linked to former promiscuity needs to beware that "the accuser of the brethren," Satan, will bring up guilt-laden accusations. The terrible toll of infertility indeed may be due to previous indiscretions, but what God has forgiven must be forgotten. The infertile couple should also beware of well-meaning but unwise Christian friends who suggest God may be punishing them for unconfessed sin. The danger of bitter retaliation exists when people callously comment, "Hang in there and keep trying."

Some automobiles come with fifty-thousand-mile guarantees, but our bodies have no such assurances. Spare parts and a lube job don't apply. Sometimes a miracle is the only answer, as it was in the case of Abraham and Sarah. But prayer without performance is presumptuous. The childless couple that wishes to conceive should explore every natural option, as they pray for God's blessing on their barrenness.

RECOMMENDED READING BIBLIOGRAPHY

Stigger, Judith A. *Coping with Infertility.* Minneapolis: Augsburg, 1983.

Stout, Martha. *Without Child.* Grand Rapids: Zondervan, 1985.

COUNSELING/INFORMATION SOURCES

Stepping Stones
Box 11411
Wichita, KS 67211
(316) 522-0954
Nonprofit Christian ministry offering encouragement and support to infertile couples.

8

Childlessness

Someone said, "Half the women in the world are hoping
they are not pregnant, and the other half are hoping they
are." Scripture bears out this blessed joy and anticipation
of childbearing.

"Children are a gift from God; they are his reward.
Children born to a young man are like sharp arrows to
defend him. Happy is the man who has his quiver full of
them," declares Psalm 127:3-5 (TLB).

What about those with empty quivers, childless
couples who cannot be fruitful and multiply? They want
children but cannot conceive. Prayerfully they wonder if
the blessedness of a full quiver means the childless are
not blessed. The emotional effect of childlessness is so
devastating, doctors report, that female patients have
been known to commit suicide after learning they could
not bear children. Their cry is like that of Rachel envying
Leah and declaring, "Give me children, or else I die"
(Gen. 30:1).

In the last chapter we looked at infertility and the
problems it brings—both before the cause is determined
(if it ever is) and while tests are being run. This chapter is

concerned with couples who are aware—either because they have been tested or because too many fruitless years have driven them to despair—that they will remain forever childless. Once infertility has been determined, recriminations emerge. The spouse whose sperm count or deficient womb is the determining factor may feel overpowering guilt. The infertile couple may blame God. Excessive compensative attention may be lavished on a cat or dog. Potential grandparents suffer dashed dreams of a heritage. Friends present an endless series of photos heralding their newest arrivals while the childless couple knows that reproductive incapacity has robbed them of parenthood. There will never be another generation bearing their name.

At this point, some childless couples try plea bargaining: "Lord, if you give me a child, I promise I'll dedicate that baby to you and do everything possible to raise the child as a Christian." What if God doesn't accept the offer? Can a Christian couple praise God in spite of their childlessness?

Historically, humanity has placed the stages of life into various categories. Adults are expected to marry and assume the responsibilities of a household, with children as part of the process. The widowed, the unmarried, or the celibate have always been among us (Mother Teresa, for example), but they are exceptions. Society expects the bearing of children and the transition to parenting and grandparenting.

But the childless couple cannot complete this pattern. Viewing procreation as a partnership with God, the barren husband and wife feel deprived of a divine process. They wonder if God has found them unworthy of entering into this most sacred communion. Where do they find an affirming family to tell them everything is OK? How can they handle Mother's Day and Christmas when there are no corsages to pin and fewer presents under the tree?

Unfortunately, "Job's comforters" may declare, "Think of all the time you have together you wouldn't have otherwise. . . . Don't worry, I know a couple who adopted and immediately had a baby of their own.... Maybe you aren't praying enough; after all, you should remember Sarah." (The latter comment may be particularly cruel in the case of a woman who has just had a hysterectomy!)

Husbands must realize the devastating effect of childlessness on their wives. Elkanah's example illustrates this well (1 Sam. 1:8). His wife, Hannah, wept over the barrenness of her womb, and, in the depths of despondency, refused to eat. Finally, in frustration Elkanah cried out, "Am I not better to thee than ten sons?" Elkanah was a kindly husband, but he just didn't understand the dimension of his wife's sorrow.

The childless woman faces a unique trauma. When she is invited to another's home for the holidays, she fears the joy of their children will increase her grief. Everywhere she goes and everywhere she looks she sees pregnant women. She bites her lip and fights tears at the announcement of each new shower. She may even wonder if her husband will divorce her in favor of a fertile woman.

Childless couples must realize that childlessness is not necessarily "less." After all, children do not *always* bring joy, as the Bible recognizes. Ecclesiastes 6:3 says, "A man may have a hundred children and live many years; yet no matter how long he lives, if he cannot enjoy his prosperity... a stillborn child is better off than he" (NIV).

Childless couples should consider the special ministry of baby-sitting or being an on-call couple whenever there is a need in the church. Without children, the doors of their homes may be more readily opened to the lonely and hurting. As in the case of Paul and other dedicated Christian singles, commitment to Christian service is another option. Childless couples also can console themselves with the possibility that God in his divine foreknowledge permitted their condition so they can parent an adoptive child.

Isaiah 54:1 offers these words of comfort to the childless: "Sing, O barren, thou that didst not bear; break forth into singing, and cry aloud, thou that didst not travail with child: for more are the children of the desolate than the children of the married wife, saith the LORD." In other words, the couple with no biological offspring can spiritually "adopt" many, many children of every age. The reproduction of spiritual offspring who have an eternal spirit allows every soul-winner the opportunity to enlarge God's heavenly family.

RECOMMENDED READING BIBLIOGRAPHY

Hanes, Mari. *Beyond Heartache.* Wheaton, Ill.: Tyndale, 1984.

Love, Vicky. *Childlessness Is Not Less.* Minneapolis: Bethany House, 1984.

Verdevelt, Pam. *Empty Arms.* Portland, Oreg.: Multnomah, 1984.

9

Adoption

With legalized abortion diminishing the number of adoptable children, childless couples are competing for healthy youngsters. Ironically, prospective parents are becoming more selective. They search diligently for healthy, white infants with no physical or emotional handicaps. Potential adoptive parents want to know if the birth mother had excellent health care or was exposed to harmful drugs during her pregnancy. In addition, they often prefer highly intelligent biological parents who were reasonably well educated. In short, today's adoptive parents want perfection.

There are forty waiting couples for every available infant.[1] In most cases, those adoptive children are far from perfect. Adoptable babies born in this country are often handicapped or the products of teenage unwed mothers who couldn't afford to keep the child. The biological parents often are not the highly intelligent types preferred by adoptive parents. This restrictive availability of desirable American infants causes some to look abroad for babies. Last year, Americans adopted more than five-thousand foreign children, the majority from Korea and Colombia.[2] Unfortunately, some adoptive parents later discover the adorable child handed to them at the airport becomes a teenager with racial identity problems.

Some childless couples turn to the black market or so-called gray market. More than thirty-five hundred black market adoptions occur each year without the knowledge of authorities and without appropriate legal documents. Black market babies are purchased outright, with the fee paid to an intermediary working outside legal channels. Medical records may be faked and the baby's age misrepresented.

Gray market babies are bartered. The biological mother chooses the couple who will pay her living and medical expenses during pregnancy and delivery. Licensed adoption agencies are avoided. The cost is considerably less than the cost for a black market baby, which ranges from $15,000 to $30,000.[3]

Increasingly, the line separating gray market from black market babies blurs; the distinguishing factor is how the money is spent. Gray market adoptions seem legal so long as a reasonable amount is paid to cover hospital fees and other birthing expenditures. But if authorities determine an actual fee has been paid for the baby itself, legal problems can arise.

Many adoptions are, of course, perfectly legal, being conducted through neither the gray or black market. But legal adoption is not what it once was. Changing mores and morals have altered the system significantly. Secrecy and rigid selection policies have been replaced by flexibility. In the past, adoptive parents could be rejected on grounds of age, religion, race, marital status, and whether the wife worked. Today the potential parent can be rich or on welfare. He can be in his twenties or fifties. He can be married or single. He can even be homosexual.

But in the midst of more openness, serious questions are being raised. Should a mother who gave up a baby because of its illegitimacy have the legal right to trace and contact her child without the consent of the new adoptive parents? Should court records be open to an adopted child who wishes to know more about his or her biological background?

Several organizations have been formed to help children uncover the identity of their natural parents, and vice versa. They go by names such as Adoptees Liberty Movement Association, Concerned United Birth Parents, and Origins. The National Committee for Adoption strongly opposes this open-record movement. It believes that once a child has been placed for adoption, the past should be closed.

What are the spiritual and emotional questions a potential adoptee must address? The adoption process can be a growth experience in understanding the love of God, comprehending the Father's acceptance of fallen humanity by spiritual adoption. The adoptive couple must be wary of harbored bitterness, thinking they have to accept second best because God denied them a biological child. A growing number of potential parents look on adoption as something they want, not something they must do if they wish to raise children. This positive attitude makes home study procedures, the investigative process conducted by adoption agencies, function smoothly and seem less like an interrogation.

The Christian adoptive couple has a perspective unavailable to non-believing prospective parents. Faith in Christ is made possible because of two beautiful instances of adoption recorded in Scripture. Moses set his people free and brought the light of God's law because Pharaoh's daughter dared to adopt him. Jesus paid the penalty for sin because Joseph adopted him, believing the message of God's angel.

Ephesians 1:5 speaks of every Christian's acceptance into God's family: "In love he predestined us to be adopted as his sons through Jesus Christ, in accordance with his pleasure and will" (NIV). God has adopted each Christian into his heavenly family through the atonement of his Son, Jesus Christ. The couple who views earthly adoption as a reflection of this divine principle gains a capacity to love that is unavailable to those outside the body of Christ.

RECOMMENDED READING BIBLIOGRAPHY

Nason, Diane. *The Celebration Family.* Nashville: Thomas Nelson, 1983.

Strom, Kay Marshall. *Chosen Families.* Grand Rapids: Zondervan, 1985.

10

Childbearing

Mark it on your calendar. September 9 is National Expectant Mother's Day. Before you rush out to buy flowers for every pregnant woman you know, it is only fair to tell you this holiday is the brainchild of the Juvenile Products Manufacturers Association, which undoubtedly has a vested interest in your purchase of merchandise on behalf of pregnant women.

Whether the idea of a National Expectant Mother's Day will entrench itself in American life remains to be seen. The potential exists, however, for a lucrative business. An estimated 3.75 million babies will be born this year, new entrants into a second-generation baby boom.[1]

Products for the newborn and their mothers have always been a lucrative business, of course. Today, even more revenue may be generated because of the late age of childbearing women. Cissy Strum, administrative officer of the Professional Association for Childbirth Education says, "Women having children older and later seem to be more hellbent that it will be the optimum experience."[2]

Sandra Steffes, a childbirth educator in Pacific

Palisades, California, says this can lead to "performance anxiety," unachievable expectations whereby people become "locked into one methodology." Steffes says, "If women need to ask for pain killers or require caesareans or feel they can't breastfeed properly, they often feel cheated or like failures."[3]

A common scriptural misconception should be addressed first. Paul's words to Timothy, "Women will be saved through childbirth" (2 Tim. 2:11-15), form one of the most perplexing passages in Scripture. Some Christians even suggest that childbearing is a means of spiritual grace regarding salvation. What is the intent of Paul's instruction?

The Greek word for *saved* in this passage is *sozo,* a term connoting wholeness rather than eternal salvation. What wholeness is the apostle defining? In 1 Corinthians 11 Paul points out that woman was made for man. But, since a man must be born of a woman, this dependency for existence balances Paul's statement about the natural order of creation. Consequently, though man was created before woman, childbearing saves woman by granting her equality with man.

Secondly, by bearing "the seed" promised in Genesis 3:15, women removed the stigma of their deception and transgression in Eden. The incarnational truth that Christ was born of a woman avenges, or saves, the disobedient state of women, since a woman first tasted of the forbidden fruit. Setting aside this potential theological stumbling block, we can proceed with more practical matters.

Frowns, first-waving, and hiccuping in utero are common. In fact, one psychologist who specializes in research on the unborn claims fetuses have a regular exercise schedule of flexing, waving, turning, and kicking.[4]

In England, Dr. Michael Clements conducted research with the unborn and found that sixteen-week-old fetuses became calm when Mozart was played and kicked intensely when they heard rock music.[5] Knowing how sensitive the unborn are, some mothers are avoiding amniocentesis. Research has shown that when a needle is used to extract amniotic fluid, the fetus tries to push the sharp object away. Some obstetricians believe that this abrupt intrusion into the fetal environment traumatically damages the emotional life of the unborn, outweighing any positive benefits of amniocentesis.

Many doctors use forceps less often now during delivery and request dimmed lights, which they believe provide a more tranquil environment in which to introduce the child. Some women have their babies by immersion in a warm pool of water. The baby is delivered submerged and kept under water for another twenty minutes to ease the transition from womb to outside world. (However, doctors warn that separating the placenta from the uterus cuts off the baby's oxygen supply, and this might not be immediately detected while the baby is under water. The dangers of drowning and brain damage make many doctors avoid such delivery procedures.)

The sensitivity of the newborn is an area of increasing concern. Researchers at the University of North Carolina tested hearing and learning abilities of three-day-old infants. The babies were offered two non-nutritive nipples. One of them was connected to a device that activated a recording of the infant's own mother. The other nipple activated the voice of an unknown woman. Within twenty minutes, the infants learned to suck at the nipple that activated their mothers' voices.[6]

Another possibility in childbearing is avoiding hospitals in favor of home birthing attended by midwives. There are about six thousand practicing midwives in the United States, and they accompany 5 percent of all deliveries. Parents who choose midwifery feel they protect the newborn from hospital germs, increase the bonding experience, and introduce the child into a less austere environment.[7]

Doctors are accused of trying to run midwives out of business. Home birthing represents a considerable loss of money to hospitals and doctors, who normally charge up to $3,000 for a delivery. Some physicians claim

midwives are practicing medicine without a license.
(Certain states allow midwives to practice without a
medical license.) In defense of their ancient art,
midwives argue that babies born in hospitals have four
times more infections and six times more fetal distress
than babies born at home. Mothers undergoing hospital
births have three times more postpartum maternal
hemorrhaging.[8]

Hospitals argue that all pregnant women run a 16
percent chance of complication during labor and
delivery. In addition, 20 percent of all expectant mothers
develop serious problems during pregnancy, such as
diabetes, hypertension, and internal bleeding. They
contend this makes a hospital birth mandatory.[9] In spite
of such warnings, many women, incensed by the
indignities of shaved pubic hair, routine enemas, jolting
journeys through hospital corridors, and unnecessary
drugs, are giving birth outside the white walls of
traditional institutions.

Another birthing trend is the husband's presence
during delivery. Today 80 percent of husbands are on the
scene, compared with only 27 percent a decade ago.
This practice has geater potential for involving the father
in child-rearing, giving him a part in the birthing process.
This participatory attitude among men often extends to
childbirth classes. Sixty percent of expectant fathers are
involved in such instruction, helping them to better
understand what a woman goes through.[10]

Other childbearing considerations include: deciding if
a birth center will be used in place of a hospital; insisting
upon natural childbirth (caesarean is performed only in
extreme instances); and choosing what changes are
needed in the mother's diet and nutritional requirements
during childbearing.

Increasing attention is directed to the phenomenon of
postpartum depression. New mothers often under
estimate how much time an infant takes. It's a twenty-
four-hour, around-the-clock job with changings and
feedings. The beautiful, long-anticipated event can turn

into an exhausting routine of responsibility. Doctors recommend that working women leave their jobs at least one week before the baby is due so they can adjust to being at home. Husbands and wives should concentrate upon talking with each other and openly expressing feelings. A wider support system of friends, relatives, and neighbors helps immensely to provide balance and to combat depression.

The executive director of COPPE (Coping with Overall Pregnancy/Parenting Experience) suggests the following to help overcome postpartum depression: (a) Arrange for help with housework and child care ahead of time; (b) line up an experienced mother or group of people with whom you can talk; (c) plan something for yourself daily, such as a soak in the tub or a walk; and (d) maintain outside interests, even if only by phone.

Regrettably, the mystery of childbirth diminishes by concentrating on these aspects of birthing. The Christian mother can have a healthy appreciation for all the modern services and innovations that comprise the process of giving birth. Yet she and her husband can, unlike non-Christian couples, revel in the knowledge that a miraculous event has occurred. Childbirth will never be *just* a mechanical procedure.

COUNSELING/INFORMATION SOURCES

Informed Home Birth/Informed Birth & Parenting
Rahima Baldwin, Director
P. O. Box 3675
Ann Arbor, MI 48106
(313) 662-6857
Helpful organization. Caution should be taken regarding certain questionable practices of visualization and affirmation exercises.

The Alternative Birth Crisis Coalition
P. O. Box 48371
Chicago, IL 60648

Midwives Alliance of North America
P. O. Box 11171
Bainbridge Island, WA 98110

The Midwifery Training Institute
P. O. Box 26174
Albuquerque, NM 87108
(505) 265-0213

11
Babies

Motherhood is in vogue again. Statistics from the National Center for Health show that nearly 500,000 more babies were born in 1983 than 1975.[1]

Older women are becoming mothers. Nearly 40 percent of women married during 1960-64 had babies in their first year of marriage, compared with only 33 percent of those married during 1970-74.[2] In addition, more of those born are wanted children. According to the National Center for Health Statistics, a wanted birth is defined as "one in which the mother intended to have a child at some point, although not necessarily at the time conception occurred." The percentage of wanted newborns grew from 86 percent to 90 percent in the years 1973-82.[3]

A new study by the Rand Corporation followed 5,284 non-parents and 5,540 new parents for three years and discovered a first baby had a stabilizing effect on some marriages. Rand sociologist Linda Waite said, "What people ignore is that after you become a parent, you have a bond with your partner through a child."[4]

The decision to bear children is an expression of hope

for humanity, a declaration of the belief that better babies will make a better world. This expression of optimism is even more crucial to Christians. That tiny, wet head thrusting into a hostile world introduces possibilities of great love, which can overcome the manifold hate surrounding us.

God so loved our world he sent his Son. Every Christian parent who holds a newborn infant says to lost humanity, "We love you, and we believe our baby has the potential for making your life worth living."

T. S. Eliot expressed it beautifully: "Issued from the hand of God, the simple soul, rising or falling, grasping at kisses and toys, eager to be reassured, taking pleasure in the fragrant brilliance of the Christmas tree." (Some parents might agree more with Shakespeare, whose view of infancy is less flattering. The Bard described helpless newborns as "mewling and puking in the nurse's arms.")

Fortunately for today's parents, rearing a child is not the chancy procedure it once was. Medical scientists know more about babies than ever. At Cambridge University, Dr. Steven N. Scott and his colleagues stumbled upon a puzzling phenomenon. Some premature babies placed in incubators were wrapped in synthetic fabrics while others were swaddled in real lamb's wool. Within a few days it became apparent those who were comfortably laid in the real thing gained weight faster. They concluded that lamb's wool calms babies, and its comforting environment positively affects their physiology.[5]

What does this mean to a mother? If the substance upon which a young baby is placed has such profound emotional effects, the values cultivated in raising an infant represent an even more sacred responsibility. Child experts say the emotional interplay between mother and child, known as "bonding," involves more than a mother's verbalization. Infants apparently understand a wordless dialogue, comprehending a mother's unvocalized expressions of love.

In his book *Bonding: Relationships in the Image of God,* Dr. Donald Joy points out that the three-hour period following delivery is one of heightened sensitivity to attachment. He suggests starting the bonding experience at this time by having both mother and father touch the infant with their skin to provide a galvanic connection. Dr. Joy writes, "No one has to write a script for a father and mother. They are programmed by the Creator to do the right things if they are given the opportunity. In those first few hours they will be aware that this is a miracle, and we have been joined by a special gift from heaven."[6]

According to Dr. Joy, bonding should be a continuing relationship that consists of at least a half-dozen daily hugs. The continuance of the bonding relationship establishes parental sexual role models to prevent children from losing balance as they develop adolescent sexual identity. In the bonding context, Dr. Joy calls mothers "encompassers," representing the unfailing attachment of God's persistent love. Fathers, on the other hand, are "engrossers," representing God's all-powerful intervention.[7]

Touching is "in"; so is breastfeeding. An increasing number of new mothers are breastfeeding their babies, which generally is more popular among the younger and better-educated. (In 1900, about 80 percent of all six-month-old babies were fed mother's milk. By 1970, that number had declined to 5.5 percent.[8]) A survey shows that 78 percent of college-educated women breastfeed, compared to 41 percent with a grade school education.[9]

The trend toward breastfeeding has government support. A 1980 U.S. Surgeon General report stated the best way to achieve sound nutrition for infants by 1990 was to have 75 percent of all mothers breastfeeding upon discharge from hospitals, with 35 percent still nursing their infants at six months.[10]

Breastfeeding seems to enhance a baby's health. According to a report by the National Center of Health Statistics, breastfed infants experience significantly fewer stomach upsets and minor gastrointestinal infections. They also develop fewer ear infections and seem better protected later in life against asthma. Nutritionally, mother's milk satisfies all a baby's needs during the first four to six months of life.[11] A report in *Science* magazine claims human milk contains numerous antibodies and an antiparasitic chemical that can prevent diarrhea.[12]

If bonding and breastfeeding are positive influences on emotional and physical health, what factors are important for developing the mind and spirit? Child expert Dr. Gerald Young of Manhattan's Mount Sinai Medical Center says, "If you want to guess what a child will be like at age seven, look first at the socioeconomic background."[13] No doubt a financially stable home, provided with adequate material resources, is helpful in nurturing mental ability.

Toys are important also. Parents must carefully choose toys that will affect a child's emotional and intellectual development. Psychologist Stevanne Auerbach has written a book called *The Toy Chest,* a review of 150,000 toys marketed by five hundred toy companies. Auerbach concluded that stimulating the child by exotic playthings is pointless. She says, "Pots and pans, nonbreakable bowls, are safe, fun and educational."[14] (Readers can probably remember their own short-lived fascination with complicated toys. How many times have you seen a child joyfully playing with the cardboard box his expensive toy came in? No wonder Tinker Toys and Lincoln Logs—and similar playthings for smaller children—are perennial favorites.)

One wonders if computer-language programs for toddlers is silly software. Why bombard a baby with Basic or Fortran when a ball and rattle are good enough? In our concern to be technologically "with-it," we may force unnecessary—and expensive—playthings on our offspring. Asking babies and toddlers to share our own fascination with sophisticated technology is probably a mistake.

Another mistake parents make is to overanalyze the developmental processes of infancy. One childhood expert says there is a normal time to demonstrate certain abilities. At six or seven months, for instance, the baby should be sitting up, and he should be standing by nine or ten months. If the infant doesn't meet the timetable, child psychologists suggest neurological testing. Many a parent becomes anxious if the child lags behind in some way.

Is such concern overreaction? Perhaps babies need to be babies, away from the watchful eyes of presumptive child experts. After all, the present generation of parents survived without the benefit of "kindergarten kollege" and video-display terminal teaching. What is gained by provoking intellectual prowess at an early age? And what could be lost by failing to behold the naiveté and sense of wonder in childhood, a vulnerability we adults lose somewhere along the way?

We do well to want our children to develop intellectual abilities, of course. But while child psychologists express concern about children's intellectual abilities, Christian couples wonder how to inculcate spiritual development in their child. They ask, "What is the right age to introduce biblical truths?"

Economists estimate the cost of raising a child to age eighteen is approximately $100,000.[15] Is that expense, to say nothing of the irritation and anxiety accompanying child-rearing, worth the investment if the offspring becomes a source of spiritual dissatisfaction? Many Christians want to assure that the child will *not* be a source of spiritual dissatisfaction. Thus they expose their children to God's Word at an early age, even reading Scripture aloud while the baby is still in the womb.

RECOMMENDED READING BIBLIOGRAPHY

Sears, William. *Christian Parenting and Child Care.* Nashville: Thomas Nelson, 1985.

COUNSELING/INFORMATION SOURCES

LaLeche League International
Mary Lofton, Assistant Executive Director
9616 Minneapolis Ave.
P. O. Box 1209
Franklin Park, IL 60131-8209
(312) 455-7730

12

Motherhood

The number of births in recent years has increased at a rate far beyond that of the seventies. Nearly 4 million babies are born each year, and the number of women of childbearing age has swelled to 51.9 million.[1]

Women in their thirties are increasingly interested in motherhood. As one said, "My mother told me that if people thought everything through, nobody would ever have children."[2] But after traveling extensively, succeeding in the workplace, and becoming upwardly mobile, many yuppie women seek what they consider the ultimate feminine experience: motherhood.

Because of the financial insecurity resulting from 1970s inflation and recession, many couples hesitated to start a family. The economy started growing in the 1980s, and inflation cooled off. Women in their late thirties and early forties reconsidered the merits of motherhood. Today, the urge to bear babies is so strong some single women deliberately stop practicing birth control without telling their lovers.

Some women intent on childbearing turn to artificial

insemination. Others advertise in the newspaper for prospective fathers. A female character in the 1984 movie, *The Big Chill,* which was nominated for an Academy Award, coaxed her best friend's husband to bed for the single purpose of procreation. Menopause loomed, and she didn't want to miss motherhood.

Why do people appreciate their mothers? A national survey by Child Trends of Washington, D.C., asked children what they liked most about mom. Their answers: she's nice and sweet (24 percent); she buys me things (15 percent); she loves me (14 percent); she lets me do things (12 percent); she's a good cook (9 percent); she doesn't get mad (7 percent). Only one percent said, "I love her."

Motherhood has always been highly regarded. Most cultures see it as almost sacred. Unfortunately, our analytically inclined world even puts motherhood under the microscope. Experts feel compelled to examine every aspect of child-rearing, and their expensive research usually leads to findings that are quite obvious. For example, psycholinguists suggest that teaching tykes to talk is an art mothers find natural. Phrases like "Mommy's little girl" and "Smile for mommy" (usually delivered in high-pitched singsong) are known to speech researchers as "motherese." These short, simple, grammatically correct sentences are frequently repeated and represent a universal language toddlers can easily emulate.[3]

With all the analysis going on, mothers still face the humdrum—and joyful—aspects of child–rearing. Whether you are thinking about having children or have recently embarked upon the mission of motherhood, you'll soon discover it's more than baby talk and cuddling. Children get older and soiled clothes pile up, sandwiches get bigger, music and sports lessons multiply, and the squeeze of our hectic society makes a mother wish she were Superwoman.

More and more mothers are becoming absentee parents. Fifty-one percent of all adult American women work outside the home.[4] Many are mothers. Psychologists are divided about what this means to the children. Most agree that the absences should be kept as short as possible. Dr. Martha Leonard of the Child Study Center at Yale University School of Medicine says, "It's important that the hours mother and baby are together be happy times. Mom should try to be relaxed, not exhausted. If possible, stay home with your baby for three months in the beginning so you can learn to recognize the baby's hunger cues and sleep patterns."[5] Many experts—especially Christians—recommend an even longer period.

One wonders if many of the women—especially career women who have no intention of leaving their jobs for an extended period—bearing children late in life are doing so for selfish motives. Many women have been conditioned to believe they can "have it all"—career, marriage, money, prestige, and, yes, even motherhood. What does it say about our society when the most natural of human instincts—the joy of motherhood—is merely an adjunct of narcissism? *Can* the busy career woman be an adequate full-time mother? We don't know. We do know it is difficult.

It is probably even more difficult for a single mother. Getting pregnant by an anonymous sperm donor through artificial insemination or jumping on the motherhood merry-go-round because everybody's doing it will not fulfill God's purpose for the family relationship. Children are a heritage of the Lord, not substitutes for a yuppie puppie. Bearing a baby should not be just another indulgence in the search for personhood.

Motherhood means bringing a separate life into the world. The attendant obligations and responsibilities should be assumed only after the most rigorous soul-searching. To some women, children are curiosities to fold into Gucci blankets as if they were Laura Ashley miniatures. Prospective parents should search their motives to insure the fruit of the womb will be "God's reward" (Ps. 127:3), not the latest symbol of success.

RECOMMENDED READING BIBLIOGRAPHY

Hancock, Maxine. *Creative, Confident Children.* Old Tappan, N.J.: Revell, 1985.

Leman, Kevin. *Making Children Mind without Losing Yours.* Old Tappan, N.J.: Revell, 1984.

THE FAMILY: SCHOOL YEARS AND BEYOND

13

Public Education

"Our nation is at risk. The educational foundations of our society are presently being eroded by a rising tide of mediocrity. If an unfriendly foreign power had attempted to impose on America the mediocre educational performance that exists today, we might well have viewed it as an act of war."[1]

Those words were issued in the early 1980s by the eighteen-member National Commission on Excellence in Education. A national debate ensued and still continues. The facts are frightening. Twenty-three percent of all adults and 40 percent of all minority youth are functionally illiterate. College Board scores have gone down 50 percent in the last seventeen years, and in most schools only one year each of math and science is required for a high school diploma.[2]

These statistics concern Christian parents who wonder if it is unscriptural that their children attend public schools. Proverbs 1:7 states, "The fear of the Lord is the beginning of knowledge." With prayer and equal access effectively denied, most Christian parents of school-age youth have determined God no longer exists in public education. Many ask, "If the knowledge of human affairs and the rights of government are not rooted in biblical mandates, how can any teacher communicate the most basic of civil truth, using a curriculum devoid of spiritual foundations?"

Such questions are legitimate. Appalling conditions proliferate in public education. In Grove, Oklahoma, a fourth-grade teacher strenuously objected to the state-mandated loyalty oath. The recalcitrant educator refused to affirm these simple words: "I do so solemnly swear that I will support the Constitution and laws of the United States . . . and faithfully discharge the duties of my office of employment."[3]

An incident in Bartonville, Illinois, was even more disconcerting. A female gym teacher showed her female phys-ed students a video of scantily clad men doing aerobics. When parents objected to this striptease demonstration, the teacher took her case to the "Phil Donahue Show," declaring her constitutional rights to "happiness in the free enterprise system" had been violated. The phys-ed instructor argued, "I believe a teacher has a right to show a film in a classroom without fear of intimidation because a few people object to it."[4]

In some cases, local boards have lost control over public schools. Incompetent teachers claim immunity from parental jurisdiction and are aided and supported by the National Education Association. Public schools are increasingly more involved in counseling maladjusted teens, unwed mothers, and drug-abusing youth. (Research indicates they are increasingly *less* involved with teaching the three Rs.)

Ronald Reagan took up the cause of concerned educators and plighted parents. The president declared, "Teachers can't teach because they lack the authority to make students take tests and hand in homework. Some don't even have the authority to quiet down their classes. We need to restore good old-fashioned discipline. We must teach the basics. Too many of our students are allowed to abandon vocational and college prep courses for general ones. If we fail to instruct our children in justice, religion, and liberty, we will be condemning them to a world without virtue."[5]

A special government report entitled "Disorder in Our Public Schools" supported Reagan's stance. According to the study, each month 282,000 students are physically attacked on school premises, 1,000 teachers are assaulted seriously enough to require medical attention, and 125,000 teachers are threatened with bodily harm. Reagan assessed the situation by announcing, "Our schools are filled with rude, unruly behavior, and even violence."[6]

Several solutions have been suggested. Some reformers favor merit pay, which would base a teacher's salary on quality rather than seniority in the classroom. The National Education Association opposes this, saying it would be unfair and patronizing. A poll by the Associated Press shows 72 percent of Americans support merit pay for good teachers, and 95 percent think teachers should pass competency tests.[7]

Standardized competency tests for nationwide use have also been considered. Opponents argue that states with lower educational budgets cannot properly prioritize their responsibilities, and their students would be penalized. Some want to institute longer class days and school years. Others argue the basics of education should be restored, including four years of high school English and three years of social studies, math, and science.

Conservative critics accuse the National Education Association of being a left-wing organization more concerned with enforcing a social agenda than graduating better students. No wonder. The 1.7-million-member teachers' union has published and distributed in high schools two controversial pamphlets. One brochure stated the Ku Klux Klan is symptomatic of "entrenched racism in our society." Another pamphlet, entitled "Choices: A Unit on Conflict and Nuclear War," represented Soviet propaganda positions on a nuclear freeze.[8]

The NEA includes in its agenda a statement regarding

"nondiscriminatory personnel policies." The edict states that "no person may be employed, dismissed, suspended, demoted, transferred or retired because of family relationships, sex, or sexual orientation." That is, the NEA would oppose firing a teacher who indulges in sexual practices forbidden by biblical standards.

Romans 1:28 says, "Since they did not think it worthwhile to retain the knowledge of God, he gave them over to a depraved mind" (NIV). An observer of today's public school system might question whether this condemnation applies to "enlightened" educators who construct NEA policy. Thoughtful Christian parents wonder if these so-called experts are qualified to teach the youth of our land.

A survey of school superintendents revealed that three-fourths oppose prayer in public schools. This denial of a providential role formulating young lives raises the specter of educational leadership opposing "the beginning of knowledge" (Prov. 1:7). Fortunately, in the midst of such bleakness, most public schoolteachers are a levelheaded lot. Ninety-one percent favor tighter graduation requirements, 87 percent support student minimum competency tests, and 74 percent favor more homework.[9]

Not every public school system reflects the appalling national statistics. There are still competent teachers around, and discipline at some schools is still fairly tight. Christian parents must decide after thorough investigation of local board policies and educational standards if public education is suitable for their family. Even under the best conditions, public education submits students to unscriptural beliefs in the biological sciences and social studies. It is the conclusion of this author that, family finances permitting, Christian children generally would be better off in a private Christian school or tutored at home. This will be discussed further in the next chapter.

RECOMMENDED READING BIBLIOGRAPHY

Gabler, Mel and Norma. *What Are They Teaching Our Children?* Wheaton, Ill.: Victor, 1985.

Garlett, Marti Watson. *Who Will Be My Teacher?* Waco, Tex.: Word, 1985.

Gow, Kathleen. *Yes, Virginia, There is Right and Wrong.* Wheaton, Ill.: Tyndale, 1985

Hefley, James. *Are Textbooks Harming Your Children?* Milford, Mich.: Mott Media, 1979.

Hefley, James. *Textbooks on Trial.* Wheaton, Ill.: Victor, 1976.

Reed, Sally. *NEA: Propaganda of the Radical Left.* Self-published, 1984.

Whitehead, John W. *The Freedom of Religious Expression in the Public High Schools.* Westchester, Ill.: Crossway, 1983.

COUNSELING/INFORMATION SOURCES

The National Council for Better Education
1373 N. Van Dorn Street
Alexandria, VA 22304
(202) 547-0645

Education and Research Analysts
P. O. Box 7518
Longview, TX 75607
(214) 753-5993

National Parent Teacher Organization
700 North Rush Street
Chicago, IL 60611-2571
(312) 787-0977

Save Our Schools
1712 I Street, Suite 1005
Washington, DC 20006
(202) 331-7223

14

Christian Schools

"I'm afraid that schools will prove to be the gates of hell. I advise no one to place his child where the Scriptures do not reign paramount. Every institution in which men are not unceasingly occupied with the Word of God must become corrupt."[1]

These words weren't spoken by the superintendent of a modern Christian school. They came from the lips of Martin Luther. We can imagine how the great Reformer would react to today's violence, drug abuse, and immorality in public schools. Echoing Luther's sentiments, many parents are disturbed by the lack of moral instruction in public schools and incensed that secular humanism predominates.

In the nineteenth century, English intellectual John Stuart Mill wrote of state-sponsored education: "It is a mere contrivance for molding people to be exactly like one another: and as the mold in which it casts them is that which pleases the dominant power in the government, it establishes a despotism over the mind."[2]

Many Christian parents today are adversaries of

government policies that seem to practice the despotism John Stuart Mill referred to. American education was established to teach children morals and competency in Bible reading, but gradually government began to consider universal free education as a right of citizenship and a means to promote public welfare. Many secular educators today see Christian schools as the creation of an arrogant, self-righteous group of Bible thumpers. They have, obviously, lost sight of the original purpose of education in America.

Whether to educate children in public or private schools is a parental decision with profound moral significance. Many evangelical parents see state-run schools as breeding grounds for moral permissiveness and insist that parents have the responsibility to scrutinize a child's education. Although they pay thousands of dollars in taxes annually to support public schools, parents consider additional investment in Christian schools well worth the cost. Conversely, other Christian parents argue that if public schools are abandoned by Bible believers, Satan will control the domain of education by default. They believe redemptive salt and light should be left in our public educational institutions.

States' rights and parents' rights rapidly converge on a collision course. While most Christians preach submission to authority, many oppose state certification of teachers in Christian schools. Legislatures in forty-seven states mandate such approval.[3] A growing movement among Christian educators insists that the command in Ephesians 6:4 (children are to be trained "in the nurture and admonition of the Lord") mandates educational instruction of children as a mission of the church.

Evidence indicates that state certification does not ensure teacher competency. Californian teacher certification tests in basic skills require only 65 percent accuracy. Thirty-two percent of those who attempted a recent test failed that minimal requirement.[4] It is rash to assume, as many persons do, that Christian schools' academic standards are necessarily lower than those of public schools. Clearly, academic standards in public schools are not always high.

The choice of private versus public education should be based on an objective appraisal of local educational institutions. Quality of teaching and the moral environment of public schools vary widely from district to district. Economic considerations should be carefully weighed.

Some parents look on their children as missionaries in the secular schools bringing the light of Christ. Unfortunately, Christian children's redemptive influence seems slight in secular schools. A Christian school usually provides quality education and a healthier moral environment. There are cases, however, when church-run schools employ poorly paid instructors whose teaching ability and academic background are not up to par. In addition, facilities may be inadequate in a high-tech age that demands computer and technical skills. Yet many Christian schools are quite adequate in this regard.

The growth of Christian education intensifies debate on several key political issues. Is a private school education a privilege or a basic right for which taxpaying parents deserve no penalty? Is education government's responsibility or the province of parents? If state certification or licensing is an issue, where is the balance between the admonishment of Romans 13 to respect authority and opposition to state intrusion into the realm of religious instruction?

Our nation's leaders should be grateful for the Christian school movement, which saves taxpayers an estimated $2 billion a year. They should also be grateful for morally conscientious students who are less prone to criminal behavior that produces a strain on the justice system.

RECOMMENDED READING BIBLIOGRAPHY

Macaulay, Susan Schaeffer. *For the Children's Sake.* Westchester, Ill.: Crossway, 1984.

Schlafly, Phyllis. *Child Abuse in the Classroom.* Alton, Ill.: Pere Marquette Press, 1984.

COUNSELING/INFORMATION SOURCES

Association of Christian Schools
P. O. Box 4097
Whittier, CA 90607
(213) 694-4797

Christian Education Association International
P. O. Box 50025
Pasadena, CA 91105
(818) 798-1124

15

Home Schooling

What do these people have in common: Robert E. Lee,
George Patton, Alexander Graham Bell, Thomas Edison,
John Wesley, Abraham Lincoln, Franklin Roosevelt,
George Washington, Winston Churchill, Agatha Christie,
C. S. Lewis, Sandra Day O'Connor, and Albert
Schweitzer? Each of these famous people was home-
schooled.

More than one million school-aged children no longer
show up in America's public classrooms. They are not
dropouts or victims of parental neglect but members of a
growing legion of home-schooled students. Instead of
boarding buses, they sit down at the kitchen table to
receive their education.

Home–schooling expert and author Dr. Raymond
Moore wrote in his book, *Homespun Schools,* "To take
little children unnecessarily out of the home and put
them into institutions before they are ready is perhaps
our most pervasive form of child abuse today."[1] Whether
it is actual child abuse or not, many parents seem to
concur with Dr. Moore.

Disillusioned with public schools and unable to afford private Christian schools, some parents find home schooling increasingly attractive. There is a precedent: It was the primary mode of education in America during the early nineteenth century. And there are obvious benefits: Home schools create an enclave that shelters youngsters from humanistic textbooks, drug enticement, and vulgar, rebellious conduct. Many parents embark on the home schooling adventure convinced that public schools waste time and that a superior education can be arranged at home.

Home-schooling curricula range from minimal book instruction to carefully organized teaching guides available from special correspondence schools. Advocates say the self-discipline and motivation instigated by home schooling outweigh all value in the socialization process of attending public school. They also believe home schooling enforces a sense of family togetherness. Proponents argue that parents better understand their children's needs than do secular institutions that morally brutalize the young.

While public schools cultivate superchildren with programs involving small children in gymnastics and computers, home-schooling experts believe such tasks are too demanding on a youngster's brain. Dr. Moore argues, "The eyes of most children are permanently damaged before age twelve. Neither the maturity of their delicate central nervous system nor the balancing of the hemispheres of their brains provides a basis for thoughtful learning before eight or nine."[2]

Those who argue that mother (or father) has insufficient time to properly instruct a child must remember the average public schoolteacher spends only seven minutes a day in direct contact with each student. Any parent can easily provide more than that. Critics also claim that home schooling deprives students of extracurricular activities and social development. Home-schoolers claim that keeping a child from these activities is less damaging than robbing him of moral teaching and the grammatical skills imperative to landing a good job. (Christians who teach their children at home are normally churchgoers anyway, so the church provides peers and social activities.)

A newspaper editorial stated, "Education is too important to be left to parental whimsy. It should not create problem children who will burden society as problem adults. That's why we should permit home-schooling only by those parents who can demonstrate they can live up to that awesome responsibility."[3]

In response to such statements, home-schooling parents quote Swiss psychologist Jean Piaget: "Even the bad parent who neglects her child is nonetheless providing much for him."[4] This is not to condone bad parents but to affirm the fact that bad parents may still provide more nurture than twelve years of bad public schools.

If you are interested in home schooling, many books are available on the subject. A visit to your local Christian bookstore should provide you with several volumes to research the subject. Some are listed at the end of this chapter.

If you feel inadequate as an educator, remember this: For fifty-eight hundred years parents have educated their offspring. Only in the last two hundred years has that responsibility shifted to outside authority (the state).

If you decide to home-school, don't do so merely because of disaffection with the public school system. Do it out of a positive desire to instill your child with adequate moral and academic instruction based on scriptural principles.

Home schooling isn't right for all children and every parent. You may feel that a nearby Christian school can do a more adequate job. You may not feel you have the time or energy or academic background that qualify you as a teacher. But if you are qualified, and if you desire a strong bond between yourself and your child, home schooling may be rewarding for both your child and you.

RECOMMENDED READING BIBLIOGRAPHY

Moore, Raymond and Dorothy. *Home Grown Kids.* Grand Rapids: Zondervan, 1981.

Moore, Raymond and Dorothy. *Home-spun Schools.* Waco, Tex.: Word, 1982.

Moore, Raymond and Dorothy. *Homestyle Teaching.* Waco, Tex.: Word, 1980.

Whitehead, John W. and Wendell R. Bird. *Home Education and Constitutional Liberties.* Westchester, Ill.: Crossway, 1984.

COUNSELING/INFORMATION SOURCES

Hewitt Research Foundation
Box 9
Washougel, WA 98671

Christian Liberty Academy
203 E. McDonald Rd.
Prospect, IL 60070

Pensacola Christian Academy
125 St. John St.
Pensacola, FL 32503

American School
850 E. 58th St.
Chicago, IL 60637

LEGAL SERVICES RESOURCES

Rutherford Institute
P. O. Box 510
Manassas, VA 22110

Home School Legal Defense Association
P. O. Box 2091
Washington, DC 20013
(202) 737-0030

16

Missing Children

Reeve Walsh didn't want to drag her six-year-old son, Adam, from one store to another as she shopped. So, she left him in the toy department while she momentarily attended to other matters on that hot July afternoon in 1981.

Mrs. Walsh was gone for just three minutes. When she returned, Adam was missing. She never saw him again. Some weeks later, after a nationwide search, Adam's severed head was found floating in a canal. The gut-wrenching story about missing children was portrayed in "Adam," a TV movie.

Maureen Gosch, whose son Johnny was abducted, has never seen her child since. Mrs. Gosch says, "In this country we have foundations to save baby seals, whales, and battleships. But there's no help for missing children and their parents. It's the burden of the parents alone."[1]

As Mrs. Gosch discovered, authorities don't take immediate action about a missing child because runaways generally return within forty-eight hours. The Gosches were told their child would be categorized as

missing for a year before reclassification to *abducted,*
after which appropriate police action could be taken.
Such delays seem unconscionable when the U.S. Justice
Department reports there are at least thirty-five known
child murderers loose in America, random killers who
lure youngsters into cars and whisk them away to death.

Every year five thousand missing children are
murdered.[2] Many have been brutally assaulted. Often
they are used for pornographic pictures and prostitution.
In a nation equipped to trace missing automobiles and
TV sets, it's ironic that officials are squeamish about
maintaining a data bank on missing children. Civil
libertarians express concern about infringement of
individual rights in respect to fingerprinting children.
While their caution is commendable, the immensity of
this horror cries out for drastic measures.

Society has barely begun to comprehend the tragedy
of missing children. Paula Hawkins, U.S. Senator from
Florida, sponsored the Missing Children Act passed by
Congress. She says more than one million children are
reported missing every year, and 100,000 are never
found.[3] The Missing Children Act requires the FBI to file
such data in its crime computer. Senator Hawkins
believes some parents encourage abduction by allowing
their children to be photographed in enticing poses
preparatory to entering beauty contests. But some
children are abducted for reasons no one understands.

Who is at fault? The playboy philosophy must bear
blame for making pornography respectable and creating
a "pederastic industry" for those who prefer children.
The perverted molester who abducts a child is perhaps
no more guilty than our permissive society, which
glorifies the satisfaction of every erotic impulse.
Negligent parents make the abductor's job easy by not
watching their children and allowing them to wander the
streets at random.

Here are ways you, as a parent, can confront the
problem of missing children and avoid the abduction of
your own child:

1. *Warn your children never to go anywhere with anyone without your permission.*
2. *Make sure school authorities will phone you at home or office if your child is absent.*
3. *Teach your child that not all adults are good people and some should be avoided.*
4. *Never leave your child alone at any time in a public place, even for a moment.*
5. *Be sure your child knows exactly what to do if he should become separated from you, including how to call any local emergency numbers.*
6. *Teach your children their full name, address, and phone number, and how to make a long-distance call.*

COUNSELING/INFORMATION SOURCES

Child Find Incorporated
P. O. Box 277
New Paul, NY 12564
1-800-431-5005

Operation Lookout
P. O. Box 231
Mountlake Terrace, WA 98043
(206) 362-7375

Child Protection Task Force
Lynchburg, VA 24514

K.I.D.S.
Data System Incorporated
P. O. Box 1505
Hermiston, OR 97838
(503) 567-1845

17

Spanking

He was eleven years old, and his parents had taken a willow cane to his bare bottom as punishment for naughtiness. The youngster ran to the local police station and reported his parents for "grievous bodily injury." Now his parents face a trial and stiff fines.[1]

It happened in Sweden, where the law forbids parents to physically chastise children. Even social workers defended the parents as loving and caring and said the boy was punished for dishonest behavior. Critics of Swedish legislation say that brats who face family discipline are terrorizing their parents with threats of legal action.

Most Americans still spank their children. The University of New Hampshire's Family Research Laboratory polled parents with children aged five to eight and found that 88 percent used corporal punishment.[2] Boards, hands, and straps are the preferred instruments. One mother said, "Other forms of punishment just don't seem to make much of an impression on a child."[3] She was probably aware, as many parents are, that long, involved explanations and lectures are wasted on small children.

Dr. Benjamin Spock opposes spanking, saying it teaches children that "the larger, stronger person has the power to get his way whether or not he is right."[4] Dr. John Knutson, professor of psychiatry at the University of Iowa, agrees, saying that spanking is "a seductively simple strategy for training children."[5]

Some experts link physical discipline to aggressive behavior in children, claiming juvenile delinquents were raised on belts and boards. Dr. Kenneth Kay, a family therapist, argues that "corporal punishment demeans both the parents and the children and presents violence as an acceptable way to solve problems...spanking is never a good substitute for communication."[6]

Many Christians take issue with this attitude. Noted Christian author Dr. James Dobson says, "Mild punishments reinforce responsible behavior."[7] Proverbs 22:15, says "Foolishness is bound in the heart of a child, but the rod of correction shall drive it far from him." Proverbs 29:15 concurs: "The rod of correction imparts wisdom, but a child left to itself disgraces his mother" (NIV).

There are those who say spanking is part of a violence-obsessed society. But how ridiculous to argue that the so-called violence of spanking will beget further violence! In a society where the average sixteen-year-old has watched eighteen thousand murders (on television) during his formative years, it seems strange to point a finger at parents. Spanking doesn't make a child vicious. It acquaints him with the reality of penalties for defiance, dishonesty, and selfishness. Corporal punishment in the hands of a loving parent can be a teaching tool that inhibits harmful behavior.

Does spanking really work? If you think punishment has no power, ask the parent who has seen the sudden change in a child's disposition after bending over father's knee. At the very least, spanking conveys the idea that improper behavior brings bad consequences.

Some parents say no matter how often you spank a child, he will repeat the offending behavior. In one of his best-selling books, Dr. Dobson says such failures result from infrequent punishment, discipline applied after an extended period of no discipline, spanking that is too gentle and doesn't hurt, and a child who is more strong-willed than the parent.

Others wonder if every child should be spanked in the same manner with the same frequency. Clearly, certain children are more emotionally sensitive than others. Proverbs 25:11 says, "A word aptly spoken is like apples of gold in settings of silver" (NIV). A word of loving care directed at a perceptive child can often evoke positive conduct. Some children may never need to be spanked, but most do.

The best Christians occasionally need chastening from the Lord. So it is with the responsive child for whom the hand instead of the lips produces correct conduct. To withhold physical discipline from a child because he is sensitive or emotional may teach him to indulge those feelings rather than control them.

Proverbs 13:24 tells us, "He who spares the rod hates his son, but he who loves him disciplines him diligently" (TLB). The Bible uses the term rod because the agrarian culture of the day was familiar with the shepherd's rod. The shepherd wielded it to protect his sheep and to guide them to better pastures. In the same manner, parents are admonished to protect their flock by not sparing the rod. Eli in the Old Testament is an example of a parent severely judged by God because he failed to restrain his vile sons.

God trains us through suffering and chastisement. Hebrews 12:6, 7 points out that discipline is a sign of God's love for us. Like God, good human parents discipline their children.

Parental authority to discipline is not derived from moral flawlessness; it comes from divinely ordained jurisdiction which God has given parents over their children. Parents should not hesitate to admit their mistakes nor avoid exercising necessary discipline because of a sense of unworthiness.

Colossians 3:20 tells children to obey their parents even

when a parent is wrong and a child is unfairly spanked because of presumed disobedience. The submissive child will adjust better in the long run because he has met God's demands for divine order. The responsibility of discipline rests with the parent, and does not revert to the child, permitting him to judge the wisdom of his parents' decision. As Lamentations 3:27 advises, "It is good for a young man to be under discipline" (TLB).

It is vital that parents control their own emotions and avoid vindictiveness while in the heat of punishing a child. Spanking to relieve a parent's frustration or to deliberately cause pain is inappropriate. We cannot believe that actual physical wounds resulting from punishment are biblically justifiable.

To be faithful to the Bible's teaching, we must recognize the difference between creative corrections and reactionary punishment when using a board on the bottom. The desire to punish may exist in your mind, but its motive should be to benefit the one you are spanking. Punishment is a human action of retribution, whereas correction has a divine intent to inhibit wrong conduct. Proverbs 29:17 says, "Correct thy son and he shall give thee rest; yea, he shall give delight unto thy soul."

Spanking should be used in cases of intentional wrongdoing to show the repulsiveness of sin. It should occur immediately after disobedience and should not be reserved for special cases of unmanageable defiance. And it should occur when the parent has said it will. It is wrong to issue constant threats and eventually give way to an angry explosion. Once you promise to do it, do it!

When a child cries after the punishment, a parent should not threaten, "If you don't stop crying, I'll hit you again." A wise parent must know when tears result from sorrow or from the desire to manipulate the parent into stopping the punishment.

A follow-up time helps when you tell the child why he was spanked and explain your feelings about his conduct. Allow your child to talk out his feelings. Hold him and explain why you were upset. Reinforce your love, but assert your right to take such action whenever necessary. Martin Luther advised, "Keep the apple near the rod." That is, balance chastisement with comfort.

Should older children be spanked? There is no clear cut-off date for changing from spanking to other forms of discipline. Spanking a teenager is usually not productive, and corporal punishment should probably taper off prior to adolescence. You can manipulate a teenager's environment by granting or withholding privileges, including the purse and the car keys.

In summary: (a) Mild spankings should begin at about fifteen to eighteen months; (b) they should be relatively infrequent and reserved for obvious disobedience; (c) it is best to administer them with a neutral object; (d) it should hurt if it's going to be purposeful; (e) spank immediately after the offense or not at all, since the child's memory may not be sufficiently developed; (f) if crying lasts more than two or three minutes, or at the most five, the child may be complaining and you might want to offer a little more of what caused the original tears.

Having considered all of this, we need to look at the legal aspects of spanking. The press has publicized cases of extreme corporal punishment in cults, such as the House of Judah group in Michigan, where a twelve-year-old boy was beaten to death.[8] After Jonestown, cries were raised that society has a responsibility to protect children from abuse, no matter what religious beliefs the parents may hold. Christians would agree that Scripture used to justify beating the devil out of someone is inappropriate. However, we should be concerned about government intrusion upon parental rights to raise their children.

Where do the rights of a parent's personal beliefs in disciplinary action end and the responsibility of the state to protect its constituents begin? English children can still be beaten lawfully, as is the case in Australia, New Zealand, and South Africa. The present situation in Sweden has been mentioned already.

Christians find a variety of biblical justifications for spanking: Proverbs 19:8 and Proverbs 22:6, in addition to passages already cited. Scripture unquestionably allows parents the option of spanking. But do these biblical admonitions extend to other adults and authority figures, including teachers and public officials?

Public educators say that students lose respect and self-control when corporal punishment is taken from the classroom. Opponents argue that spanking is ineffective and encourages the very behavior it seeks to eliminate, to say nothing of precipitating child-abuse cases. Those opposed to spanking say there is no such thing as reasonable and appropriate physical violence against children. Each year one million public school students are paddled for breaking school rules. Some say it's not necessary, since restricting activities and denying the privileges of students is just as effective. (The practice of spanking in schools depends, incidentally, on the local school boards. In many schools systems spanking is strictly prohibited.)

Irwin Hyman, director of the National Center for the Study of Corporal Punishment and Alternatives in Schools, goes so far as to say, "It prevents children from acquiring internal controls based on the moral belief that one should behave properly because it's the right thing to do—rather than because of fear of punishment."[9] His attitude is common among educators, and the results are obvious: undisciplined schools. No wonder many Christian parents teach their children at home or send them to Christian schools where spanking is used in discipline.

Regrettably, many parents and teachers have abused the privilege of spanking. We can't ignore instances of child abuse cited by social workers who oppose corporal punishment. But too often they cite isolated and extreme incidents in order to cast all corporal punishment in a bad light. These extreme cases are given wide publicity, and many parents are led to believe that all spanking is brutal and cruel. Right now there is a strong possibility that the state may eventually mandate that parents cannot spank their children. Christians may soon have to decide if they will disobey authority to heed the higher law of God as pronounced in the Book of Proverbs.

RECOMMENDED READING BIBLIOGRAPHY

Dobson, James C. *Dare to Discipline.* Wheaton, Ill.: Tyndale, 1970.

————. *Dr. Dobson Answers Your Questions.* Wheaton, Ill.: Tyndale, 1982.

————. *The Strong-willed Child.* Wheaton, Ill.: Tyndale, 1978.

18

Child Abuse

British researcher Roy Meadow was the first to identify it
in a 1977 article. He called it *Munchausen's syndrome by
proxy*. Those afflicted with Munchausen's syndrome
constantly manufacture illnesses. They crave the attention
given by concerned doctors and health attendants.
Munchausen's syndrome by proxy is present when the
parent receives indirect attention because of a sick
child—a child made sick not by illness but by parental
abuse.[1]

Medical researchers have discovered that a child's
sickness is sometimes created by the parent.
Munchausen's syndrome by proxy causes a parent to
give his child large doses of tranquilizers, laxatives, or
other medicines until the child is incapacitated. When
mysterious medical symptoms appear, the parent hurries
the child to a doctor, professing ignorance of its illness.
Just as sufferers of Munchausen's syndrome repeatedly
attempt to hospitalize themselves, the abusing parent
(who suffers this disorder by proxy) makes sure the child
is always sick. After the child is hospitalized, the parent
may even assist in the recovery of his offspring.

Munchausen's syndrome by proxy is one of the rarer forms of child abuse. More common is the use of physical violence. Such violence is often excused by an ironic twisting of fact. Abusive parents believe if their children were taken away to a foster home, the progeny would be in a worse environment. After all, don't parents know what is best for their children? How could someone else raise them better?

Such arguments obscure the horror of child abuse. Extreme cases may involve cigarette burns on the tongue, backs scarred with human bite marks, and telltale spiral fractures, small bone breaks caused by twisting a spindly arm. Other children suffer from buttocks bearing marks of electrical cords and bodies tortured with ropes and chains. Some children are even refused food and toilet facilities.

The story of Elizabeth Manning's three-year-old son Michael is a tragic case in point. Little Michael was crying, so Manning's boyfriend Daniel Arevalo took the child into the bathroom and shut the door. For hours he beat the lad with a large belt buckle. Finally, Elizabeth heard a thud. When she opened the door, she saw Daniel with his foot on Michael.

The more Michael cried, the more Daniel hit him. Finally, little Michael turned pale and died. His mother and her boyfriend wrapped the tiny body in a blanket, tied it together with a clothesline, and hid it in a heating vent. The apartment windows were kept open to permit the putrefying body odors to escape. At last, Daniel Arevalo buried the body in a field near the apartment complex.[2]

Most parents are sickened by stories of such incomprehensible cruelty. Yet some of these same parents angrily grab hairbrushes, rolling pins, cooking spoons, and straps to mercilessly beat their own children who have disobeyed household rules. Sometimes, in a frustrated state of emotional intensity, parents unintentionally inflict permanent scars.

An estimated one million children suffer each year from such abuse. Two thousand to five thousand of them die annually. Seventy percent of child abusers are biological parents and 50 percent of violent cases occur with children under the age of one.[3] Hairline fractures, bruises, and broken bones are often explained away as the result of falls, bumps, and household injuries.

It's impossible to categorically profile child abusers. They represent both sexes, all economic strata, every race, and many religions. Some abuse springs from misdirected anger intended for their own mothers and fathers. In other instances, parents see childhood clumsiness as a commentary on their own parenting skills rather than an expression of normal adolescent ineptness. They respond by lashing out at the child.

Abuse often occurs when the child is tired and more demanding, or the parent is exhausted at the end of a long day. Parents may fail to understand the developmental states of childhood and perceive offspring as more mentally and physically advanced than they actually are. The parent consequently sees the child's failure to perform properly as an act of disobedience, and responds violently.

Not all child abuse involves a violent parent and a cowering child. There are other ways to abuse innocent victims. A child may be verbally degraded, called horrible names, and told he is worthless until self-esteem is utterly destroyed. Some children are emotionally tossed back and forth between parents when a marriage disintegrates, husband and wife immaturely using their children as pawns to vent their own anger and resentments. The parent who has visiting rights takes advantage of being with the child, forcing upon the youngster everything he wanted to do for months or weeks. Such intense situations become cauldrons of boiling abuse.

Analyzing the rise in child abuse, one doctor commented, "We've lost the comfort of the extended family. Religion is less of a guide than it used to be. We seem preoccupied with material things. All of this undermines the serenity of the family."[4] Those are the words of none other than Dr. Benjamin Spock. Critics charge his advice is two generations too late! They say his permissive child-rearing attitudes ripped apart the fabric of postwar homes, tearing at the fragile lives of the most vulnerable members.

Parents who berate their children at the end of a hard day must defuse such frustrations before things get out of hand with a blow to the body producing permanent damage. The cycle of violence must be broken, or it will break both parent and child. Parents who were themselves abused as children need to be especially wary. (Studies show most abusers were battered children.)

The child abuser isn't a monster. He or she is generally a normal parent, overwhelmed by stress, who hasn't learned effective coping skills. Christian friends can fulfill the scriptural command of Galatians 6:2 to "bear one another's burdens" by providing baby-sitting services. If you know a frustrated mother facing the possibility of domestic violence, provide that mother an escape. Watch the child for her so she can be alone for awhile, away from the demands of her baby. Breaking this cycle of tension is necessary to afford the potentially abusive parent a chance to get a grip on things again.

Angry parents should consider if their reactions to the child are based upon undisciplined patterns in their own lives. If you find yourself getting angry, ask someone else to look after the child and get away for a few moments. Behavior can't be corrected by beating it out of the child. Don't expect more of a child than he can give. A three-year-old who spills his food on the floor is clumsy, not rebellious. Parents should learn to distinguish between a child's act of contempt and accidents resulting from underdeveloped physical skills.

If you abuse your child, take this matter prayerfully to the Lord. Confess your errant behavior to the abused child. Say you are sorry and admit he did nothing to deserve this kind of punishment. Be honest. Admit you have not acted in accordance with conduct that pleases the Lord.

A *Time* magazine report about child abuse stated

eloquently, "At stake is simple human dignity. If wolves and bears and birds take meticulous care of their young, why are human beings subjecting theirs to whippings and punches? Child abuse is the ultimate crime, the ultimate betrayal."[5]

The Word of God agrees. "Suffer little children . . . to come unto me," Jesus said in Matthew 19:14. Christ declared it is a grave offense to hinder a child from approaching his kingdom. What better way to keep a child from reaching out to his heavenly Father than by forcing him to see his earthly father as the perpetrator of cruel punishment? The abused child who has been hurt and robbed of self-esteem will find it hard to trust God, because the earthly father he does know represents pain and rejection.

Not all abuse is active and violent. One form of abuse is neglect. Some abused children are never beaten or physically tortured. They are simply ignored by parents who provide the good things of life but avoid the necessary personal attention to make a house a home. This is common in households where both parents are caught up in their own careers and hobbies. Active church members can be guilty of overloading their calendars with church meetings. Commitment to any group—even if it is part of the church—should never lead to neglect of one's parental responsibilities.

More than 50 percent of all major crimes are committed by children under eighteen, a price we pay for an abusive society. If abusive parents continue to offend or neglect these little ones, the children will strike back the only way they know how—by hurting others as they were hurt.

COUNSELING/INFORMATION SOURCES

The National Committee for the Prevention of Child Abuse
Box 2866
Chicago, IL 60690
(312) 633-3520

Parents Anonymous
1-800-422-4453
Call local number for information. Chapters in most large cities.

National Coalition Against Domestic Violence
1500 Massachusetts Ave. N.W.
Suite 35
Washington, DC 20005

19
Child Molestation

He was a respected Catholic priest who delivered
spellbinding funeral sermons and won local accolades
for rescuing a man who was trapped under an
overturned tractor. Women in Louisiana's Vermilion Parish
were impressed with his charm. But there was a secret
side to Father Gilbert Gauthe. Over an eleven-year span
Father Gauthe committed sexual acts with at least thirty-
five boys.

Child molestation incidents appear to be on the rise.
Charges that 125 children were raped and sodomized at
the McMartin Preschool in Manhattan Beach, California,
opened floodgates of suspicion. Gradually, the public is
becoming aware that the stereotypical sleazy old man in
a trenchcoat is an uncommon child molester. More often,
the man or woman who indecently fondles children is an
authority figure with a sterling reputation.

In her book *The Silent Children,* Linda Tschirhart
Sanford claims that 60 percent to 90 percent of victims
are girls, and that men are molesters in 97 percent of
reported cases.[1] Every two minutes in America a child is
sexually molested.

Each year more than a half-million molestation victims are reported. Unfortunately, they represent only about one-third of the actual total.[2] For every case of adult rape reported, approximately twenty children are molested. Half of all young girls will be molested before they emerge from childhood.[3] Statistically, the perpetrator will abuse an average of 68.3 victims.[4] Only one out of ten molesters is ever caught. One of ten will be convicted. If convicted, only 10 percent will ever spend time in jail.[5]

In two-thirds of pedophilia cases, the victims and parents know the assailants, who may be relatives and even respected church members.[6] Individuals with a position of trust prey on a child's vulnerability. Unsuspected intentions provide unhindered access to the molester.

The prophet Zechariah spoke of a time when children would freely walk the streets of any city without fear of mistreatment. "The city streets will be filled with boys and girls playing there" (8:5, NIV), he declared. Such safety is a far cry from today's cities with their numerous pedophiles.

Not everyone is bewailing this situation. NAMBLA (North American Man-Boy Love Association) is an organization dedicated to pedophilia. Its active members call themselves part of a "political and educational organization" with a "libertarian, humanistic outlook on sexuality." NAMBLA argues that adult society has no right to limit a child's selection of sexual partners. Members believe *they* are the victims of discriminatory laws, insisting that sex with children is an educational tool that destroys childhood myths regarding adult sexual roles. NAMBLA wants nothing less than legal approval for adults to have sex with any consenting child.[7]

The Rene Guyon Society, a tax-exempt propedophile organization, adopted as its slogan, "Sex by eight or else it's too late." In England, the British Pedophile Information Exchange is lobbying for a drop in the age of legal sexual consent to four years of age![8] Such goals may sound ludicrous, but not long ago the aims of pornographers and homosexuals also seemed outlandish.

Western culture has believed for generations that children should be protected from temptation until they are old enough to determine right from wrong. Today that moral principle is threatened by activists demanding recognition for their perverted "rights." As Christians, we have an obligation to protect our children from such perversity.

Knowing the facts about child molestation can help parents protect their children. Watch out for any unusual behavior from your child without being overly inquisitive. Tell your children not to keep secrets, particularly about someone giving them candy or gifts. If you suspect molestation, immediately contact an expert who knows the correct way to question a child. Don't underestimate the extent of child molestation. It is the most often committed serious personal crime in America, and it is the least frequently punished.

Though most attention is focused on the male molester, women also commit such crimes. For this reason, every parent should be cautious when choosing a baby-sitter or day-care center.

Teach a child that it's OK to not like being touched. A child must know the parts of his body that are off-limits. No one has a right to lay a hand on those places in an inappropriate manner. If it happens, tell the child to scream, kick, and run. To the rule, "Don't ever take candy from a stranger," should be added the warning, "Don't talk to strangers or let them touch you!" Experts recommend taking the child through a possible scenario, determining in advance how to handle molestation situations.

Experts who counsel molested children say it's best to believe childhood claims of abuse, for such accounts are seldom fabricated. Don't be surprised if the victim is very young. Records show that children of nine and ten months have been molested. One account was given of a father who molested a baby only two hours old. (If that isn't sufficiently shocking, another convicted child molester, a Scoutmaster, admitted to more than three thousand victims!)

Teach your children to avoid unsupervised amusement parks, arcades, and schoolyards where molesters hunt for victims. So many parents are content to let their children roam for hours in such places, where the only adults present may be the most undesirable sort.

The best advice to parents is this: Love your child and express that love physically. One child molester justified his perversion by saying, "I'm giving children the love and attention their parents do not." There is a measure of truth in his statement. Some parents unconsciously invite molestation by not spending enough time with their children, holding them and reassuring them. Lack of affection can render a child vulnerable to advances of the pedophile who exploits the absence of parental love. In the words of one researcher of pedophilia, "Have you hugged your kids today? If not, a child molester will."[9]

RECOMMENDED READING BIBLIOGRAPHY

Berry, Joy. *Sexual Abuse.* Danger Zone Series. Waco, Tex.: Word, 1984.

Hyde, Margaret O. *Sexual Abuse: Let's Talk About It.* Philadelphia: Westminster, 1984

COUNSELING/INFORMATION SOURCES

Little Ones Books
P. O. Box 725
Young America, MN 55399

C.A.P.
Box 3584
Bakersfield, CA 93385
(805) 589-0520

Society's League Against Molestation
Consult local chapter.

20

Teenage Sex

Jerome Lanier, age thirty-eight, admitted having repeated sexual encounters with an unnamed twelve-year-old girl. Florida's Dade County Attorney Janet Reno brought indecent assault charges against Lanier, citing the girl's status as a minor. A three-judge panel ruled that no felony had been committed because the girl was not a virgin and admitted consenting.[1]

The lesson of the court decision seems clear: Teenagers or prepubescent adolescents who willingly indulge in sex cannot expect the law to defend a chastity they've surrendered. Unfortunately, a lot of teenagers have given up moral purity. The statistics are stunning: 40 percent of girls become pregnant in their teens,[2] and by the age of 19 only one-third say they have retained their virginity.[3] Last year, there were 1.2 million teen pregnancies.[4] For every three live births, there were five abortions.[5] Only 17 percent of babies born to teen mothers were conceived after marriage.[6]

The decline of America's morals has been gradual. Servicemen returning from World War I brought back a loose, more European view of sex. Then came the automobile with its backseat and unchaperoned privacy. The birth control pill and the playboy philosophy followed. Vietnam's importation of easygoing Asian morality and Joseph Fletcher's supposedly Christian "situation ethics" accelerated the moral decline. With the threat of nuclear war screaming doomsday from newspapers and TV, the accompanying cry seems to be, "Eat, drink, and have sex now before you're atomized tomorrow."

Sleeping with someone is a matter of technique, not an intimate experience to be shared in the marriage bed. Young people see hundreds of movies and TV programs extolling casual, overnight encounters. Most have never heard the proclamation of 1 Corinthians 6:18 "Flee from sexual immorality. All other sins a man commits are outside his body, but he who sins sexually sins against his own body" (NIV). Somewhere along the way the idea of *sin* got discarded.

Strangely enough, there is evidence that teens aren't obsessed with sex. In a recent study by a UCLA psychologist, a group of teenagers was requested to rank a list of five activities including athletics, good grades, sex, friendship, and having a steady date. When the order of importance was compiled and analyzed, boys listed sex last and girls ranked it next to last.[7] Why this gap between preference and performance?

Peer pressure is a significant factor. Too many kids today believe, "There's something wrong with me if I'm a sixteen-year-old virgin." There is also pressure from the person one is dating. More than one young lady has succumbed to the solicitation, "You would do it if you really loved me" or "You're the only one in the class who doesn't." And girls now use the same lines on boys.

In the midst of a culture obsessed with lust on TV and eroticism on Hollywood screens, the biblical view of immorality is stern: ". . . the sexually immoral . . . their place will be in the fiery lake of burning sulfur" (Rev. 21:8, NIV). God's dim view of sexual sin has no room for euphemisms such as "lover" or "paramour." The Bible doesn't speak highly of being "involved with" someone or sleeping with another person. Scriptural language is plain: sexually immoral persons risk eternal damnation.

But what constitutes sexual immorality? Or, to ask the conscientious teens' earnest question, How far is too far? Drawing that line by anatomical restrictions is helpful, but youth needs a comprehensive understanding about the emotional momentum of sensual arousal. It's not merely a matter of where to touch or not touch. It's a matter of understanding just how degrading lust is and how destructive promiscuous sex is. Promiscuity is a way of denying self-worth. To be promiscuous is to say, in effect, "I'm so worthless that I'm willing to let my body be used by different people. I have got to get my kicks through sex instead of through schoolwork, clubs, hobbies, and social encounters."

Emotions and sex were not meant to be separated. Regrettably, the promiscuous person may come to believe that his sex partners feel more emotion than they actually do. (It isn't possible to feel too deeply if one has several partners.) He may see sex as both emotional and physical—even though his relationships are primarily physical. Once the emotional feelings associated with sex are lodged in the consciousness, the powers of memory and suggestion will always be useful tools for Satan.

In an age of self-expression, the chaste young person needs to cultivate the art of self-discipline. If self-control can be mustered for education and athletics, surely the most tempting urges aroused by our sinful society can be overcome. The Lord's moral requirements are reasonable because his concern is mankind's long-term welfare.

As promiscuity tightens its grip on our young, parental responsibility increases. Opposing sex education in public schools isn't enough. Mothers and fathers should inform their children at an early age about the full range of sexual responses. Telling children about the facts of life involves more than explaining the mechanics of sex. Parents should emphasize the spiritual and emotional significance of life's most intimate relationship.

It may be advisable in some cases for a father to tell his daughter the facts of life and a mother to inform her son. Hearing about sex from a parent of the opposite sex can communicate a better understanding of how the other sex approaches intimacy. (In some families this obviously will not be possible because of parental inhibitions.)

Caution and wisdom are necessary when introducing the facts of life. I was approached in a counseling case by a youth pastor who had an affair with a girl in his church. His wife had been raised in the home of a well-known minister, who writes volumes of advice for young people. But, when it came time to tell his own daughter about "the birds and the bees," he commissioned his wife to perform the task. One evening, the mother entered her daughter's bedroom in darkness and abruptly asked, "Do you know how babies are made?" When the girl responded affirmatively, the mother left without saying another word.

The daughter married as a virgin, but her knowledge of sex was limited. Sexual dysfunction developed, causing her husband to look elsewhere for the excitement and emotional fulfillment his wife could not provide. His immoral behavior is inexcusable. This case illustrates, however, that the circumstances under which a person first learns about sexuality profoundly influences the ability to relate in a healthy, uninhibited fashion after getting married.

Several other parental cautions should be noted. If a teenager says "I'm in love," don't mock him by responding, "You're too young to know what love really is." Such derision may drive him into promiscuity to prove he is in love. Also, don't allow fear of your child's sexual involvement force you to suggest birth control devices to avoid possible pregnancy.

If your church does not have a sex education program as part of its instructional curriculum, you may wish to recommend it. It's ironic that parents who usually oppose sex education by claiming, "That sort of thing belongs in the home," do nothing about it in the home and ignore the subject altogether.

21
Teenage Pregnancy

Faye Dunaway and Jessica Lange did it. Then Farrah
Fawcett did it. Many movie stars and Hollywood
personalities have decided that motherhood and
marriage need not go together.

Having children out of wedlock has become
fashionable. Those who have done so include Monaco's
Princess Caroline, rock star Grace Slick, actresses Ursula
Andress and Nastassja Kinski, and basketball star Kareem
Abdul-Jabbar. Rock-and-rollers have been doing it for
years, including Sting of the Police and Mick Jagger of
the Rolling Stones.

Melody Thomas of the soap opera, "The Young and
Restless," proved her sexpot screen character was no
mere image. Of her illegitimate pregnancy she says,
"Judging from the reaction around the country, it's not
something that should be kept in the closet." What will
she say when the baby is old enough to ask questions?
"I'll explain that she was born out of wedlock," Melody
says. "I don't anticipate any problems when that occurs.
Times have changed so much."[1]

They certainly have. In New York City, unmarried

women give birth to more than one out of every three children.[2] According to the latest statistics, less than 50 percent of American female college students are virgins, and 74 percent of engaged couples of college age engage in intercourse.[3] As more babies are brought into the world without legitimate birth certificates, motherhood becomes less affiliated with matrimony. Shotgun weddings are out of style, and fewer marriages are forced on unwed mothers to save family reputations.

Consider the following case study. Arlene Pfeiffer gets up at six o'clock every morning to start the day with her five-month-old daughter, Jessica. She prepares her own breakfast along with Jessica's milk bottles. Sometimes she's wide awake and ready to start a busy day. At other times, she's bleary-eyed from Jessica's all-night crying episodes. Like any mother, Arlene loves her daughter and hates leaving her with someone else during the day. At seventeen, Arlene is in high school.

Arlene Pfeiffer has been the focus of national publicity regarding a discrimination suit she filed recently. When she became illegitimately pregnant, Arlene was kicked out of her high school National Honor Society. School officials explained that candidates for the organization are evaluated on the basis of scholarship, leadership, and character, and the last attribute necessitated her dismissal. In response, Arlene filed a sex discrimination suit.[4]

In a similar case filed by another member of the National Honor Society, unwed mother Loretta Ward found a favorable verdict. U.S. District Judge J. Waldo Akerman ruled that her dismissal from the Society violated federal civil rights laws and equal protection guarantees of the Constitution.[5] Arlene and Loretta are but two unwed mothers who chose to keep their babies rather than aborting them or putting them up for adoption.

Since World War II, the number of children born out of wedlock has doubled. The stigma of illegitimacy is fading fast in America. Single mothers are no longer seen as sinful scarlet women. Many young mothers forsake marriage and keep the consequences of their conduct. Some high schools have established special programs for unwed teenage mothers.

Mental health authorities are concerned that single motherhood creates an unhealthy dependence between mother and child. In some cases, this mutual dependency is fostered by feminists wanting babies for selfish reasons, even bearing them out of wedlock, asking a man to father a child so they can participate in life's procreative processes.

Not all social experts believe it's bad that unwed mothers keep their children. Martha Kirkpatrick, a Los Angeles psychiatrist, studied thirty children of single mothers and says there is no reason to fear that such children will suffer sex-role confusion.[6] Unwed mothers, however, should address the question of the biological father's identity. Ignoring that issue can confuse the child about life's origins and create emotional distress as the child observes his peers with two parents.

The social tragedy of mothers keeping their children is demonstrated by the growing market of bartered babies. South Carolina has the most liberal adoption laws in the country, permitting people to run classified ads in order to buy babies. Family court judge Mendell Rivers, Jr., of Charleston says, "Even if baby-selling does exist, what's so horrible about that? If the child is going to a home with good parents who can give it all the love and security it will ever need, why should we care if the parents paid $50,000 for the privilege? The child is happy, the parents are happy, so what is the harm?"[7]

Unwed mothers are targets for those who traffic in the exchange of human life. There is a new breed of "ambulance chasers" called "bassinet hounds." They pursue unwed mothers all the way to the delivery room in some cases and talk the frightened young lady into relinquishing her baby for a tidy sum. They prey on the frustrations of childless couples and the economically vulnerable unwed mother.

Some see baby-selling as a victimless crime, which allows an unwed mother to have her baby and experience the joy of childbirth while bringing happiness to couples longing for the love of an infant. One Los Angeles entrepreneur, Ronald Silverton, even planned to set up a cottage industry in the Caribbean. There, pregnant girls who answered his ads would live in comfort during pregnancy, being promised that the baby would be turned over to prospective parents willing to pay ten thousand dollars each. The scheme was stopped only after a resourceful district attorney dug up a 1901 antislavery statute and applied it to Silverton's plans.

As potential adoptive parents know, there are fewer babies available legitimately. Today, 96 percent of all unwed teenage mothers keep their babies.[8] Believing they are being discriminated against, the fathers have retaliated by forming an organization called the Free Men. Free Men protests the mothers' complete control over the child they fathered, control that extends to granting or denying visitation rights. Organizers of Free Men contend they, too, have rights, and a pregnant girl who refuses marriage should allow the biological father access to his child.[9]

Social and economic questions are raised by this trend of unwed mothers keeping their children. Taxpayers are being asked to provide increasing welfare support for single-parent family units. Some see this as a subsidy of illegitimacy that encourages immorality. Others accuse unwed mothers of selfishness, being financially and emotionally incapable of looking after a child. Opponents of unwed motherhood say it would be better to place the baby in a traditional family.

The strain on an unwed mother is great. She is concerned about holding down a job, providing adequate day care, and wishing someone else were there to share the joy of parenting. When the baby cries all night and responsibilities await the next day, she wonders if it was worth it. The bonding experience, however, can knit mother and child together in a fulfilling relationship. Still, it must be admitted that teens make inadequate parents, expecially since those who conceive out of wedlock are, mentally, mere children themselves.

What can concerned Christians do about unwed teens having babies? First, parents can instill in their children a healthy attitude toward the body and sex. Parents should make it clear that sex is to be enjoyed freely within marriage, but not outside of the marital bond. Second, if one's son or daughter is involved in a pregnancy, insist that he or she take responsibility for the action. This rules out abortion, which makes the innocent unborn child take the rap for the carelessness and selfishness of its two unwed parents. As mentioned above, shotgun weddings are out of style, a fact we should probably welcome, since teenage marriages have little chance of success. Probably the best alternative is to put the child up for adoption. Don't encourage the mother to follow the lead of celebrity women who brazenly bear children out of wedlock. Such women have the financial resources that teen mothers lack. And while these women have the material means to rear a child, their motives for doing so are questionable. A child needs two parents, not one.

Above all else, be supportive. You can let your son or daughter know that the conception was irresponsible and immoral, but now that new life has begun, condemnation won't solve the problem. Work constructively with both parents (assuming the father is known, and available) to do what is beneficial for the unborn. Emphasize God's grace and our human capacity to accept his forgiveness, also forgiving ourselves.

RECOMMENDED READING BIBLIOGRAPHY

Roggow, Linda, and Caroline Owens. *Handbook for Pregnant Teenagers*. Grand Rapids: Zondervan, 1984.

22

Teenage Runaways

Deborah's father lost his job. He wasn't exactly a model single parent to begin with, and unemployment made things worse. At first he didn't talk. Then he started knocking Deborah around. One night he brought home a friend. Both were drunk. They forced Deborah to lie on the floor and have sex. That's when she ran away.

All alone in New York's Times Square, she met a man who offered her a place to stay in exchange for her body. Soon he was hiring her out to other men. Sixteen today, Deborah says she tries to turn a trick at least five times a night. She charges extra if a guy includes his wife or wants to take pictures. Deborah misses her family but says she'll never go back home. Prostitution is her life.[1]

More than a half-million teenagers like Deborah leave home each year to escape the tensions of marital problems, drug- or alcohol-dependent parents, and school difficulties.[2] Ninety percent of runaways return within forty eight hours.[3] Fifty thousand never go back.[4] Like Deborah, most turn to prostitution as a means of support. America has one million teenage prostitutes fourteen years of age or younger.[5] Most are runaways. Every twelve months five thousand teenagers are buried. They die or are killed, and no one claims their bodies.

Those who counsel teenage runaways say that only 10 percent qualify as spoiled brats, rebels without a cause who leave out of spite or boredom.[6] Half of the runaways are kicked out by parents who think they can no longer cope. In some cases, parents actually dump their children at local shelters.

Other runaways fit the Huck Finn stereotype: teenagers in search of adventure, Hansels and Gretels no longer welcome at home in an age of disposable diapers and throwaway pop cans. Many runaways are disposable children, too young to be on their own and too burdened to bear the innocence of childhood.

Counselors often hear runaways say of their parents, "I love them, but I don't like them." What do they mean? The natural human instinct of love is undeniable. But after years of being told (with words or with actions) by their parents, "I hate you! Get out!" they believe the demand has to be fulfilled.

The cost of runaways is enormous. One hundred sixty-six federally-funded shelters are maintained at taxpayers' expense.[7] But the cost doesn't end there. Forty percent of runaways are school dropouts who can barely read and become a drain on the resources of society.[8] They fill juvenile halls, detention centers, and welfare rolls. Many support themselves by shoplifting and other illegal activities.

Most runaways turn to prostitution. Its proceeds momentarily fill their pockets, but money from sex stops when youthful innocence disappears. Cruising homosexuals and profiting pimps no longer find them attractive. Society eventually pays the bill for their health services and illegitimate children. It would be cheaper for all if parents of potential runaways said, "I love you. Please stay home."

The fragile condition of modern marriage lends the impression that adults play games with life. Divorce and its repercussions leave many teenagers with adultlike freedoms and childlike feelings. It's little wonder they rebel by running away, as if crying, "Help me! I need stability in my life." At a time when strong role models are crucial, teenagers find in their parents a narcissistic "me first" attitude.

If you are a parent of a teen who seems unhappy at home, the best advice is this: Express love, and show that your own life is not governed by selfishness. If you are counseling a potential runaway, remind him that the unpleasantness of home may be far better—and at least more predictable—than life on the street.

23

Throwaway Children

With his light brown hair and sprinkling of freckles, Roger Lindsey looks like a typical fifteen-year-old. He's not. Roger's father kicked him out of his Portland, Oregon, home two years ago. Today he services male homosexual clients for $30 to $250, depending on particular sexual requests. Roger is a "chicken," the object of homosexual "chicken hawks" who cruise Sunset Boulevard. ("Chicken hawks" are gays who seek out extremely young sex partners.) To cope with his avocation, Roger first requests that a customer give him enough money to buy drugs so he can forget what he's doing.[1]

Roger Lindsey is one of an estimated 300,000 throwaways, children nobody wants. He says, "If only people would get the message that having children is serious business and that people who want to become parents have to give lots of love. If they did, there wouldn't be throwaways like me."[2]

A *U.S. News and World Report* article about throwaway children detailed the account of several youngsters who were booted out by their parents.[3] Jim refused to obey his father until the elder could no longer tolerate it and told Jim to leave. Brenda's father molested her, then forced her out when she resisted. Sammy's mother committed suicide, and he was raised by his older brother, who finally decided he didn't want the responsibility. Barb was the child of alcoholic parents who split up and didn't want her as part of their separate lives. Jack was gay, and after confessing his homosexual activity, his parents demanded, "Get straight or get out."

What makes parents turn out their own offspring? Why would a mother or father force a child to hit the streets where he is likely to end up in prostitution or drug dealing? In some cases, throwaway children come from broken homes where neither parent wants custody. A frustrated teenager may turn to sex or drugs as he watches his parents' marriage deteriorate. The parents usually react by saying, "After everything I've done for you, look what you're doing to me now. I can't take it any more. Get out!"

The growing incidence of incest and child abuse generates throwaways. A recent federal study showed that 20 percent to 40 percent of runaway kids had been physically assaulted, and 8 percent had been sexually molested.[4] One girl complained that her stepfather was fondling her. When the girl's mother was informed, she sided with the new husband and told her daughter to leave. In Boston, a study at a runaway counseling center showed that 54 percent had been abused until they were forced to leave.[5]

In 2 Corinthians 12:14, Paul tells us, "Children don't pay for their father's and mother's food—it's the other way around" (TLB). Paul is addressing the importance of *spiritual* children caring for those who led them to Christ, but his message applies to all parental responsibility. The Bible clearly affirms that mothers and fathers must look after their offspring and provide life's necessities.

Dr. James Gordon, a psychiatrist at Georgetown University School of Medicine in Washington, has studied the phenomenon of throwaways and declares, "Many of them were involved in long-term conflicts with their parents, and they were given subtle but strong messages saying, 'We don't want you interfering with our life.'"[6]

Materialistic parents are less willing to invest time and energy in their children. Today's instant society makes parents feel children ought to respond more quickly to their direction. Frustrated when they don't, they sometimes boot kids out the door.

Increasing divorce is turning many children into throwaways. When a disintegrating marriage is pushed to the breaking point, children sometimes get shoved aside. Statistics show that 30 percent to 35 percent of America's runaways left because of marital conflict in the home.[7] Remarriage can also create throwaways. One social service representative says, "When there's reconstitution of a family, when a mother or father takes on a new spouse, the youth often fall through the cracks."

In the animal kingdom a mother will die for her young, fighting off a predator or offering herself in exchange. The bondage of sin can make humans worse than animals. Spiritual indifference can cause mothers and fathers to forsake their natural God-given parental instincts. By throwing away their own children, parents admit their spiritual neglect by removing the evidence. Such behavior has no place in a Christian home.

In fairness to parents, it must be said that some children are thrown out of the home for legitimate reasons. Some parents, having tried every possible solution, conclude that the presence of a child in their home is making life unlivable for other members of the household. While parents can often be blamed for their children's rebelliousness, they are not always at fault. A rebellious youth, especially one whose association with questionable peers causes constant difficulties, may have to leave, at least temporarily. There comes a point when total disregard for parental authority and lack of concern for the welfare of the home becomes unbearable. In such cases, the children can hardly be called throwaways. Needless to say, loving parents will cautiously make every effort to integrate such a rebellious youth into the family again, if he is repentant.

24

Teenage Suicide

"Is there any way out of life?"

The question was posed by James Stalley, an Arlington, Texas, high school senior. Before his teacher could respond, a classmate jokingly replied, "Well, you could kill yourself." Everyone chuckled.

Then, James Stalley stepped onto the stage of a drama classroom, placed a chair in the center, and methodically set a stool in front of the chair. Taking a shotgun from a briefcase, he smiled, put the .410 gauge sawed-off shotgun to his right temple and fired a single shot. A classmate observed later, "We thought it was fake. We just couldn't figure out where he got all the stage blood."[1] It wasn't stage blood.

Each year 6,000 teenagers kill themselves.[2] Another 600,000 try but fail.[3] Among those aged fifteen to nineteen, suicide is the leading cause of death after traffic accidents—and many traffic accidents are suspected suicides.[4]

A recent survey conducted by *Teenage* magazine showed that one out of six youths had attempted suicide. Fifty percent said they had thought seriously about it.

Some mention should be made here of autoerotic asphyxiation, which may be the cause of as many as a thousand deaths annually. Accompanied by pornography and/or sexual devices, a youngster ties a piece of rope to his neck and jumps off a chair, tightening the noose. As the oxygen supply diminishes, an altered state of consciousness induces sexual pleasure. Masturbation usually accompanies the procedure. A knife to cut the rope is nearby, but in many cases unconsciousness occurs before the teen can reach the knife. Death ensues in minutes. Many of these deaths are accidents, but many are probably planned as suicides, and certainly the whole bizarre practice is, as the teens who do it are well aware, a flirt with death.

Alfred Dell Bello, the former New York lieutenant governor who served on the National Committee on Youth Suicide Prevention, estimates the toll to be even higher, with as many as 180,000 teenagers a year committing suicide.[5] Whatever the correct statistics, the suicide rate among youth climbed 41 percent in the last decade.[6]

Why? Some blame the pressures of drug and alcohol abuse, free sex, fragmented families, and fewer limitations on adolescent behavior. Television tells our youth that every problem has a solution, the solution is immediately accessible (a pill for every ill), and some mechanism can resolve every crisis be it a gun or helicopter. Teens have grown up with the notion that there is always an "out."

Rock-and-roll music also contributes to the problem. Dr. Robert Litman, head of the Suicide Prevention Center in Los Angeles, points out that 75 percent of popular songs are about the rejection of love, a contributing factor of suicide.[7] A teen suffering from a broken romance will hardly get inspiring messages from the local rock station. A few years ago, the heavy metal group Blue Oyster Cult sang, "Don't fear the reaper." An album by the rock group W.A.S.P. (which stands for "We Are Sexual Perverts") contains a song entitled "The Torture Never Stops," which some consider a thinly veiled reference to teenage suicide.

Marital conflict in the home is a major suicidal influence. A profile of adolescent suicide-prone victims reveals these interesting insights: 84 percent have a stepparent; 72 percent have at least one parent absent; 52 percent say the precipitating events that led to an attempted suicide were related to marital problems of the parents.[8]

Parents should watch for these warning signs:

1. *Verbal*—It's a myth that people who talk about committing suicide never do it. Statements like, "I wish I had never been born" could be distress signals. Seventy-five percent of those who commit suicide talked about it in the past.
2. *Behavioral*—Changes in eating or sleeping habits may be signs of trouble. A teenager contemplating suicide may give away prized possessions or take risks like driving recklessly. Teachers should be alert for a drop in performance at school.
3. *Situational*—Suicide sometimes is attempted after the loss of a friend or parent, or after the breakup of a romance. A drop in self-esteem brought on by failures at school or other factors can trigger suicidal impulses.

If your child confides that he is thinking about ending his life, take him seriously. Don't respond with comments like, "Wait until you grow up and see what problems really are." The anguish he's facing right then is the most devastating dilemma of his life. To make light of it only complicates his inability to cope.

If there are guns or pills in the home that could be used as devices of death, put them away or get rid of them. Remember, 80 percent of people who successfully commit suicide have made one or more previous attempts.

Remind your teenager who has thought about suicide that pressure at school, problems in the home, or preoccupied parents don't have to push him over the edge. There is light at the end of the tunnel. The black night of depression won't last forever. Ecclesiastes 11:9

speaks directly to teens: "Be happy, young man, while you are young" (NIV).

Teens need to be reminded that death is irrevocable. If a person kills himself, he leaves behind innocent, heartbroken victims of his self-induced death. He selfishly bequeaths untold suffering to them. For the rest of their lives, they will agonize about what they could have done to avert the tragedy.

Ending one's emotional pain only dumps the grief on the broken shoulders of family survivors. Before ending it all, a person owes those he loves one final effort to deal rationally with his despair. Consider the words of Psalm 30:5: "Weeping may remain for a night, but rejoicing comes in the morning" (NIV).

A friend, a suicide hotline counselor, a pastor or teacher can help a teen view more objectively his sense of hopelessness. Such persons can help him see that the self-murder he contemplates is not an expression of dignity, but an abject failure of the will to survive. Even misery can create long-term benefits if a person develops coping mechanisms that build character from adversity.

25

Empty Nest

"Free at last, God almighty, free at last!"

Martin Luther King, Jr., said it, but so have many parents whose children have left home. They have saved or received enough in benefits to retire early and are known as empty nesters. Their children are gone, and now they have time and money to spend. Their dilemma is what to do with these new-found liberties. They may perceive themselves as pitiful parents with vacated bedrooms and empty chairs at the dinner table.

Opinions of social experts and psychologists are divided as to whether the empty nest is a time of boredom or burgeoning opportunity. Dr. Bertram J. Cohler, Ph.D. at the University of Colorado, claims the "empty nest blues" is a myth. In fact, says Cohler, most parents feel *increased* morale and satisfaction with both their marriages and their children when the kids leave home.[1] But researchers at the University of Minnesota in Minneapolis revealed different conclusions through interviews with 169 couples whose sons or daughters were college freshmen. Fathers said the change caused more stress.[2]

Probably both sets of findings are correct. Some families enjoy the new situation while others don't. Most, however, have trouble coping with it. By middle age, some fathers are beyond the demands of early career-building years. Finally, they have more time to spend with their children. Then, just as they have time, the kids leave home. The result is a depressed dad. On the other hand, many mothers tend to see the empty nest as a period of life heralding less stress. If nothing else, work around the house is reduced because the kids are gone.

Barbara Highland, who has written a book about the empty nest, says the syndrome can bring anger and loneliness. Of her own empty nest experience she writes, "I felt abandoned. Women have to learn how to redirect their lives and let their children move on to new things. This is a hard lesson for lots of women to learn."[3]

Ms. Highland describes the empty nest as similar to the situation facing a retired corporate executive. Empty nesters have centered their lives around their children and can't bear being without them. Feelings of abandonment and resentment sometimes follow the departure of children. Some parents become so depressed they weep, wishing those little feet were once again stomping down the hallways. Christian parents sometimes retreat into a state of fearfulness, worried that years of spiritual training will produce disappointment once the offspring faces life on his own.

But in some cases, empty nests are filling up again. Increasingly, parents are being asked to rescue young adults pressured with problems ranging from divorce and drug abuse to increased housing costs and rising unemployment. Parental compassion can wear thin when their offspring brings back a baby long after cribs and diapers had been relegated to the past. (On the other hand, the parents may enjoy feeling needed again.)

When drug abuse or alcoholism propels grown children back to the doorstep, the result can be explosive. Mom and Dad are ready to retire and spend winters in Tucson, but suddenly they are saddled with the burden of an adult enslaved to addictions. Few parents possess the ability to take a firm stand, saying, "When you left you were on your own. Don't come running back to us."

Some children return to the nest to escape hardships for which they were inadequately prepared. They retreat to the womb of parental protection. The parent in this situation should avoid becoming a cushion for the inability of his offspring to cope with reality. He should show compassion while at the same time encouraging independence and a return to the "real world" outside the home.

Is the parent's responsibility for a child finished when the child leaves home? The father of the prodigal son invited his wayward child back to the nest. That attitude should influence Christian parents who have a repentant child who wants to start life over again. The returning child, however, should be told that he must respect household disciplines and responsibilities.

The return of children to the nest can be coupled with taking in elderly parents. Sociologists have coined a new phrase—"The sandwich generation"—referring to those in the middle years who must lend a hand to aging parents as well as adult children. Only about 5 percent of the elderly live in nursing homes.[4] Most live with their families. If that situation is coupled with a son or daughter having returned home with a child after divorce, the "sandwich" can turn into something less than a delectable morsel. The situation is not unbearable, however. It is helpful to remember that the nuclear family—father, mother, and children—living under one roof is not a biblical mandate, nor has it been the norm throughout human history. Extended families—more than two generations—living in one house are workable, and the situation can even be rewarding as generations learn from each other.

If you expect to have an empty nest in the near future, determine when your child walks out the door that he is gone for good, barring tragic intervention. When it is time for children to go, don't devise ingenious schemes to hold on. Look forward to filling your empty nest with new opportunities for Christian service, free from the restrictions of parental responsibilities.

26

Mid-Life Crisis

"I'm thirty-three and I'm longing for someone. I want to have a mad affair. I want the heat and the rush and the fire of new flesh, but I also want my marriage. Does anybody know what's wrong with me?"

That's the question Susan Squire posed in a *Redbook* magazine article regarding the female mid-life crisis. Miss Squire points out that some women turn to abuse of food, alcohol, or drugs as means of forgetting the frightening emotions of mid-life. She concludes, "The more central your looks have been to your self-esteem throughout life, the likelier you'll seek sex outside of marriage as a way to ward off the aging process. Some women, desiring to be dominated by a more powerful male, may seek out an affair with a man whose status of life supersedes that of her husband. Others look for a younger man who will convince them that no matter what the body clock says, they've still got it."[1]

A woman in mid-life crisis fights the urge to chuck it all and hop on a plane to anywhere. She fantasizes about falling into the arms of someone who appreciates her as a woman, not just a married mistress.

Dr. Pepper Schwartz, a sociologist at the University of

Washington, studied twelve thousand men and women facing identity crises. Dr. Schwartz concluded that many extramarital affairs are triggered by the feeling "you're in the last stages of being able to walk down the street and turn men's heads."[2]

Men in mid-life crisis face similar situations. At a time in life when more maturity is expected, they act like adolescents, playing out bizarre teenage roles of rebellion. Feeling trapped because their futures no longer hold the promise of riches and fame, mid-life men become filled with guilt and frustration. The result may be an adulterous affair to assuage nagging doubts of adequacy.

A hundred years ago, no one paid any attention to mid-life crisis. Even at the turn of this century, only ten percent of the population was middle-aged. The total portion of the population of mid-life, however, increased 200 percent in this century. Many mid-life men and women ask themselves, "I've achieved my goals, but am I fulfilled?" In a frantic quest for fulfillment, middle-aged men and women may adopt behavior patterns more appropriate for adolescents than for adults.

The Apostle Paul said, "When I was a child, I reasoned like a child. When I became a man, I put childish ways behind me " (1 Cor. 13:11, NIV). Conversely, the man in mid-life crisis reverts to postpubescent longings. He may buy a new wardrobe and turn into a shirt-unbuttoned-to-the-navel, draped-in-gold-chains absurdity. He may even have his face lifted, his hair transplanted, his chin tucked, and his gray locks dyed. He laments a stale marriage and a nagging wife. His female counterpart becomes prey for every advertiser offering renewed youth via skin creams, quick weight-reduction schemes, designer clothing, and hair care products. Like the male, she seeks to conceal every external indication of aging.

How does the Christian man or woman face mid-life crisis? Is there a way to cope with bodily change, deal with sexual temptation, and revitalize a stale marriage? Can mid-life marriage avoid demolition on the rocks of insecurity?

The man in mid-life crisis must learn to deal with unrealized dreams of what he had hoped to become. He must accept who he is and avoid sexual fantasy as if he were an adolescent or a mid-twenties macho male. He must avoid self-pitying depression and the search for unreasonable affirmations of his masculinity. Coping with male menopause means being a strong father to adolescent children as well as advisor to aging parents. The mid-life male who faces life with renewed vigor and purpose can make these years satisfying and productive. The crisis is easier to face with a supportive wife who affirms his masculinity and sexuality.

Women in mid-life crisis should face their biological boundaries, knowing their sexuality should be enhanced, not diminished. Passing forty and encountering unovulating ovaries isn't the end of passionate love. The woman in mid-life can set her hormones aglow with renewed affection for her husband. Her life's flame can be rekindled with desire to shape the lives of younger women, compelling them to be diligent followers of Christ.

RECOMMENDED READING BIBLIOGRAPHY

Conway, Jim. *Men in Mid-Life Crisis.* Elgin, Ill.: David C. Cook, 1978.

Conway, Jim and Sally. *Women in Mid-Life Crisis.* Wheaton, Ill.: Tyndale, 1978.

Conway, Sally. *You and Your Husband in Mid-Life Crisis.* Elgin, Ill.: David C. Cook, 1980.

COUNSELING/INFORMATION SOURCES

Mid-Life Dimensions
P. O. Box 3030
Fullerton, CA 92634
(714) 680-3660

FAMILY PERILS
AND DIVORCE

27

Adultery

If you want to cheat on your husband, Cynthia Silverman, a forty-three-year-old psychologist, has a workshop just for you. She teaches wives how to have extramarital affairs. To justify her actions, Silverman says, "The frequency of women having affairs is now almost as great as that of men. The goal of my workshop is to educate women to make a meaningful decision so they don't hurt themselves or their families."[1]

Silverman offers practical advice on covering absences with excuses a husband can't check out and resisting the temptation to confess what is happening. The workshop advises adulterous wives to have affairs with married men because they are more likely to be discreet about adultery.

Silverman has plenty of clients willing to pay $7.50 for two hours of instruction per week. Why? *Playboy* did a survey and found that 34 percent of its married female readers have had affairs.[2] In a similar *Cosmopolitan* survey the percentage was 69 percent.[3] Sociologist Ira Reiss of the University of Minnesota studied adulterous women and came to the conclusion that wives today "see affairs as an option, not as being unfaithful."[4] A *Time* magazine article regarding infidelity declared, "Marriage has become a breakable alliance between self-seeking individuals."[5]

A woman interviewed on infidelity said, "I do everything else for my husband and children. I do this for me."[6] Adulterous women may be seeking relief from boredom. One woman described her affair with this analogy: "My lover was Beethoven, while my husband was television and beer." British researcher Shirley Eskapa, author of *Wife Versus Mistress,* discovered that some women are so absorbed in their careers they would rather have a relationship with a man who is married. That arrangement ensures that career advancements are not threatened by a man looking for a wife.[7]

Not all women want an affair. Some are too busy coping with adulterous husbands. For women whose husbands are having an affair, Gigi and Ron Moers operate a business with the slogan "Women helping other women." They help suspicious wives find out if their husbands are two-timing them. The Moer's detective agency, Wives Infidelity Service, offers a $75, five-week course entitled "How to Be Your Own Investigator." Gigi says, "If he usually smells like old shoes and dresses like a dock worker and suddenly he's all Jordache jeans and Old Spice, you're on to something."[8]

The Moers tell clients to watch for unexpected phone calls and abrupt changes in spending patterns. They show wives how to ask a hotel manager for his register, and how to wear a wig and walk past one's husband and mistress on their way to a liaison. Other instructions offered in the course include: snooping in an unnoticed car borrowed from a girlfriend; operating recording devices and cameras with telescopic lenses; and bursting in on an errant husband while he's with his lady friend.

Statistics indicate the Moers have plenty of potential clients. Depending on whose survey you believe, anywhere from one-half to three-fourths of all married men indulge in extra-marital affairs. A study by a Florida State University researcher indicated that 43 percent of all men who commit adultery have had from three to nine partners.[9]

The old double standard still prevails in American society. In the opinion of many, men are entitled to be married and enjoy forbidden fruit on the side. (Ironically, research reported in a 1983 *Psychology Today* survey found that 75 percent of male respondents prefer sex in the context of a stable love relationship in marriage.[10])

How does a good marriage go wrong? What makes a man or woman look elsewhere for sexual satisfaction? Immorality doesn't grow in a vacuum. A good marriage is based on communication, compatibility, and commitment. An affair is often a desperate plea for help, not just a sign of sensuousness. When adultery occurs, one of the marriage partners usually has failed to meet a need or displayed emotional immaturity regarding adult responsibilities.

Unfaithfulness may be the result of a deliberate attempt to taste forbidden fruit. It also occurs when one of the spouses expects marriage to deliver what it can't provide. The man who wants a mother to attend his every need and the woman who wants a father to respond to her every whim are candidates for adultery. No mate can meet such unreasonable demands.

An alarming number of men—including many Christians—rationalize affairs while appearing to maintain family responsibilities. In some cases, men malfunction in the marital bed and compensate by abandoning all inhibition in their extramarital involvement.

A study at Illinois State University concluded the biggest reason men have affairs is to boost self-esteem.[11] In addition, some men can't prevent an immediate reaction to an attractive woman from distorting into sinful fantasy. Proverbs 22:3 says, "A prudent man forseeth the evil, and hideth himself: but the simple pass on, and are punished." It is wise to consider sexual sin as a looming possibility and to remove easy temptation.

If you are the offended victim of an adulterous spouse, be careful about shutting off your mate sexually and confronting him or her with evidence. It probably won't help. Let life continue normally for awhile. Give yourself a chance to cool off and objectively consider what is happening. Don't harangue your unfaithful spouse with questions like, "Where do you go with him (her) on dates? How many times have you been together? Don't you care about the kids?"

Adultery is a state of emotional disorientation. Don't expect logical answers from a mate living in spiritual rebellion. Beware the temptation to repay evil with evil. Giving your adulterous spouse a taste of his (or her) own medicine will only insure the demise of your marriage. Focus on the good experiences of your relationship. Concentrate on what can be done to resurrect what caused you to first love each other.

If you are tempted to commit adultery, remember the words of Jesus in Matthew 5:28: "But I tell you that anyone who looks at a woman lustfully has already committed adultery with her in his heart" (NIV). Don't let Satan tempt you with thoughts about unmet needs, or fantasize about that other person satisfying you emotionally and physically. Instead, persistently refuse to give up on your marriage. Adultery is best combated by the proof of faithful vows steadfastly obeyed.

RECOMMENDED READING BIBLIOGRAPHY

Petersen, J. Allan. *The Myth of the Greener Grass.* Wheaton, Ill.: Tyndale, 1983.

28

Incest

She was his sister, but it made no difference. He desired her sexually. An equally evil man, his cousin, devised a plan. "Pretend you're ill," he suggested. "When she comes to bring you food, grab her as she enters your bedroom."

It seemed like a good idea. After all, he was convinced he truly loved his sister. The plot worked. But the sister was less than willing. She pleaded with her brother to stop.

"Don't do this!" she cried. "You'll shame me. What you're doing is evil."

Her brother wouldn't listen. When she refused to give in, he forced her to yield. He was puzzled afterwards by his emotions. For months he had lustfully craved his sister. Now he hated her. He threw her out of his bedroom and locked the door. Humiliated, shamed, and fearful, she fled.

Her older brother suspected what had happened and quizzed her. When she admitted it, he determined to avenge her honor. When the time was right, two years later, he murdered his brother.

It sounds like a soap opera plot, and it's as contemporary as a psychotherapist's patient list. This story occurred nearly three thousand years ago. The incestuous brother was Amnon. His sister was Tamar. The avenging brother was Absalom. All of them were children of King David.

This account of incest in 2 Samuel 13 is not the only instance this familial moral crime is mentioned in the Bible. Abraham married his half-sister. His brother Nahor married the daughter of his brother Haran (Genesis 11:29). In Genesis 35, Reuben seduced his father's concubine. Amram married his aunt (Exodus 6:20), and Moses and Aaron were born of the union. But once God called forth his chosen people and communicated his moral law in written form, he made plain his hatred of incestuous relationships.

Leviticus 18 contains a long list of shalt-nots governing sexual conduct, prohibitions that end in verse 29 with God commanding the death penalty for violators. Specifically, God forbade intercourse with the following familial persons: father, mother, father's wife, sister, stepdaughter or stepson, niece or nephew, aunt or uncle, brother or daughter-in-law, and a brother's wife.

In contrast to God's Word, Wardell Pomeroy, coauthor of the original Kinsey report, says, "Incest can sometimes be beneficial to children."[1] Sociologist Floyd Martinson of Minnesota's Gustavus Adolphus College advises against jail sentences for incestuous parents. He says, "Intimate human relations are important and precious. I'd like to see as few restrictions placed on them as possible."[2]

Psychologist Douglas Powell of the Harvard Health Services says, "I have not seen anyone harmed by this so long as it occurs in a relationship with somebody who really cares about the child."[3]

The book *Incest: A Family Pattern* by Jean Renvoize points out that in every society investigated by anthropologists a taboo exists against incest. A few cultures have allowed members to commit incest for certain reasons, as when ancient Egypt permitted brother/sister marriages to preserve the purity of dynasties. But after Christianity swept the world, incestuous marriages among all people were forbidden.[4] Incest has continued, but only under the veil of secrecy. In contrast to the psychologists quoted above, most persons still see incest as immoral. And many have spoken of its devastating effects.

Katherine Brady, author of the biography *Father's Days*, writes regarding her nightmare of incest, "I didn't understand what the word incest meant, although I had a sexual relationship with my father for ten years. I thought I was the only person who'd ever had such an experience. It was something that had happened in the past and remained there finished. I've learned that by looking at it, releasing it from the prison of the past, letting it rise to the present, I could at least leave it behind." Ms. Brady admits turning to lesbianism as a means of coping with her father's behavior.[5]

Ms. Brady's experience is not isolated. Dr. Finkelhor of the Family Violence Research Program at the University of New Hampshire says between 15 percent and 34 percent of all girls and between 3 percent and 9 percent of all boys are victims of incestuous sexual abuse.[6] A San Francisco study of 930 randomly selected women revealed that 28 percent of females will be sexually abused before age fourteen, and 38 percent will have at least one such experience before age eighteen.[7] Unfortunately, most victims are never known. A 1981 survey of sexually abused college students revealed that 63 percent of the girls and 73 percent of the boys told no one what happened.[8]

Whether brother assaults sister, two brothers or two sisters indulge prepubescent curiosity, mother seduces son, or father violates daughter, incest is an all too frequent crime. According to the Kinsey report, one of four girls suffers sexual abuse before age eighteen.[9] Three-fourths of the time she knows her abuser, and 34 percent of the time it's a member of her own household. A study of two hundred prostitutes revealed that approximately 30 percent were incestuously assaulted.[10] An analysis of drug treatment patients uncovered the fact that 40 percent of drug-addicted women are victims of incest.[11]

The American Psychological Association estimates that 12 to 15 million Americans have experienced incest in degrees ranging from fondling to intercourse. Eighty-one percent of these victims are twelve years of age or younger. The Harbor View Sexual Assault Center found that only 17 percent of cases of intrafamily abuse consist of a single incident. Another survey revealed 75 percent of runaways fled to escape incestuous abuse.[12]

Sibling incest is estimated to occur five times more frequently than parent-child incest. Incest between father and son is the third most frequent kind of family sexual behavior.[13] Far more common is father-daughter incest.

Society has only begun to face the problem of father-daughter incest. Researchers say that incestuous fathers with bad marriages are often drawn to their daughters. The desire for emotional support or the frustration brought by a frigid wife makes close companionship with a daughter seem like a solution. Once warmness and closeness turn to intercourse or assorted sexual acts, the rationalization begins.

The father may tell himself, "I'm teaching her the facts of life," or "She's a tease and I'm only accommodating her needs." Sin twists the mind until daddy's little girl becomes an in-house mistress. "Don't tell your mother" begins as a request and continues as a threat. Each episode is followed with resolutions of "Never again!" But it does happen again, and the denial goes on.

The frequency of incest should not surprise us. The break-up of the family is a major source of incestuous conduct. Abortion, birth control, and a soaring divorce rate have bred tolerance toward all kinds of sexuality. Many modern households consist of members who came from divorced or separated families. Because they do not share a biological relationship, incest between stepchildren who live as a family without the benefit of bloodlines is increasing. Too often, incest is part of a general pattern of family chaos, which includes violence, alcoholism, neglect, and criminal behavior. The ensuing sexual psychopathology is merely part of an overall morally anarchistic environment.

All of society bears some blame for incest. Child models from five to fifteen are trained to seductively sell blue jeans, underwear, soap, and perfume. We've grown up with the prepubescent packaging of sex by Jodi Foster and Brooke Shields. Why, then, should we be shocked by sexual abuse of children? American culture encourages daily eroticism, declaring that little girls are sexy. Society sows seductiveness, and innocent victims tragically reap the whirlwind of incestuous abuse. But society cannot shoulder all the blame. It is individuals who commit incest, and perpetrators and victims must find constructive ways of coping.

If you are a perpetrator of incest, face the self-centeredness of your perversion. You exploited innocent displays of affection and turned them into self-gratifying encounters designed to bolster your depleted self-worth. If your marital relationship verges on disaster, incest won't hold it together.

"It's better than going to a prostitute," some incestuous fathers argue. Don't believe that lie. And incest is indefensible by any claim that you must satisfy your daughter's sexual needs. Beware that self-disgust creates a compulsion to continue. Don't console yourself if your wife fails to acknowledge what's going on. Her need to protect the family and her own self-esteem can't excuse your conduct.

If you are a victim of incest, you must understand it wasn't your fault. Don't feel incriminated by any pleasure you may have felt. Former victims of incest often say they were torn between poles of fear and satisfaction, tormented with guilt because they sometimes enjoyed it. Some eventually use sex as a tool to get things from their fathers. Incest can also be used to capture the attention of a father who otherwise refuses to notice a daughter.

God can give you the ability to forgive your father for his heinous deeds. Remember, the only thing worse than blaming yourself is hating him. If possible, go to him prayerfully. Confront him with what he did, and extend the forgiveness of Christ.

In most cases, it's advisable to share the trauma of your past with your husband, especially if you experience sexual dysfunction or frigidity as a result. If your husband is unaware of your past, he may think you find him repulsive. Calm his fears of rejection by being honest and open about what you suffered. Then, he can help you cope with the innate fear of men you may have developed.

If your mother knew and refused to act, nothing can be gained by continued resentment toward her. By forgiving everyone concerned and establishing a positive sexual relationship with your husband, you can turn the ashes of incest into the beauty of sexuality God intended.

RECOMMENDED READING BIBLIOGRAPHY
Ricks, Chip. *Carol's Story.* Wheaton, Ill.: Tyndale, 1981.

COUNSELING/INFORMATION SOURCES
Scope Ministries
700 N.E. 63rd St.
Oklahoma City, OK 73105
(405) 843-7778

Parents United
Box 952
San Jose, CA 95108
(408) 280-5055
Secular organization headed by Dr. Henry Giarretto, psychologist.

29

Battered Wives

Actress Dominique Dunne had a promising Hollywood career until John Thomas Sweeney got his hands on her and choked her to death. Sweeney had witnessed his father beating his mother and couldn't shake the trauma. He was obsessively jealous of his paramour.

At the height of a quarrel on August 27, 1982, Sweeney grabbed the budding actress by her thick hair and yanked so violently that handfuls tore out by the roots. Even then, Dunne returned to live with Sweeney until that fateful day when he lunged at her and his hands closed on her throat. Sweeney says he doesn't remember what happened. He only recalls finding himself on top of Dominique with his hands around her neck.[1]

Battered wife syndrome, the silent crime of domestic violence hush-hushed for so many decades, is center stage in the public mind. Several cases of wife-beating have dramatized the horror of such abuse.

In March of 1981, Francine Hughes poured gasoline around her husband's bed and started a fire. As the house burst into flames, she herded the family into an automobile and drove away. She was tried for murder, but the jury returned a verdict of "not quilty by reason of insanity."[2]

In Morgantown, West Virginia, Lorraine Moman grew tired of being bruised and bloodied. When her husband knocked down the front door of her house and charged toward her, she shot him.[3]

In Lakewood, Colorado, Patricia Nordyke shot her husband to death with a rifle. Patricia testified her husband had bloodied her nose and lip and butted his head against her. She grabbed for a gun, and it fired when he fell toward her.[4]

Leslie Ann Meick shot to death her sleeping husband. During their five years of common-law marriage, he had beaten her, branded her, sexually attacked her, and hung her from a makeshift gallows. On the evening of the shooting, Leslie's husband had said, "I'm going to kill you, the children, and myself in the morning."[5]

A New York State attorney general's task force recently heard the testimony of a wife who described her husband throwing boiling water on her, beating her, and slitting her throat with a switchblade.

Family violence is an American epidemic. The statistics are chilling. One-third of all female murder victims are killed by husbands or boyfriends.[6] Each year, 6 million wives are abused by their husbands and approximately four thousand are beaten to death.[7]

Police say they spend a third of their time responding to domestic calls.[8] Such violence is responsible for 40 percent of all police injuries.[9] Twenty-five percent of suicide attempts by women are triggered by battering.[10] In fact, more women are beaten senseless by their husbands than are injured in automobile accidents, rapes, or muggings.[11]

In his book *Behind Closed Doors: Violence in the American Family,* author Richard Geeles says his findings reveal that 15 percent of married couples say one spouse has thrown something at the other sometime in their marriage.[12] Ten percent claim a spouse has used an object for physical abuse.[13] Four percent admit using a gun or knife to threaten a partner.[14] A study by the Justice Department shows that 75 percent of all violence reported between spouses takes place when divorced or separated women become victims of retaliation from rejected husbands.[15]

Why has the American home become a battleground? Social experts who study domestic violence stress that our generation was raised on television violence. Those subjected to such mayhem are likely to see physical battering as a way to resolve conflict.

Murray Straus, Director of the Family Research Laboratory and professor of sociology at the University of Michigan, is a recognized expert on family violence. He believes that abusive family behavior comes from a social philosophy that "the marriage license is a hitting license in a male-dominant household."[16]

America's social attitude desperately needs change. Wife beating bore legal sanction throughout U.S. history, and no law prevented it until 1871. Eighteenth-century wives were considered little more than property. Even though feminism has affected society profoundly, many husbands still see wife abuse as "no big deal." And some women seem to have the attitude that a violent husband is better than no husband.

All Americans must awaken to the dimensions of this tragedy. During the Vietnam conflict between 1967 and 1973, 39,000 soldiers died. During the same period, 17,570 women and children died on the home front from family violence.[17] Now that Vietnam is behind us, it's time to put family violence in front of us. (Unfortunately, the battered wife is not the only family member to suffer these brutal attacks. In 13 percent of wife abuse cases, children have also been assaulted.[18])

While solutions are being sought, bruised victims conceal cheek discoloration with makeup and dread each visit to the hospital emergency room. Too often, battered wives are financially dependent on spouses and silently absorb their punishment. They desperately want to hold their families together and have no confidence that courts or social agencies will protect them.

Is there a solution? The government wants to spend millions to create shelters for battered wives. Conservatives argue these feminist-controlled safe houses will encourage women to end their marriages and sacrifice the family. (The U.S. has three thousand shelters for stray animals and only seven hundred for battered wives.[19])

Is the church doing enough to help battered wives? Too often ministers view marriage with a cursory reference to Ephesians 5, insisting that wives be subject to their husbands in spite of physical abuse. Sadly, erroneous emphasis on biblical submission turns some Christian wives into bloodied and bruised punching bags. Some Christian women unnecessarily submit to family violence because they see themselves as their husbands' saviors. They are driven by a maternal instinct that says the husband will be eternally lost if she packs up and moves out. Sadly, many Christians encourage such wives to stay.

Is this right? Should an abused wife refuse involvement in pornography and subsequent sexual acts, or should she participate at the risk of battered breasts and bruised eyes? In Luke 4:18, Jesus clearly stated he came to "release the oppressed" (NIV). The time is overdue for congregations to offer safe harbor to women who are victims of violence. A portion of the budget could easily be directed toward establishing abuse shelters. Churches should set up temporary sanctuaries for the immediate safety of its more helpless members. Jesus commended such concern in Matthew 25:45 when he declared, "Whatever you did not do for one of the least of these, you did not do for me" (NIV). If evangelical churches don't take the initiative, they concede by default that province of human affairs to the federal government.

You can also do something as an individual. Encourage a battered woman to flee after the first beating. The woman who doesn't leave or seek help passively encourages continued violence. A good woman cannot necessarily change a bad man. This misplaced altruistic motive usually leads to desperate submission from which the only escape may be murder or suicide.

Most battered women were physically violated by their husband-to-be while dating. The man who hits his girlfriend during the courting period will almost certainly bash his wife after he walks down the aisle. Encourage a woman who is dating to ask a prospective mate if his history includes childhood abuse. Eighty percent of abusive partners witnessed the abuse of their own mothers.[20]

Tina Turner, whose song "What's Love Got to Do with It" became a pop hit, says her former husband Ike Turner beat her and threatened to kill her. Is it any wonder she sang with such fervor, "What's love...but a second-hand emotion?" Tina Turner turned to Buddhism and occultic chants to soothe her spirit and escape the horror of her past. Christ is a better place of refuge to escape the savage beast inside a battering husband.

One final word of warning to the battered wife who is reading this chapter: Today's bruises and minor lacerations may be tomorrow's skull fracture and broken back. Alone, you cannot compensate for your husband's low self-esteem and his traumatized memories. Get out. Get help. Your scriptural responsibility to your body as the temple of God's Holy Spirit is greater than any misplaced acquiescence to erroneously defined biblical submission.

RECOMMENDED READING BIBLIOGRAPHY

Della Courte, Betty. *Sheltered from the Storm*. Glendale, Ariz.: Villa Press, 1985.

Green, Holly Wagner. *Turning Hope to Fear*. Nashville: Thomas Nelson, 1984.

Olson, Esther Lee. *No Place to Hide*. Wheaton, Ill.: Tyndale, 1982.

COUNSELING/INFORMATION SOURCES

AMEND (Abusive Men Exploring New Directions)
2205 Forest
Denver, CO 80207
(303) 420-6759
Chapters nationwide.

Coalition for Battered Wives
1500 Massachusetts Ave.
Room 35
Washington, DC

Abusive Partner: An Analysis of Domestic Battering.
Edited by Maria Roy. New York: Van Nostrand Reinhold,
1982. (Lists forty-five organizations in twenty-four states
treating abusive relationships.)

30

Abused Men

"Take it out."

The voice was insistent. The knife at his throat emphasized the urgency of the demand.

"Take it out, I said. If you want to live, you'll do what I say."

The victim reached for his billfold when the voice angrily interrupted, "That's not what I want. Take out your ———."

The attacker was female. What she wanted wasn't money, but sex. Minutes later it was over and the victim, Doug, an advertising executive in Connecticut, had been raped by a woman.[1]

Occurrences of reverse rape have increased dramatically in recent years. Homosexual gang assaults constitute most instances of male rape. One out of every four reported male rapes, however, involves a woman rapist.[2] Considering marital rape, incestuous relationships, and the sexual abuse of younger boys by older women, the number of reverse rapes is astounding. To date, no male rape victim has ever won a court case.

Experts say the rape of a woman is an angry, violent act

not performed for sexual gratification. Likewise, reverse rape is an angry attempt by a woman to hurt and humiliate a man. The aftermath of male rape traumatizes men who think of sex as an act emphasizing masculine control. It can cause many kinds of sexual dysfunction.

Reverse rape is just one aspect of the abused male phenomenon. While the battered wife syndrome is well-publicized, little interest has been shown assaulted men. A study conducted by psychologist Daniel O'Leary of the State University of New York at Stony Brook reveals that women are as likely to assault their future spouses as men are to batter their fiancées. In findings presented to a meeting of behavioral therapists, O'Leary revealed that research on 369 engaged couples showed 37 percent of women had physically assaulted their fiancés at least once. Abusive men generally perpetuate behavior they witnessed in their own families. The O'Leary study shows that women engaging in violence against spouses have an overall pattern of aggression not limited to the marriage.[3]

Though men are more likely than women to hit or threaten their mates with a weapon, female tactics include slapping, pushing, shoving, or kicking. More than half of the participants in the O'Leary study said they had assaulted their fiancés once or twice. In 3 percent of the cases, the violence involved a threat to life. Increasingly, men are enduring slaps and denigration from what they had presumed to be the weaker sex. In an age of feminism, the head of the home too often becomes a punching bag. With their liberated freedom, some females feel freer to kick and punch.

It is not easy for men to speak about traumatizing experiences. Though women may lock such incidents deep in their emotions, they respond to therapy and Christian counsel in a tearful, open manner. Men find such overt displays of sensitivity difficult. If you have been physically assaulted by a woman or homosexually molested, share these frightful experiences with a mature Christian counselor. Face the doubt regarding your sexual identity. You can be a *real* man and confront the unfortunate circumstances of your past. Resolution of these hurtful memories can make you the father and husband you long to be.

RECOMMENDED READING BIBLIOGRAPHY

Getz, Gene. *The Measure of a Man.* Ventura, Cal.: Regal Books, 1974.

Payne, Leanne. *Crisis in Masculinity.* Westchester, Ill.: Crossway, 1985.

31

Impotence

"A disease like cancer makes you feel inadequate, but this makes you feel clumsy and stupid. You simply can't perform as a man. It's driven me to the brink of suicide." So said a victim of impotence.[1]

Literally, impotence means "without power." It represents to a man inability to deal with the most intimate aspect of life. According to estimates, there are at least 10 million impotent men in America; half of them are impotent because of physiological reasons.[2]

Relief from this humiliation has been sought for centuries, and cures range from the exotic to the ridiculous. Until recently, men were told, "It's in your head." Doctors know now that deficiencies in male hormones, hardening of the arteries, injury and nerve damage, and medication side effects can impinge upon male sexual performance. Other causes of impotency include diabetes, sickle-cell anemia, Parkinson's disease, epilepsy, pituitary tumors, kidney or liver failure, prostate cancer, and drugs. Experts believe at least 50 percent of new cases are attributable to marijuana and alcohol usage.[3]

Impotence can terrify the man who wonders if he is homosexual or lacking virility. Wives may wonder if they are poor lovers or simply unattractive. In this erotic age, it's strange that impotence should be a major problem for the American male. Counselors point out that guilt over past promiscuity can cause impotence and can also result from efforts to obscure adulterous relationships. In effect, more sex may actually mean less sex.

The issue of impotence raises questions about mannishness. Psychologists claim the father affirms the sexual identity of a child. Though the mother nurtures the young early in life, the knowledge of separateness of the sexes comes from the father, who affirms femininity in the daughter and models masculinity for the son. Unfortunately, some males never learned from their fathers what it means to be a man, a deficiency that influences sexuality.

In her book *Crisis in Masculinity,* Leanne Payne, a Christian counselor, suggests that some impotent men may have to renounce childhood oaths regarding their fathers. For example, the male child who said, "I'll never grow up to be like my dad," may become impotent as he approaches middle age. The ensuing spiritual oppression causes estrangement between himself and the source of his masculine identity. Forgiving his father will facilitate renewed understanding of true masculinity, solving the psychological root of impotence.

The Christian male must assiduously avoid the temptation to cure impotence by resorting to carnal therapy. One Christian husband used mirrors in his bedroom and experimented with erotic fantasies to overcome impotence. Afterwards he said, "To communicate sexually, I had to pretend I was another man when I made love to my wife." As might be expected, pornographic fantasies were unable to reaffirm his maleness.

Impotent men sometimes think X-rated videos and sexual devices are answers, but pornographic aids sever a person from his true self as he acts out a role. That other personality may experience heightened sexual responses, but sexual dysfunction of the real person remains unresolved. Adulterous affairs can't overcome impotence. Extramarital liaisons probably make the condition worse. Engaging in sex beyond marriage to induce erotic stimulation only buries the real problem, further complicating sexual communication within marriage.

Understanding impotence necessitates a search for the meaning of sexuality. Sex is communication, not just a physical act. Those suffering from impotence should not abandon sex. Making love isn't always genital intercourse. It can be sharing life's most intimate moments with one's beloved regardless of physical activity. Talking, nongenital loving, and expressions of care and concern should continue even when emotional and physical frailties inhibit sexual performance.

The impotent man should see a doctor. Deficiency of the male hormone testosterone can be detected by a simple blood test and corrected by injections. Arteriosclerosis restricts blood flow and can be corrected by an artery bypass operation. In addition, more than 75,000 men have undergone the penile implant operation that introduces a rigid or semi-rigid inflation device to assist intercourse.[4]

Since an estimated 20 percent to 50 percent of all cases of impotence are psychologically caused, the Scriptures should be consulted for an understanding. "As he thinketh in his heart, so is he," Proverbs 23:7 reminds us. Bitterness toward an authority figure, such as a father, can cause impotence, and hostility may be subconsciously transferred to the wife. Thus, the failure to forgive others becomes a spiritual and psychological hindrance in the marriage bed. Instead of impotence being the end of a man's measure, it can be the beginning of uncovering cares to be cast upon the Lord.

RECOMMENDED READING BIBLIOGRAPHY

LaHaye, Tim and Beverly. *The Act of Marriage.* Grand Rapids: Zondervan, 1976.

COUNSELING/INFORMATION SOURCES

Impotents Anonymous
5119 Bradley Blvd.
Chevy Chase, MD 20815
(301) 656-3649

32

Divorce

Hallmark now markets cards with messages to "Mom and her husband" or "Dad and his wife." A Los Angeles card firm offers one product line showing a bride and groom perched on a high wire with a message inside declaring, "So far, so good! Happy anniversary."[1]

Divorce, in case you haven't heard, is quite common. A study at the University of Wisconsin reveals that half of all divorces occur within seven years after the wedding.[2] The average length of marriages in the United States is now only 9.4 years.[3] Divorce has become so acceptable to our society that some therapists pride themselves on dissolving marriages as painlessly as possible. Thomas Clark, president of the American Association of Marriage and Family Therapy, says, "I think the profession has matured enough that in some cases a good and capable therapist will work just as hard at ending some relationships."[4]

The purpose of a new service called Divorce Mediation is to alleviate the trauma of divorce. It advocates direct negotiation between husband and wife with a neutral third party to help arrange a fair bargain.

The process can last six to eight sessions and up to twelve hours, and deals with everything from who gets child custody to who gets the goldfish. Those who have used Divorce Mediation say it's cheaper than lawyers and strikes the best deal available in a bad situation.[5]

There is proof for those convinced that modern marriage is going to the dogs. One judge awarded a childless couple joint custody of their beloved and pampered dog, a cockapoo named Runaway. Rex and Judy Wheatland quarreled over the precious pet until a judge finally intervened. Rex offered his wife $20,000 to buy out her share in the dog, to which Mrs. Wheatland responded, "She's my baby. I wouldn't give her up for anything."[6]

As with the Wheatlands, who gets what is often the biggest battle. Generally, the partner who dominated the marriage also dominates the parting. Thus, the reticent spouse gets left holding an empty bag. Bargaining can get sticky. Personal belongings become implements of revenge. Bickering over an expensive antique is one thing, but a $50 chair can become a point of contention if it is a spouse's favorite piece of furniture. Family memorabilia and photographs become matters of hot dispute. Parting couples resort to duplicate copies of photos so everyone retains a record of the family that was.

What about mutual friends? Who gets them and whose side will they choose? The custody of children is easier to determine than the custody of friends. Those divorcing blame each other, and friends hesitate to take sides. Friendships usually dissolve along with the divorce. What was harmonious for four doesn't work for three.

Children are victimized. Though most divorcing couples would never think of violently striking their children, they commit an even more serious form of child abuse. The offspring are used as instruments of communication and hurt, and weapons of warfare as the marriage disintegrates. A psychiatrist at the University of Montreal studied teenagers in divorced families and discovered they are "less optimistic and have more psychological problems than those whose parents stay together."[7]

In her book *Growing Up Divorced,* author Linda Francke points out that children follow a series of reactions when the marriage dissolves: shock, depression, denial, anger, low self-esteem, and, among younger children, guilt.[8] Even when an appropriate custodial arrangement is reached, Francke warns that anger may be directed against the custodial parent who is perceived as keeping the child from his biological mother or father. The divorced parent may attempt to relieve his own guilt by appeasing children with overindulgence, and children may become emotional supports to assuage pangs of guilt from a bad marriage.

In spite of all this, divorces keep right on happening, and the process is made even easier by no-fault divorce laws. Proponents of no-fault divorce say it removes finger-pointing, and neither partner becomes the bad guy who digs up dirt about the other. But judges still have a difficult time ruling on such things as potential earning power and the value of homemaking. Some critics feel that no-fault divorce establishes a dangerous precedent by dismantling a marriage and assigning responsibility to neither partner.

No-fault divorce is not painless. A Stanford University researcher says the losers in no-fault divorces are women and children. As proof, he cites these statistics: 53 percent of women who are awarded child support don't get the payments; women and children average a 73 percent standard of living decline the first year after divorce, while men average a 42 percent increase; if a man makes $1,000 a month, only $300 goes to his ex-wife and children.[9]

No matter how easy society makes divorce, it is a tragedy that should require every divorce lawyer to caution, "Warning! Divorce is dangerous to your health." It's true. A report in the *New York Times* reveals that heart disease, cancer, sclerosis of the liver, high blood pressure, and accidental death occur more frequently to the divorced than the happily married.[10]

As more marriages fail, Christians fall victim to the trend. Divorce and remarriage are almost as common in the church as in secular society. The excuses are similar: "We don't love each other any more; the flame has gone out." "I prayed about it, and the Lord showed me that I could be of greater service in his kingdom by being married to someone who shares my faith and could work together with me to win souls." "We've tried everything, and it just won't work. Why should we go on living miserably together when we could be happy apart and remarried to someone else we really love? After all, a good divorce is better than a bad marriage."

These excuses show that too many people don't even understand what marriage is. Marriage is more than feeling. It is a conscious decision to unite with another person for better or worse. It is a covenant before God and his church, a promise that flies in the face of our throwaway society in which even people are expendable. It is a recognition of the relationship between man and woman, which is an even deeper bond than that of parent and child. The latter is genetically based, whereas the former expresses the mystery of oneness in spiritual union.

In Malachi 2:16, God proclaimed his hatred of divorce. He, too, knows the agony of adultery. Israel, to whom he was espoused, forsook him. In Ezekiel 16:32 he described his chosen people as an "adulterous wife" that preferred "strangers to your own husband" (NIV). Israel's adultery (serving other gods) became so bad that Jeremiah 3:8 tells us God "gave faithless Israel her certificate of divorce" (NIV). For God to be reconciled to his people, it cost him the death of his Son. When Hosea was reconciled to his wife, Gomer, a prostitute, he had to buy her back. Such dimensions of reconciliation are seldom emphasized in today's Christian counseling.

While acknowledging that God hates divorce, we wonder if there are biblically permissible grounds for divorce. How far should a believing spouse go to retain the relationship with an unbelieving spouse? When is remarriage permissible by God's standards? An often-quoted portion of Scripture that speaks of divorce is 1 Corinthians 7:10-16:

To the married I give this command (not I, but the Lord): A wife must not separate from her husband. But if she does, she must remain unmarried or else be reconciled to her husband. And a husband must not divorce his wife. To the rest I say this (I, not the Lord): If any brother has a wife who is not a believer and she is willing to live with him, he must not divorce her. And if a woman has a husband who is not a believer and he is willing to live with her, she must not divorce him. For the unbelieving husband has been sanctified through his wife, and the unbelieving wife has been sanctified through her believing husband. . . . But if the unbeliever leaves, let him do so. A believing man or woman is not bound in such circumstances; God has called us to live in peace. How do you know, wife, whether you will save your husband? Or, how do you know, husband, whether you will save your wife? (NIV).

Many questions arise from these verses. Paul teaches that a believing spouse should not divorce an unbelieving spouse. But what about severe abuse or a situation where the unbelieving spouse refuses to make the house any kind of a home? What about the partner who didn't want a divorce and tried to prevent it, while the other partner proceeded to legally dissolve the marriage? Is the one who resisted divorce free to remarry? What about cases of physical abuse and the desertion of affection, as well as failure to supply living provisions? The passage from 1 Corinthians does not answer all these questions.

The Pharisees assumed that divorce for any reason was permissible, as long as it was legally justifiable. In Matthew 19:8, 9, Jesus pointed out that infidelity was the only exception: "Moses permitted you to divorce your wives because your hearts were hard. But it was not this way from the beginning. . . . I tell you that anyone who divorces his wife, except for marital unfaithfulness, and

marries another woman commits adultery" (NIV).
Commenting on this passage in his book, *Divorce and
the Christian,* Robert J. Plekker writes, "At best, divorce
is a gracious allowance to the innocent, given as a
balm."[11]

The parallel passage in Mark 10:10-12 is the same—
except that here Jesus does not list infidelity as grounds
for divorce. In fact, he names no grounds for divorce.
This is also true for Luke 16:18. These differences
between the Gospels are difficult to account for, and
debates about which Gospel takes precedence over the
others are usually fruitless.

Two other portions of Scripture pertaining to divorce
need our special attention:

*Matthew 5:32: "Anyone who divorces his wife, except
for marital unfaithfulness, causes her to commit
adultery, and anyone who marries a woman so divorced
commits adultery" (NIV).*

*Romans 7:2, 3: "By law a married woman is bound to
her husband as long as he is alive, but if her husband
dies, she is released from the law of marriage. So then,
if she marries another man while her husband is still
alive, she is called an adulteress. But if her husband
dies, she is released from that law and is not an
adulteress, even though she marries another man"
(NIV).*

According to these passages, only death dissolves the
marriage bond. Some believe that any remarriage, except
in the case of death, is an act of adultery, regardless of
circumstance. Others point to 1 Corinthians 7:28,
suggesting that remarriage is permissible. In his book
Marriage, Divorce and Remarriage, Dr. Jay Adams
asserts this position. Plekker, on the other hand,
proclaims, "Christians are not permitted to remarry after
divorce." Referring to 1 Corinthians 7, he maintains,
"Separation is allowed in verse 15 and celibacy is
expected after the unbeliever leaves."[12]

Most evangelical Christian leaders maintain a compassionate but intolerant position toward indiscriminate divorce. That viewpoint could be summarized as follows: Divorce and remarriage are permissible when (a) the marriage and divorce occurred prior to salvation (2 Cor. 5:17), (b) one's mate is guilty of sexual immorality and is unwilling to repent and live faithfully (Matt. 19:9—"except for marital unfaithfulness"), and (c) one mate is an unbeliever and willfully and permanently deserts the believing partner (1 Cor. 7:15—"not under bondage").

This chapter is not intended to be the last word on divorce for Christians. Couples differ in their abilities—and willingness—to cope with problems and each other's idiosyncracies. One wife may find it impossible to forgive her husband's one extramarital fling, while another easily forgives several instances of adultery. A believing husband may feel such devotion to his unbelieving wife that he determines to make the marriage last. Another believing husband may yearn to have a wife who is a spiritual partner, so he may divorce his unbelieving wife to begin his search. Regardless of personal differences, however, all Christians do have the ability to forgive others and to seek reconciliation. All have the desire—if they are truly living under God's will—to make marriage last and to view divorce as a painful alternative. All have the capacity to understand the forceful and direct statement in Malachi: "I hate divorce." If we know God hates divorce, we will do whatever is necessary to prevent it. And we will encourage our friends to avoid becoming part of the divorcing trend in this society that seems to have little regard for marriage.

RECOMMENDED READING BIBLIOGRAPHY

Dahl, Gerald L. *Why Christian Marriages Are Breaking Up.* Nashville: Thomas Nelson, 1979.

Plekker, Robert J. *Divorce and the Christian.* Wheaton, Ill.: Tyndale, 1980.

Smoke, Jim. *Growing through Divorce.* Eugene, Oreg.: Harvest House, 1976.

Divorce, Coping with the Pain (pamphlet). Focus on the Family, P. O. Box 500, Arcadia, CA 91006.

COUNSELING/INFORMATION SOURCES

The Academy of Family Mediators
111 Fourth Ave.
New York, NY 10003
(212) 674-7508

Born-Again Marriages
P. O. Box 8
Council Bluffs, IA 51501

Christian Marriage Enhancement
Colorado Springs, CO
(303) 633-6700

Renewal Ministries
4500 Campus Dr.
Suite 662
Newport Beach, CA 92660-1830

33

Children of Divorce

Virgil Everhart had a badly damaged chain saw after
sawing his house in half. Virgil, age fifty-seven, was
getting a divorce from Janet, his thirty-six-year-old wife.
So, to divide things up equally, he took a chain saw to his
Central City, Kentucky, home and cut a six-inch gap
through the flooring and walls. Like Virgil's house,
America's homes are literally coming apart at the seams.
For every 1,000 marriages in the U.S. there are 490
divorces.

Of all the persons affected by divorce, children suffer
the most. Today, 20 percent of all children live in a
single-parent household. One million children a year
suffer through the break-up of their parents.[1] Forty-five
percent of all children will live with only one parent
before they are eighteen.[2] The number of children
involved in divorce has tripled in the past twenty years.[3]
Half of the children of divorce have not seen their father
in at least a year.[4] Tragically, three out of four children
who suffer parental divorce are doomed to repeat the
problem in their own marriages.[5]

What price must society pay for having nurtured selfish

parents who care more for pleasure than the future of those they created? In 1970, 85 percent of children lived with both parents. Today that statistic has dropped to 75 percent. The public is titillated by accounts of what goes on behind bedroom doors in Tinsel Town. Millions flock to TV sets to watch with curious speculation those actors and actresses currently flaunting their infidelities. But it's not funny when the marriage at stake is your own, and the children who cry at night are your flesh and blood.

A recent study at Stanford University examined 6,710 adolescents and found that deviant behavior was considerably more prevalent among teens living with one parent.[6] Researchers report that children from broken homes are overly cautious about choosing mates, often flitting from lover to lover looking for a surrogate father or mother. Girls seem to suffer most. A study of five hundred outpatients at the Psychiatric Youth Service of the University of Michigan revealed nearly two-thirds of the adolescent daughters from divorced homes had problems with alcohol, drugs, or promiscuous sexual activity.[7]

Judith Wallerstin, a psychologist at the University of California at Berkeley and founder of the Children of Divorce Project, says the idea "more happiness comes from divorce" is an adult argument construed to rationalize the break-up of the family. She discovered that 37 percent of children in divorced homes were "consciously and intensely unhappy and dissatisfied with their life in the post-divorce family."[8]

Some social experts point out that ten years after divorce some children resent their parents. The offspring feel they were unfairly burdened by the pressures thrust upon them. Although most children finally forgive mom and dad for failing to stick it out, they often repudiate the sexual liberalism that preceded the divorce.

A tragic consequence of divorce is the tug-of-war that occurs when children are caught in the cross fire of embittered ex-spouses. Divorced couples use the kids to get even with a former mate or pump the children for information. A child's self-esteem can suffer permanent damage if he sees himself as the pawn in a continuing conflict. Children may even blame themselves, believing they caused the cleavage.

Some experts believe divorce can sometimes be better for children. Thomas Langner, a Columbia University professor who traced two hundred children of divorce over a sixteen-year time span says, "Divorce by itself does not damage kids. A conflict-ridden home is as bad—or even worse—for children in the long run."

But other child psychologists aren't so sure it's better to live peacefully with one parent than to live in constant chaos with both. A bad father may be better than no father. Perhaps a terrible mother could be preferable to the total absence of a mother figure.

Most children do, of course, feel an attachment to both parents. Because of this, many children of divorce go through a stage of believing their parents will somehow get together again. Experts say it is all right to indulge children in this hopeful feeling without deliberately perpetuating the fantasy. Their hope is a sign they haven't given up on an evil world. Sooner or later, they will face reality and acknowledge the marriage is over. It is important then that they forgive their parents for having divorced and accept them as humans who failed.

After a divorce, some children seek a surrogate mother or father, an older man or woman to look after them. Such yearning can lead to promiscuous sexual activity. Children may also engage in frantic spouse-hunting on behalf of the newly single parent. A child may also exhibit antisocial behavior as a way of getting back at a divorced parent. In response, the parent must demonstrate understanding and realize it was his failure that triggered such conduct.

If your marriage is coming to an end and you are certain it can't be salvaged, counseling experts say you should truthfully explain to the children what is happening. Though the partnership with your mate may be terminating, your responsibilities as a parent don't end. If you don't love each other, at least tell the children they are loved. Reassure them that both of you are concerned about their welfare. Make sure they don't blame themselves. Avoid any negative comments about your spouse that force your children to choose sides. In a divorce, each child identifies with one of the parents, and negative statements about that parent wounds the child.

Some marriage counselors today discard the old idea of staying together for the sake of the kids. So do many parents. They say that a broken home can be better than an unhappy home. That may sound good on paper, but tell it to the child who feels like a discard from a failing marriage. Holding the family together until the kids are grown may not make a house a home, but it could counteract the pervading sadness America reaps today from the lives of children of divorce.

RECOMMENDED READING BIBLIOGRAPHY

Tickfer, Mildred. *Healing the Hurt: Help for Teenagers Whose Parents Are Divorced.* Grand Rapids: Baker, 1984.

34

Stepparenting

"The American family has changed more in the last thirty years than in the previous 250 years." So say University of Washington sociologists Drs. William Blumstein and Pepper Schwartz in their landmark study entitled, *American Couples.*[1]

One sign of this shift away from the traditional nuclear family is the phenomenon of stepparenting. Families find themselves coping with ex-spouses, former in-laws, stepchildren, and stepparents. Each day divorce and remarriage create thirteen hundred new stepfamilies with children under age eighteen.[2] More than a half-million stepfamilies form each year.[3] Thirty-five million Americans live in stepfamilies, and one child out of six lives with one stepparent and one natural parent.[4] According to a study by the School of Sociology at Johns Hopkins University, by 1990 stepfamilies and single-parent families will outnumber traditional families consisting of two biological parents and children.[5]

Marriage increasingly joins two sets of children, as well as two adults. Regrettably, the optimistic "Brady Bunch" portrait of stepfamilies is unrealistic. Too often, a stepparent oppresses the natural children of his spouse. Television sitcoms portray merging families facing minor irritations that are easily solved by an outpouring of mutual love. The real picture is often quite different.

In a traditional family, children enter the home after the formation of the marriage partners' relationship. With stepparenting, children are thrust into an environment where established parent-child bonds precede new matrimonial arrangements. Sparks can fly. Some stepparents worry so much about the kids they neglect the new marriage relationship.

A stepparent should make it plain that instant love can't be created. He cannot replace the biological parent, and the stepparent must be cautious of going overboard to prove how much he cares about the stepchild. It's also wise not to disparage an absent natural parent. Respect for both the absent biological parent and the stepparent must be stressed for the child's emotional development.

It's difficult for stepfathers to discipline children who retaliate with, "You're not my real father. You can't tell me what to do." Consequently, stepfathers tend to do too much or too little to prove their love for the stepchild. Sometimes stepfathers change diapers and pay college tuition out of guilt because they feel they neglected their biological families. A stepfather who sired no children with his first wife may resent sharing his new wife's center of attention.

Stepmothers have difficulty nurturing values in children not their own. They may pass off children's indiscretions as indications of the biological mother's failure. Stepmothers often feel guilty about spending time with their stepchildren while separated from their natural children. As for discipline, the stepmother faces a stepchild who may recognize only the authority of its biological parent. Thus, it is important that stepparents present a united front concerning matters of discipline.

Stepchildren are caught in an equally difficult bind. The new union sabotages the secret wish that Mom and Dad will reunite some day. Even if the natural parent is dead, children may feel disloyal switching affections to

the new stepparent. Stepchildren may see the new
parent as evil and uncaring.

Stepchildren become part of a reconstituted family
with new brothers and sisters thrust upon them without
warning. Just about the time they learn to cope with the
divorce, they must face the challenge of accepting a new
Mom or Dad, not to mention new siblings they must
relate to as brothers and sisters.

The situation is further complicated when one
stepparent has been a single parent for an extended
time. Accustomed to making all decisions for his
children, he must learn to consider the new spouse. An
equally touchy issue is how to handle discussions about
the natural parent. Even if the former spouse's conduct
was and is reprehensible, the new stepparent must not
criticize and, thus, avoid creating resentment in the
stepchild.

With eight grandparents and a host of new in-laws, the
burden of stepparenting can be unbearable. In fact, 58
percent of marriages with stepchildren eventually
dissolve. Many stepparents become frustrated and
withdraw from an active parenting role because they feel
rejected by the newly acquired stepchildren.

If you are a stepparent, avoid the pitfalls pointed out in
this chapter and heed these warnings: Don't worry if the
stepchild feels guilty because he isn't enthusiastic about
the new marriage. Befriend him instead of trying to
replace his natural parent. Allow love and trust to
develop. Permit the stepchild to maintain close contact
with all grandparents and thereby diminish the
threatening prospect of having to form new relationships.

Stepparents face unique problems of responsibility for
household chores and concepts of discipline that are
alien to the stepchild. Stepparents are often surprised to
learn that the natural parent's signature is needed for a
medical procedure or permission for a school trip.
Adoption by the stepparent is not always advisable, since
this procedure can make the stepchild feel he is
abandoning love for his natural parent.

Stepparents should consult an attorney regarding the

legal status of their blended family. Stepchildren and stepparents in some states cannot inherit from each other except by specific bequests in a will. A destitute stepparent has no right to support from grown stepchildren. Unless stepchildren are adopted, the stepparent is not accountable for feeding, sheltering, clothing, and educating the stepchild. Furthermore, stepparents should be careful about granting certain kinds of permission without the consent of the natural parent. In an actual case, a stepmother allowed her stepdaughter to pierce her ears and was sued by the natural mother for assault and battery.

Psychologists suggest a stepparent should be considered more an in-law than a father or mother. A stepchild may want to keep the last name of his biological father. Family experts advise stepparents to remind themselves that their stepchildren are not and never will be truly theirs. In the midst of today's divorce dilemma, a stepparent assumes an uneasy role requiring patience and consummate social skills. Stepparents need the grace of God to fully integrate the blended family into a cohesive unit with proper parental authority.

RECOMMENDED READING BIBLIOGRAPHY

Frydenger, Tom and Adrienne. *The Blended Family.* Grand Rapids: Chosen Books, 1984.

Lofas, Jeannette, and Dawn Sova. *Stepparenting.* New York: Kensington, 1985.

COUNSELING/INFORMATION SOURCES

The Stepfamily Foundation
333 West End Ave.
New York, NY 10023

The Stepfamily Association of America, Incorporated
28 Allegagny Ave., Suite 1307
Baltimore, MD 21204

35

Child Custody

A couple divorced after seven years of marriage. The father did not want custody of his six-year-old daughter and moved seventy miles away. Three years later he learned the child's mother was involved in a lesbian relationship. He sued for custody, stating, "I am a real man and can offer the child a stable home."

The daughter testified she rarely saw her father. Teachers said she was well-adjusted. Neighbors claimed the mother was a loving parent. Psychiatrists testified the daughter was functioning well with her mother and living with the emotionally unstable father could be harmful. A judge awarded custody to the father.

In the much-publicized Betty Batey case, Frank Batey, Betty's homosexual ex-husband, was given custody of young Brian.

At the initial court hearing, Frank, who admitted living with a lover, brought in expert witnesses to testify that Brian would be more endangered by living in a strict Christian environment. After hearing her son's repeated pleas to be taken away from his father's homosexual lifestyle, Betty kidnapped her child and went into hiding for nineteen months. Eventually, Brian Batey was awarded to neither parent.

As more and more marriages break up, courts must decide which parent is best suited to raise the children. The psychological health of a custodial parent is taken into consideration. The courts also view gender as important, presuming that boys want to live with fathers, girls with mothers. Parental sexual behavior used to be a major consideration, a concern reduced by today's widespread moral laxity. Most judges now feel little reluctance to grant custody to a parent with a live-in lover.

The Uniform Marriage and Divorce Act of 1970 (Part V, Section 401) states the following: "The court shall determine custody in accordance with the best interests of the child. The court shall consider all relevant factors including: (1) the wishes of the child's parent or parents as to his custody, (2) the wishes of the child as to his custodian, (3) the interaction and relationship of the child with his parent or parents, (4) the child's adjustment to his home, school and community, (5) the mental and physical health of all individuals involved."[1] Nothing in this act addresses the child's spiritual welfare.

In his book *Getting Custody,* Robert Woody, who holds a Ph.D. in clinical psychology, advises courts on the top twenty factors to determine who should be the best parent. The mother's list runs from quality of relationship with the child through mental health, intelligence, and education. Religion is nineteenth. For fathers, Dr. Woody considers personality, stability of residence, and vocation. Religion ends the list.[2]

Under the tradition of common law, the father was entitled to the custody and services of his children. The practice changed at the turn of this century when the "tender years presumption" was devised. It was based on the notion that a suckling child should not be taken from its mother's breast.

In the mid-1920s, laws were passed giving mothers rights equal to fathers regarding custodial preference. Gradually, mothers took precedence in custodial decisions. Until 1970, custody was given to the father if the mother was proved unfit, which usually meant she was a chronic alcoholic or prostitute. A growing men's lib movement in the 1970s argued the tender years philosophy was sexist and discriminated against fathers. The result is a wide variety of custodial practices in today's divorce-prone culture.

Sole custody is the most common arrangement. The parent with whom the child lives makes most of the decisions. In split custody circumstances, one or more children live permanently with the mother and the other children with the father. Divided custody requires a child to spend half his time with one parent and half with the other, an uprooting that occurs every six months. (Since courts don't want the school year to be disrupted for children whose divorced parents live in separate locales, they often arrange for a "nine-three" custody, where the child spends the three summer months with one parent.) Joint custody arrangements give both parents equal rights and responsibilities, granting superior rights to neither party. Any custodial decree can be contested when the child periodically lives with a parent whose moral behavior is unacceptable. Some Christian parents kidnap their children to change court jurisdiction and to prevent the child's living with an immoral ex-spouse.

Today, eighteen states offer divorced couples the option of sharing custody, and another thirteen states regard it as preferential.[3] An imperfect solution, the arrangement has unique problems. Good-byes are painful, and so are the frustrations of a child's spending half his life with a spouse the former marriage partner considers undesirable. Critics call the scheme "Ping-Pong parenting." They argue that couples unable to hold their marriage together are seldom mature enough to share parental responsibilities. A Solomonic solution is impossible. You can't cut a kid in half. When both are bad parents, the court is asked to make what is referred to as the "least detrimental alternative," which places the child with the best of two undesirable parents.

If you have gone through divorce and child custody

rights are a major concern, here are some things to consider: Insist that both sets of grandparents be allowed visiting privileges. Ex-spouses can become so involved in their own disputes they forget about grandparents' loving concern. Avoid loyalty tests to determine if the child loves you each time he visits. Don't perpetuate the bitterness of the divorce settlement by deploying children as weapons on opposing weekends.

At holiday time, try balanced visitation so the child spends half of the day with one parent and half with the other. Avoid the trauma of distorting a special day into a focus of emptiness. Be careful not to use toys or material possessions to compensate for possible insecurities. You can't bribe your offspring into allegiance. Above all, ask God to give you grace to place the welfare of your child above your own selfish feelings.

36

Child Support

"How much money is in your pocket?"

"Eight dollars," the defendant responded.

"Let's have it," the judge ordered. "And give me that gold ring on your finger, too."

This exchange took place in the chambers of Judge Charles McClure, a Tallahassee, Florida, judge who is disgusted with delinquent dads. The suspect owed his former wife $1,070 for support of their three children. Though the defendant argued he had a second family to support, Judge McClure was adamant.[1]

Of five million men ordered to make child support payments, more than half pay nothing. Some fathers argue that their visitation rights are vengefully withheld, and they resent paying for children they can never see. But to the courts, it's a moral matter. If you bring a child into the world, you're obligated to provide support. Well-publicized police roundups of deadbeat dads have resulted in cars, boats, and jewelry confiscated to pay off delinquent child support debts.

"We aren't deadbeat dads. We are ordinary men retreating from the hurt and torment that has become our relationship with our children. We are treated as a wallet and must pay child support and any other expenses the mother feels is necessary."[2]

That's the way a member of the Equal Rights for Fathers organization expressed his indignation toward a new federal law addressing the issue of delinquent child support. On the other side of the issue, Judy Goldsmith, former head of the National Organization for Women, says, "Child support payments ought to be as well-collected as car payments."[3]

The intent of child support was to create a humane way of coping with the tragedy of divorce. Wives who had no substantial means of gainful employment and children who stayed with their mothers would be cared for by their absentee father. But with 1.2 million divorces each year in America, half involving at least one child, the system of child support has deteriorated to a cruel mockery of justice.

More than eight million women are raising children alone.[4] Only 59 percent of them have legal orders for child support.[5] Among these, less than half have received the full amount due them. The shortfall in legally mandated child support amounts to $4 billion a year.[6] The children for whose care those billions were intended were literally cheated by the men who fathered them. The average annual amount of child support is only $1,800; welfare picks up the rest. Eighty percent of all Aid to Families with Dependent Children is caused by absent parents who ignore child support.[7] No wonder former Health and Human Services Secretary Margaret Heckler called the current child support situation "a national disgrace."[8]

Studies show that the standard of living of women and their children declines 73 percent in the first year after divorce. The standard of living of men, single after divorce, increases 42 percent during the same period.[9] Typically, a woman needs about 80 percent of the family's former income to maintain the same standard of living. Court orders generally provide 30 percent of the father's take-home pay if he was the sole wage earner.

Consequently, the single parenting mother has a 50 percent income gap even if the father does pay.[10]

Marian Edelman, president of the Children's Defense Fund, says, "More than half of children who live in households headed by women are poor. All divorced women, whether working or not working, have a right to child support from the father."[11]

The common law system assumed in the past that economic responsibility accompanies procreation. That legal approach worked well in a society with low divorce statistics, but today 20 percent of all children live with one parent. A significant portion of their economic livelihood should come from their fathers, since 95 percent of those ordered to pay child support are men.[12]

President Reagan signed into law a measure requiring states to garnishee wages and place liens on property to collect unpaid child support. Some feel that federal child support legislation is another example of Uncle Sam interfering with the family. Psalm 82:3 says, "Defend the poor and the fatherless: do justice to the afflicted and needy." This Scripture can be interpreted as providing a biblical mandate for government action regarding child support, since justice is the function of a duly ordained state.

Not everyone is sympathetic with court-ordered child support. Fathers have legitimate complaints. Absentee fathers can be unemployed or deep in debt, or they may refuse to pay because of unfair visitation privileges. Some fathers say they no longer have the satisfaction of parenting and see no reason to foot the bill for their kids.

As a result, some men use child support as a tactic to insure access to their offspring. James Cook of the National Congress for Men, a fathers' rights advocate group, asks this question: "Can we level responsibility on fathers to pay child support without an equivalent right, the right of access to the child?"

Other injustices occur. For instance, in some cases a wife earns more than a man, but the man must pay child support. Some feel a woman should pay child support when the father has custody and she has sufficient income. In other instances, the father's child support money pays for the mother's drugs or is used to support an immoral life-style, while the children are left ill-clothed and ill-fed. The father argues, reasonably enough, "I love my child, but why should I pay for my ex-mate to live in a self-gratifying manner?"

One father's rights advocate said, "A self-confessed killer has more rights in court than a father or his child ... many divorced fathers are victims of a judicial system that is corrupt, irresponsive, and biased against them."

One hundred thirty-five divorced men's rights groups distill the anger of disenfranchised fathers who feel they have been relegated to second class parenthood.[13] Many feel that fathers should have custody of children as a means of fulfilling responsibilities of parenthood.

The issues of child support are not easy to resolve. With more than one million couples each year becoming grist in the divorce mill, many Christian families must confront dilemmas of divorce decrees. A Christian father may ask if he is obligated to honor a child support mandate if his money is used for immoral purposes. Most divorced Christian fathers feel they should obey the courts no matter what the mother does with the money. But others believe the father should not be required to pay a continuing subsidy when dissolution of the marriage wasn't his fault, having occurred because of an adulterous wife.

The divorced Christian woman may feel justified to force child support by preventing her ex-husband from seeing his children. If the father isn't paying up, the Christian mother should conceal that from the child and do the best she can. It would be unscriptural to teach the child to resent his father, no matter how delinquent he may be.

The Bible states plainly in 1 Timothy 5:8, "If anyone does not provide for his relatives, especially for his immediate family, he has denied the faith and is worse than an unbeliever" (NIV). The responsibility of obeying this Scripture can't be rationalized to mean the obligation ceases with the broken marriage bond. When a divorced father neglects to support his children, he disobeys the commandment in Ephesians 6:4, "Fathers, do not exasperate your children" (NIV). He can cause resentment in a child who is innocent concerning what his parents did. Children should look on Psalm 27:10 as God's promise to take care of them in spite of irresponsible fathers, "Though my father and mother forsake me, the LORD will receive me" (NIV).

37

Alimony

Even in his sixties, he still reigns as the glitter king of the
show biz circuit. He performs at a candelabra-graced
piano in rhinestone-studded suits. But the glow and
glitter has faded since Liberace faced a palimony suit
filed by his former chauffeur-bodyguard, Scott Thorson.[1]

Such legal action by Thorson, who claims to have been
Liberace's homosexual lover, is only slightly less
shocking than the Vickie Morgan/Alfred Bloomingdale
scandal several years ago. Bloomingdale, a founder of
Diners Club and the retail store chain which bears his
name, died leaving nothing to his mistress, Vickie
Morgan. She promptly filed a $10 million "palimony" suit,
claiming she had been promised lifelong support in
exchange for twelve years of sexual services. The case
never came to court. Before Morgan could face
Bloomingdale's widow from a witness stand, her lover,
Marvin Pancoast, beat her to death with a baseball bat.[2]

The hubbub over palimony—live-in lovers suing their
former cohabitants—began when California attorney
Marvin Mitchelson became Michelle Triola's lawyer.

Triola sued actor Lee Marvin for half his estate when their seven-year relationship ended. A precedent was established. Today the palimony pattern intrudes upon middle America. A Michigan attorney says, "This is no longer a matter for celebrities. We get people coming to our offices all the time to discuss it."[3]

The idea that a cohabitating relationship carries with it economic responsibilities after the glow is gone is a new concept, the legality of which has not been adequately tested. No doubt the legality will be tested, since sociologists estimate that 10 percent of adults live together without marriage. Many of them enter into non-nuptial agreements that limit division of property if they separate. From Hollywood to Providence, Rhode Island (where a recent case was filed), women sue former lovers, claiming property rights and financial contributions through palimony.

Palimony isn't all that common yet. *Alimony,* however, continues to be an issue in millions of households. Millions of divorced women check the mailbox each month for the court-ordered alimony payment. Most don't arrive. One angry ex-wife expressed her frustration this way: "I worked two jobs to put my husband through eight years of college and graduate school. Now, after the divorce, all I have to show is a stack of bills and an ex-husband with a new wife who will never have to worry about money."

In an age of equal rights, alimony paid to women is a subject of dispute. Advocates of men's liberation suggest there should be no gender identification connected to alimony payments. They argue that women should be as accountable to financially underwrite ex-spouses as men traditionally were required to do.

A recent poll in *Glamour* magazine asked: "Should alimony be the guaranteed right of a divorced woman?" Ninety-three percent of the respondents weren't sure. They said it depended on the situation and felt alimony should be reserved for a handicapped spouse incapable of working. Another national survey revealed that 50 percent of people polled feel a man should not automatically be required to pay alimony. Fifty-six percent of those surveyed said the spouse—either wife or husband—whose earning power is greater should assume economic liability.[4]

For decades, *Corpus Juris Secondum* has been a standard legal reference work on American law. Under the title "Duty of Husband," it states: "At common law under various statutes, the husband is bound to support the wife. No obligation rests on the wife to support the husband unless a duty is imposed on her by statute." In two-thirds of the states, a wife is not required to support her husband even when he cannot support himself. In short, the law obligates men to support their wives. But an increase in divorce and a near passage of the Equal Rights Amendment shifted public opinion away from *Corpus Juris Secondum.* Many people doubt that an ex-husband should in every case have to provide his ex-wife's economic needs.

The Bible states that a man who does not care for his own family is worse than an unbeliever. Even though man capriciously writes a divorcement, God views the marriage unit as a continuing relationship unless broken by adultery or desertion. Consequently, a Christian man divorced under non-biblical circumstances must support his ex-spouse until she remarries, whatever the courts decree. Even a brief marriage does not diminish the responsibility of a divorced Christian male to provide for his defunct family.

Palimony? This is an issue for Christians only when a live-in lover becomes a Christian while the relationship is going on or after it ends. (Someone who is already a Christian should not—obviously—be involved in a live-in relationship, so palimony cannot be a problem.) The newly converted Christian male may be obligated to pay palimony if he insisted on the live-in relationship. This is particularly true if his ex-lover had to forego educational opportunities and is unable to support herself.

Converted Christians cannot expect immunity from consequences of a sinful past in an age of live-in love and easy divorce. The biblical injunction, "Let him that stole steal no more" (Eph. 4:28) may denote particular importance to a recently born-again Christian man who stole the virginity and earning opportunities of a woman he no longer loves.

38

Single Parenting

The image bears scant resemblance to reality. The single parent is perceived as a liberated swinging parent who enjoys multiple love relationships, all the while knowing the satisfaction of motherhood or fatherhood. But, in truth, many single parents feel like failures.

They worry about remarriage and contemplate the difficulties of providing emotional support for a child lacking a maternal or paternal role model. They struggle with loneliness and feel guilty that they receive insufficient emotional satisfaction from their child. "Shouldn't my baby be enough for me?" they ask. Resentment can simmer subconsciously toward the child whose presence discourages potential mates.

Some credit the Dustin Hoffman film *Kramer vs. Kramer* for elevating public consciousness of single parenting. Today, unrelated single people constitute 25 percent of all households in America.[1] Since 1970, the number of such households has soared. (Ironically, a study shows that 75 percent of all divorced persons think less than a year later the divorce was a mistake.[2])

Single parenting also contributes to American poverty.

The U.S. Bureau of Census reports the number of poor families is growing, as divorce creates one-person households with lower incomes than traditional husband/ wife families.[3]

The burden of single parenting falls most heavily on women. The number of one-parent families headed by an unwed mother has risen by a startling 367 percent in the last decade. And the problems of single parenting involve more than the immediate parent-child relationship. After the breakup of a marriage, the single parent seldom maintains a continuing relationship with former in-laws. Also, in order to escape the censure of nearby relatives, the parent may move to another part of the country, thus depriving the child of an extended family. Without an extended family, no aunts or uncles, grandpas or grandmas provide stability for the family unit.

Some children of single parents develop psychoses and abnormal fears. They may hide under beds or in closets until mother or father gets home. Even more tragically, some turn to incest or other forms of sibling sexual abuse because of boredom or frustration.

A debate currently rages in family counseling circles as to whether the child of a single parent is better adjusted than if he lived in a home where marital strife is present. A University of Washington study indicates that children who get along with a single parent demonstrate fewer psychosomatic illnesses and less delinquent behavior than children living in an unhappy home.[4] Other studies imply the pressures of parenting mount when faced alone. Evidence suggests that single parents die earlier, spend more time in the hospital, and have more emotional problems.

Single parents must realize they ride a horse headed in two directions. A child demands time and emotional energy, while the parent struggles with sexual urges and loneliness, problems the child may not understand. There is great temptation to become involved in casual sexual relationships. These create problems for both parent and child, since they usually frustrate the parent's need for a long-term relationship and also give the child a distorted view of what male-female relationships should be like.

The single parent who believes two make a family must realize the home is incomplete without a spouse. A loving child meets certain needs, but the single parent cannot expect a youngster to provide the necessary emotional support to combat loneliness. The grace of God is an indispensible ingredient to the single parent who must handle the hurt created by a broken home.

RECOMMENDED READING BIBLIOGRAPHY

Bustanoby, Andre. *Being a Single Parent.* Grand Rapids: Zondervan, 1985.

39

Latchkey Children

Employers call it the "three o'clock syndrome" because of the time after which productivity decreases for working mothers. The mothers know their children are home alone, and they wait for the reassuring phone call: "I've arrived safely." Often they are on the phone, trying to supervise children from a distance or attempting to assist in the minor tragedies of sibling rivalry, slight injuries, or unexpected illnesses.

This cultural phenomenon is known as *latchkey children.* Every year, one million children experience the breakup of their parents. Today, 25 percent of all children in America live in single-parent households. As many as fifteen million are known as latchkey children.[1]

By definition, latchkey children are youngsters routinely left unattended for part of each day, sometimes seven days a week. The term *latchkey* refers to youngsters who must literally unlock the door to get inside their own homes. With latchkeys in pockets or dangling around necks, they return from school to wait long, lonely hours, day after day, for working fathers or mothers.

Lone latchkey children are bored and frightened. They must fend for themselves, worry about encroaching darkness and about whether to answer or ignore knocks at the door. They fear fire or a break-in and they dread someone following them home. Some become angry with their parents for forcing them to shoulder adult responsibilities. Some parents burden latchkey children with overwhelming chores to occupy them, greatly straining adolescent coping abilities.

Parents of latchkey children often go through a denial process. They don't want to know about their children's fear and anger. It's difficult to admit that their job, vital as it is, creates trauma for their child. They are torn between economic necessity and the fear that catastrophe will strike their child.

Christian parents of latchkey children must pass the responsibility to God, knowing his angels are watching. But even with this assurance they wonder which is the lesser of two evils: failure to provide financially or the anguish of inflicting injury on the latchkey child.

How does the single parent handle fears that little ones left alone may feel physically and emotionally abandoned? Psychologists familiar with these problems suggest that single parents leave their children alone for short periods and gradually increase the length of the absence as a training tool.

The problem of latchkey children isn't going away. More than half of all women with young children have jobs. As more working mothers enter the job market, their children will be left unattended for long periods each day. Congress has considered legislation providing money for the supervision of latchkey children. The funds would go to schools and community agencies. Many conservative Christians, however, fear it as governmental intrusion into a familial realm beyond Uncle Sam's economic jurisdiction.

For the present, while the burden of the children's safety rests with the parents, consider these safety guides for latchkey children:

- Teach your child to wear the key around his neck beneath his clothing.
- Hide a backup key in an unlikely place outside the house.
- Ask a neighbor to keep a key and try to have that neighbor meet the child each day as he arrives home.
- Prepare the child for his response in the event of an emergency, such as fire or a medical problem.
- Post a list of phone numbers he can call for help.
- Child-proof the home against dangers of sharp objects or anything that could cause injury.
- Prevent boredom by planning constructive activities such as reading or doing small chores. Don't allow your child to fill up his own time, using the television as a surrogate baby-sitter.
- Pets—especially a dog or a cat—can help forestall loneliness by greeting your child when he comes home. Dogs are also protective and may frighten away some potential intruders.
- Instill a sense of spiritual trust in the Lord so your child knows that God looks after him in lieu of human company.

HEALTH AND FITNESS FOR THE FAMILY

40

Stress

Nuclear war. Unemployment. AIDS. A U.S. president nearly assassinated. Poisoned Tylenol. A jumbo jet shot out of the sky. Every day newspapers and telecasts scream fearful headlines. No wonder ours is a stressful age that sets teeth on edge, jolts the adrenaline, and activates sweat glands. And it's no surprise that the three best-selling drugs in America are an ulcer medication, a hypertension drug, and a tranquilizer.[1]

The American Academy of Family Physicians claims that two-thirds of all office visits to family doctors are prompted by stress-related symptoms.[2] Health experts believe stress is a major contributor in the six leading causes of death in the United States: heart disease, cancer, lung ailments, accidental injuries, cirrhosis of the liver, and suicide.

Even farmers are falling victim to stress, though agrarian living has long been seen as idyllic. Apparently, the good-health image of living harmoniously with nature, eating fresh eggs, and dringing real cow's milk is erroneous. A University of Nebraska study disclosed that the nation's 3.7 million farmers suffer more stress than citified high-level executives. Of the farmers surveyed, 22 percent feel excessive irritability, and 19 percent complained of nervous stomachs.[3] It can't be the physical demands of farming that cause such stress. In fact, the physical aspects of a job cause less stress than matters of bureaucracy. Police officers admit they get more uptight pushing paper than by physical dangers on the street. Air traffic controllers worry more about work schedule changes than inherent occupational hazards while protecting human lives.

What makes people nervous? Psychologists developed the Holmes-Rahe scale to measure stress. Death of a spouse tops the list. Next comes divorce, marital separation, imprisonment, and death of a close family member.

Other causes of stress range from the immoral to the humorous. A nationwide poll by New York University found that the greatest source of societal stress among married men and women aged eighteen to sixty is the changing attitude toward sexual permissiveness.[4] At the University of Washington, biopsied human tissue revealed to a psychiatrist cellular damage occurring from *talking* about a mother-in-law's impending visit.

Stress would be enough of a problem if it only affected adults, but teens and even children complain of stress. Teenagers bemoan their primary stress factor as the pressure to indulge in sex. A study conducted by the Stress and Cardiovascular Research Center of St. Petersburg, Florida, revealed that girls don't know how to say no, and boys feel unduly pressured to make girls say yes. Students compensate for such stress by turning to alcohol or drugs.[5]

A recent report in *Pediatrics* magazine reveals that stress is so serious for teenagers that some of them mistake chest pains for heart attacks. Half of one hundred youths studied thought they were contracting cardiovascular disease. Doctors theorize that teenagers see themselves as adults with vulnerability to adult ills.[6]

Children are prone to stress also, which is not surprising, considering some of the family problems already discussed in this book. Even a "normal" family can create stress for children, however, often by overemphasizing perfection and achievement. A report in the *New England Journal of Medicine* claims that some children develop such stressful fear of obesity that they are borderline anorexics. Obsessed with slimness, they skip meals and thus stunt growth and delay puberty. They survive on a diet of candy and convenience food.[7] Another study at Johns Hopkins Medical College indicates that a major factor of youthful mental illness and suicide is "the lack of closeness to parents."[8]

Is America's youth being consigned to a future of tranquilizers, ulcers, and heart attacks? Who is at fault for wanting children to be geniuses by five, sexual adepts by thirteen, and fashion experts by sixteen? It's too easy to blame Hollywood, TV advertisers, and irresponsible rock stars. Granted, they all played their part in encouraging youthful stress, but parents must take responsibility for trying to mold a child into a mini-adult to please their own egos.

Experts' evaluation of stress reveals that *recurrent, prolonged stress is more physically damaging than initial reaction to a single crisis.* Two months after the death of a spouse, many widows and widowers become vulnerable to disease through a severely diminished immune response. In other words, it isn't what happens to a person as much as how one handles it over the long haul.

Psychologists say the best means of coping with stress are being in control of one's life, having friends in which one can confide, and possessing a sense of hopefulness. Each of these coping mechanisms is mentioned in Scripture.

The promise of Romans 8:28—the promise that a loving sovereign God watches over us—certainly provides a sense of comforting control. Fellowship with the saints of God provides emotionally supportive friendship in times of crisis. Christian companionship is indispensable in our stress-prone age. And more than any earthly hopefulness, an abiding confidence in Christ's return offers *the* blessed hope that makes life bearable.

If you are laden with stress, physically exhausted, chronically depleted of hopefulness, God's remedy is certain and simple: "Thou wilt keep him in perfect peace whose mind is stayed on thee" (Isa. 26:3).

RECOMMENDED READING BIBLIOGRAPHY

Congo, David and Janet. *Less Stress: The Ten-Minute Stress Reduction Plan.* Ventura, Calif.: Regal Books, 1985.

Collins, Gary. *Spotlight on Stress.* Santa Anna, Calif.: Vision House, 1982.

41

Workaholics

If you want to see him, you must make an appointment. Sometimes you load the kids in the car and spend a Saturday afternoon with him at the office. A Type A personality, he's driven, always in a hurry. No matter what anyone else does, he must do it better. He complains of chest pains and occasionally drinks Maalox like water. You're worried that he might have a heart attack. He's a compulsive workaholic, and he's your husband.

Wives of workaholics generally are confident of their husbands' love. But it still hurts when sexual intimacy is treated like another task on a daily checklist. Children suffer, too. The daughter's piano recital is forgotten, or the father fails to show up at his son's baseball games. The workaholic usually provides well, but that doesn't prevent familial fragmentation. A unique lot, Christian workaholics attend church every Sunday but treat spiritual matters with the same methodical attitude given a job assignment.

Researchers David Boyd and David Gumpert analyze entrepreneurialism. Gumpert is an associate editor of *Harvard Business Review*, and Boyd is associate professor at Northeastern University School of Business Administration. Their findings show that workaholics suffer from back problems, insomnia, headaches, and indigestion. From 55 percent to 65 percent of the 450 entrepreneurs they surveyed are afflicted with such maladies. Although workaholics derive enormous satisfaction and stimulation from their activity, the stress that is the cost of achievement exacts its physical toll.

The workaholic suffers more than a damaged body. He experiences loneliness but cannot communicate with company colleagues because emotional proximity to those who depend on him for their livelihood is unacceptable. Even though the workaholic may be financially well off, he works long hours and puts off taking vacations, fearing the slightest letup will be disastrous.

Researchers of problems in high-pressure jobs discovered that stress is addictive. Sky divers get hooked on jumping, executives purposely arrive late at the airport, businessmen schedule one too many appointments. Workaholics make impossible commitments. Unlike the diligent worker who slows down when pressure is off, the workaholic keeps going, driven by an inner need to succeed. In the process, he goes beyond hard work and becomes a compulsive achiever. Whether the motive is personal fulfillment or materialistic gain, the result is the same.

Women have joined the workaholic ranks. Wives of compulsive achievers often overcompensate by becoming workaholic housewives. They compete with their husbands by ironing socks and giving the garage white-glove treatment. Some overwork because romance fled the marriage, and harried activity is one way of coping with a house that isn't a home. Rather than face a stressful evening of unsuccessful communication, the workaholic housewife indulges in her own round of chores.

A recent study indicates women workaholics burn out quicker than men. They also feel marriage problems more deeply than their male counterparts. Sometimes the woman workaholic is driven to help support the family. Sadly, such employment often renders the wife a casualty of stress. Her attempt to achieve success in the work world destroys her mind and marriage.

The Bible does condemn idleness and commends activity. "If any would not work, neither should he eat," declares 2 Thessalonians 3:10. The Proverb writer tells the lazy sluggard to consider the busy ant as an example of the work ethic (Prov. 6:6). (It might be argued that nobody asked *Mrs.* Ant her thoughts concerning all that frenetic activity.)

The Bible warns that a man who does not provide for his family commits a sin as serious as unbelief. But Christians should take care these scriptural injunctions don't evolve into dictums commanding eighteen-hour days, boring vacations, ruined health, and marred marriages. Neglecting church attendance in the name of industriousness is no virtue. Neither is it a virtue to become so involved in an endless round of church activities that a large share of non-working time is spent away from the family. Too many workaholics extend their habits into their church life. They become busy—and respected—church workers. They also can become neglectful in spending enjoyable, meaningful leisure time with their families.

Psychologists say the workaholic is less a noble creature than a product of undeserved praise lavished upon him as a child. As an adult, he is compelled to live up to the image. Experts who treat workaholism say the afflicted should learn to network with other active business people to combat loneliness. They also counsel workaholics to get away from work, even for a few hours, to break the vicious cycle of compulsive work. The self-driven worker should seek satisfaction outside the office through unrelated hobbies or activities.

If you are a workaholic too frazzled to function, quit cramming your calendar with commitments two people couldn't keep. Learn to say no and mean it. Don't be driven by supposed altruistic motives, thinking you are looking out for others and failing to look out for yourself.

(You might just be selfishly feeding your drive to take on more work.) Leave your work at the office. Don't dump its frustrations on your family. Before you lose both family and job, shut off—at closing time—the adrenaline that pumps nine to five.

42

Burnout

He was a man of God who dearly loved his wife and
children. He worked hard as pastor of a small suburban
church, especially since he had no staff to help.
Everyone in the congregation thought he loved his work.
For the most part, he did.

He mowed the grass, took care of the plumbing,
painted walls, and cleaned the sanctuary in addition to
visiting the sick and dying. It was all part of his job
description, or so the congregation thought. Only his
doctor knew all wasn't well.

He couldn't confide in fellow pastors. That would be a
sign of weakness. On that particular Sunday morning, he
was excited about the sermon he had worked on the
previous night. He went through the outline over coffee
with his wife, then it was time to walk from the parsonage
to the sanctuary.

His wife thought he was going to the bathroom to
shave or brush his teeth, until she heard the earsplitting
bang. "Something must have exploded," she thought.
Then she saw blood, his dead body on the floor, the gun
in his hand.

The story is true. The dedicated pastor was a victim of burnout.

Burnout could be described as a condition of physical, emotional, and mental exhaustion. It is marked by physical depletion, chronic fatigue, feelings of helplessness and hopelessness, and by development of a negative attitude toward self, work, life, and other people.

Herbert J. Freudenberger, the New York psychologist credited with coining the term *burnout* in the late 1960s, has a simpler description: unrelieved stress. Freudenberger says, "The person who is susceptible to burnout is a high achiever, an individual who is success-motivated, a compulsive person who has a hard time delegating authority and wants to do it all himself."[1]

Dennis Jaffe, a lecturer at the UCLA School of Medicine and author of a book entitled *From Burnout to Balance,* describes burnout this way: "It's a complex response to life in which a person becomes apathetic, things become meaningless, energy is depleted, he does thing to avoid or escape work. He becomes dysfunctional."[2]

In short, the person who has burned-out is one whose get-up is gone. The effects of burnout are revealed in the increasing number of compensation insurance claims filed for mental occupational hazards. Last year, 11 percent of the workers filing compensation claims did so because of stress. Obviously, some lawyers see this trend as a gold mine, since it is difficult to define burnout through work trauma.

A nurse who claimed she was burned-out performed poorly on the job and was fired. The dismissal destroyed her self-esteem to such an extent she was unable to find any other kind of work. She filed a claim for compensation and won. A state trooper in the Northeast claimed his sex life was ruined because of on-the-job stress and resultant burnout. He, too, submitted a successful claim.

Inefficient handling of priorities can cause burnout. A worker blames job stress when his own time management is at fault. Some who have experienced occupational burnout believed the myth that working long hours automatically gets them ahead. That's not always true. Sometimes a person succeeds because he has the right breaks or right brains. It's dangerous to think you will automatically be successful if you work long enough and hard enough.

Burnout can happen in any profession, but it is most acute among idealists who approach their work with unrealistically high expectations. Maladaptive response to stress in the workplace comes in three stages. First, the victim feels chronically drained and emotionally exhausted. Second, burnout triggers cynicism and insensitive regard toward others. The final stage of burnout occurs when he believes he is a total failure. Depression affects the body's immune system, possibly leading to physical problems.

Burnout isn't a disease you catch, it's something you do. Elijah was burned-out after his Mount Carmel conquest. Moses was chronically fatigued and ready to give up because of the discontented people he led. Elijah sat under a juniper tree, burned-out and fearing the death sentence of Jezebel. How did each of these men spring back? How can the burned-out regain joy of life?

Psychologists who have studied burnout say its effects aren't necessarily permanently traumatizing. They suggest that self-renewal is the key to recovery. Christians, however, have the comfort of God's solace for their suffering. While thinking "I can't take another day of this," resilience can be revived and hope rekindled by believing God's promises.

Burnout isn't the end of the world. It can be a turning point, forcing positive changes that lead to a more rewarding life. If burning out causes one to reorder spiritual priorities, the victim can overcome depression and serve the Lord zealously. Even in the midst of burnout, Christians are called upon to "rejoice in the Lord alway" (Phil. 4:4).

The most unique victims of burnout, the clergy, find it difficult to effect a cure. Psychologists call pastoral burnout "the disease of the overcommitted." One in five parish pastors suffers such chronic stress. It's ironic that dedicated pastors who love the Lord and would do anything for the flock are highly susceptible to burnout.

All members of the helping professions confront burnout. After all, they're supposed to help *others* overcome fear, anxiety, and depression. Ministers are supposed to be especially other-centered. And doesn't God give them special grace? Isn't the minister a man of prayer who studies the Word? Yes, but too often the insensitive layperson sees the minister only on Sunday morning; he ignores the other eighty hours of a pastor's typical work week.

Ministers are in constant contact with the suffering and bereaved. They must study intensively to try to prepare exciting sermons that compete with the drama and thrills their parishioners see nightly on TV. In addition, a pastor's home is often a counseling center where the pastor's wife and children serve as volunteer staff. And the minister is *always* on call.

If you are a pastor and wonder whether you are burning out, consider these signals: Are you having frequent physical illnesses because your body is overloaded? Do you find yourself so exhausted and overcome with depression you can't comfort others in times of death and difficulty? Do you crave abnormal amounts of rest? Are you reaching the point where you feel you can't take it any more?

Like all burnout, the pastoral variety creates feelings of failure and a sense of helplessness. Apathy replaces idealism, and the man of God may even question his calling. What can be done? If you are a concerned Christian and wonder if your pastor is headed for burnout, consider these points:

1. *Ask the church board to review the pastor's salary to assure financial needs are met by a salary commensurate to his professional responsibilities.*
2. *Avoid intruding upon your pastor's personal life. Allow him time alone, away from the office and the concerns of the congregation.*
3. *Make certain he hasn't excessive demands on his*

*time. He may not mind mowing the lawn, but
someone else in the church can do the job as well.
Don't insist that he speak at every church meeting.
Let him focus on services that touch the most
people.*
4. *Encourage laypeople to help minister to shut-ins and
those facing times of trouble. Don't insist the pastor
call on every person with a problem in the church.*

If you are a pastor suffering burnout, exercise regularly
to combat your sedentary profession. Look for a pastor in
whom you can confide and who will be *your* pastor.
Acknowledge your humanity. Don't be afraid to say "I
don't know" if you don't have an immediate answer.

Approach the Scriptures in a new, personal way and try
consulting Bible translations that expose other insights.
Protect the privacy of your home. Hire an adequate staff.
Don't be afraid to ask for a raise or to request a needed
sabbatical.

For those in secular employment, be alert to your
personal identity linking too closely with your job. The
successes and failures of nine-to-five can distort your
sense of self-worth. Management experts say the danger
of burnout is especially dire in cutthroat professional
competition. Don't hang around with other workaholics
or aggressive subordinates who covet your job. Follow
the scriptural command of Philippians 2:3: "Consider
others better than yourselves" (NIV).

An aid toward leaving work at the office is to list the
next day's tasks, an act that steers your mind (when
you're at home) away from tomorrow's demands. Put your
least stressful task at the end of the day so you can wind
down. When you get home, don't tell your mate
everything. Relate only parts of your day so the pressures
of the workplace aren't dumped on her or him.

If you are burned-out, admit it! Look at your body and
heed what it says through allergies, hives, acne, and
ulcers. These are warning signals designed by God.

The words of Jesus in Matthew 6:25 address the issue
of burnout caused by materialistic concerns. "Don't

worry about things—food, drink, and clothes" (TLB). To brood oneself into burnout is foolish and sinful. Tomorrow has its own problems. Care for each day and prepare for the future. Don't burn-out with fear and fretful anxiety.

43

Depression

Clothes designer and arbiter of fashion, Yves Saint Laurent is a household name. He sees a therapist five times a week and regularly swallows tranquilizers. He freely admits the cause is depression.[1]

Menachem Begin, former prime minister of Israel, has become reclusive. He sees or calls almost no one. Begin has grown a beard, subsists on rice, cottage cheese, and eggs, and watches television all day in robe and slippers. Since the death of Aliga, his wife of forty-three years, Begin has been a victim of depression.[2]

Like his famous brother Ernest, Leicester Hemingway was a writer. Like Ernest, he also shot himself. Severe circulatory problems threatened amputation of both legs. After a period of deep depression, he committed suicide.[3]

Yves Saint Laurent, Menachem Begin, and Leicester Hemingway were (or are) victimized by depression. The despair of depression is not unique to the twentieth century. Hippocrates was the first to identify depression. He called it melancholia and presumed its cause was body absorption of black bile (one of the four *humours*—

body fluids—that determined personality). Other historical personages afflicted with depression were Moses, Jean-Jacques Rousseau, Abraham Lincoln, and Sigmund Freud.

Medical experts estimate depression afflicts 25 percent of the population, and at least 10 million are acutely affected.[4] A University of Pennsylvania study discovered depression costs Americans at least $5 billion a year in lost work and medical bills. It contributes to broken marriages, troubled children, suicide, and homicide. Women are more subject to its emotional consequences.

What is depression? Sadness, despondency, hopelessness, pathological guilt, nihilistic delusion, insomnia, loss of appetite, decreased sexual urges, and diminished interest in external events are all associated with it. Psychologists condense depression into two basic categories: *endogenous depression,* caused by physiological changes in the metabolism of the body, and *reactive depression,* caused by events unacceptable to the victim.

Christians would add two categories: depression brought on by sin-produced guilt that cannot be rationalized away, and demonic oppression (or possession) causing supernatural behavior modification that induces altered mental and emotional states.

Whatever the source, depression manifests physical and emotional disturbances: high blood pressure, asthma, obesity, headaches, backaches, arthritis, allergies, ulcers. Depression can strike with or without stress and occurs any time from cradle to grave. It manifests itself in the elderly through aches and pains for which there is no physical evidence.

The young are not immune to depression. The American Academy of Child Psychiatrists estimates that 400,000 of the 21 million children aged seven to twelve in the United States suffer from depression.[5] Some exhibit sleep disturbances, dramatic changes in scholastic performance, and feelings of despair. Others mask depression with antisocial behavior, such as stealing, drug use, and setting fires. Experts on child depression point out that the most frequent causes of childhood despair are death, home relocation, and divorce. Depression has even been diagnosed in babies whose mothers are absent or who sense depression in the mother.

The poor and downtrodden are not the only sufferers of depression. A study of Harvard students shows that during four years of schooling 40 percent eventually have psychological problems severe enough to warrant psychiatric help. In fact, depression is the most frequent diagnosis for Harvard students with emotional difficulties.[6]

If you or someone you know suffers from depression, understanding its three stages will help combat despair:

Subacute Major Depressive Disorder. This first stage of depression involves feelings of worthlessness and memory impairment. Suicidal thoughts can surface.

Acute Major Depressive Disorder. Isolation increases, and in some instances, hallucinogenic visionary experiences may occur.

Depressive Stupor. By this stage, the victim is bedridden and may refuse to eat or speak. Some must be fed intravenously. Time and place disorientation occurs, and close relatives may not be recognized. In its most severe stages, elimination processes cease, and the victim enters a vegetative condition.

What can be done? One logical step is to uncover the cause. Proverbs 13:12 points out a major cause of depression—hopelessness: "Hope deferred makes the heart sick, but a longing fulfilled is a tree of life" (NIV). A sense of futility or purposelessness can make one believe there is no escape. This sense of futility can be dispelled if there is hope that present conditions will improve or that life does, contrary to appearances, have purpose. *Hope* is necessary. Hope should, of course, be based on more than wishful thinking. Biblical hope is the positive assurance that no matter how bad things are, all things work for good in the lives of God's people (Rom. 8:28). Our hope is also hope in the return of the Lord Jesus (Titus 2:13).

It is reassuring to know that God promises solace to the depressed. When King David learned the Amalekites had taken his family captive during his absence, 1 Samuel 30:4 says he and his men "wept, until they had no more power to weep." Verse 6 tells us David was greatly distressed, or, in psychiatric terms, depressed. David found a solution. The Bible tells us he "encouraged himself in the Lord his God" (1 Sam. 30:6).

Christians should know that depression can be beneficial if it compels one to alter negative circumstances leading to despair. It may prompt us to lean on God for comfort and to pray more fervently for his aid. Philippians 4:6, 7 tells us to seek God's assistance "with thanksgiving." Gratefulness toward God is perhaps the best antidote for depression.

RECOMMENDED READING BIBLIOGRAPHY

LaHaye, Tim. *How to Win Over Depression.* Grand Rapids: Zondervan, 1974.

Poinsett, Brenda. *Understanding a Woman's Depression.* Wheaton, Ill.: Tyndale, 1984.

44

Gluttony

Mary Taylor operates a San Francisco computer dating service, but, unlike similar enterprises, her questionnaires don't emphasize svelteness. Miss Taylor's customers are overweight men and women looking for similarly obese lovers. Finding clients shouldn't be a problem, since America has an abundant supply of gluttonous citizens.[1]

Seven million Americans are severely obese, 13 million are moderately obese, and 80 million are overweight. Medical experts say that about 10 percent of this gluttonous group fights fat because of genetic factors. The other 90 percent became overweight simply because they ate more than they burned as body heat. In other words, most people are obese because they let themselves be obese.

In the United States the average person devours in one day as many calories as most world citizens consume in a week. The United Nations latest edition of *World Statistics in Brief* says the world average caloric intake per day is 436. The average in the United States is 3,576.[2] American standards of classifying such weighty matters have changed. According to the ideal weight tables compiled from insurance industry mortality statistics, 45 percent of American men and 33 percent of women weigh more than their top average in any height range.[3]

Why is this so? One young man who once weighed 485 pounds said, "Food is the cheapest recreation of all in this country." It's true. We eat better than kings. Henry VIII and Louis XVI never had thirty-one flavors of ice cream or nacho cheese chips. They also were never exposed to endless repetitions of advertisements for foods that are more fattening than nutritious. (Ironically, the same media that persuade us to eat, eat, eat, also sing the glories of slim, youthful bodies.)

Obesity is not a sin, but the Bible does have disapproving words on gluttony. In Job 15:27, Eliphaz describes the wicked obese man as one whose "face is covered with fat and his waist bulges with flesh" (NIV). The Proverb writer (23:21) proclaims, "The drunken and the glutton shall come to poverty." Early in the same chapter he warns, "Put a knife to thy throat, if thou be a man given to appetite!" (v. 2). Homosexuality was not the only reason God destroyed Sodom. Ezekiel 16:49 tells us, "This was the iniquity of thy sister Sodom, pride, fulness of bread, and abundance of idleness." If fire and brimstone rained on the overweight in Sodom, what must God think about the American surplus of Whoppers, Big Macs, and fries?

Surveying an average Sunday morning evangelical congregation would expose excessive weight in both pulpit and pew. Because many Christians avoid places of sinful amusement, food is often used as the main means of social interaction.

Overweight Christians believe, "I can do all things through Christ who strengthens me." They control the desire to indulge in such sinful activities as drinking, but they eat what they please. Railing against smoking, drinking, and other bodily abuses, their waistlines bulge hypocritically.

Christians should look well as well as behave well. Alcohol temperance and non-smoking shouldn't be the

only qualifying restrictions for evangelical leadership.
Ignored too long, obesity has taken a backseat—a large
one at that! Is sexual promiscuity any worse than constant
gastronomical oral gratification?

Christians may not worship idols made by hands, but
Philippians 3:19 does speak of those "whose God is their
belly"; they are enemies of Christ. Too many trips to
Taco Bell may well be a form of idolatry. How many more
souls could be saved if money spent on late night snacks
was given to missionaries?

Just as people pray for deliverance from their addiction
to drugs and alcohol, overweight people should pray that
they be delivered from the constant desire to eat.
Christians should pray for temperance in eating, so as to
set an example for others, including their own children.
It is commendable that a Christian parent discourages
foul language, but it is disgraceful to indulge that child's
unrestricted diet of soft drinks and sweets.

45

Dieting

Tongans are not offended by fat. To these plump Polynesians, thick arms and legs exemplify the body beautiful. The average Tongan woman is five-feet-four-inches tall and weighs 163 pounds.[1]

The big names in dieting—Atkins, Pritikin, Scarsdale, and Cambridge—wouldn't have much success in Tonga. But they do in America. Ten billion dollars a year are spent convincing people that unsightly pounds can fade fast with pills, powders, liquids, and nutrient bars. Each year more than twenty million Americans go on some kind of diet.[2] Those who are really serious about losing often undergo a gastric bypass operation, sealing off most of the stomach.

Critics of diets claim they accomplish little. Doctors report that people who lose pounds through crash dieting quickly regain the same pounds. Even those with surgically altered stomachs can stretch back to original size by gorging, then regain what weight was lost.

Dr. Blackburn of the Blackburn Center for Nutritional Research says, "There's no quick fad-fix diet—only quick loss of water, vitamins, minerals, and electrolytes such as potassium, which can cause heart rhythm abnormalities, inflammation of the gastrointestinal system, hormonal and metabolic change, other diseases or cardiac arrest."[3]

Yes, diets can be dangerous. Recent reports show at least of one-third of all high school and college women use diet pills that seriously endanger their health. Worse, many of these dieters double and triple the manufacturer's recommended dosage. In their zeal to be "lean, mean machines," many succumb to teaching of the instant-everything society, which glorifies the quick-fix. People want to be self-satisfied and happy in our narcissistic age. And if being happy means being slim, anything is worth the price—as long as it happens overnight.

Nowhere is this narcissism more evident than on bookstore shelves that feature over three thousand volumes on dieting. In *The Carbohydrate Craver's Diet,* Dr. Judith Wurtman says you can have your cake and eat it too. She recommends constant moderate snacking to shut off the inner responses of the body. Instead of crunching celery, you tap without guilt the nearest vending machine for a gooey goodie, so long as no single snack exceeds two hundred calories.[4]

The Southampton Diet claims that sexual gratification can substitute for food. Its exponent, Dr. Berger, recommends masturbation as a method of weight loss.[5] Only slightly more zany is the starch-blockers fad, which was supposed to inhibit digestion of starchy foods and allowed a dieter to consume any quantity he wished.

Looking at the state of dieting in America, one sees an interesting patchwork of physical danger, pure silliness, and, sadly, many wasted dollars. In their frantic attempts to lose weight, people forget some crucial findings of the medical profession. Medical researchers claim the body has a "set point," a mechanism for stablizing weight loss for long periods of time within a narrow range. The difficulty with dieting occurs when a person has been overweight a long time, thus establishing a high set point. Food consumed under that set point makes him feel starved.

Some people do manage to lose weight. Usually these

are the ones who have to come to recognize that the body has a set point and that weight loss takes time. In other words, those who lose weight and keep it off are the patient, dedicated ones. These people usually testify to an increased feeling of well-being and self-worth. They find that, as the doctors have been telling us, we feel better when we control our appetites and maintain a sensible body weight.

What does this mean to Christians? If our bodies are the temple of the Holy Spirit, does that mean we should obsessively strive to be as skinny as a *Vogue* model or as muscle-bound as a steroid-enhanced shot-putter? Hardly. Gluttony is a sin to avoid, but so is trendy conformity to a youth-obsessed culture. We do well to care for our bodies and exercise temperance in eating. But we don't have to jump from one faddish, instant-success diet to the next in an attempt to look like TV idols. In fact, our motivation for avoiding obesity is to bring honor to God, not to show our idolatry of youth and slimness.

Christians wishing to give their gluttony to God should remember that 1 Corinthians 10:13 tells us we will not be tempted beyond endurance. God will provide an escape so we can bear it. That escape may not be Cambridge diet powder or expensive carbohydrate snacks. The path to self-delivering diets is the principle found in Ephesians 4, that we be renewed in our minds and thereby control our appetites.

46

Bulimia

Dave Hoffman is the ultimate junk food junkie. In his book, *The Joy of Pigging Out,* he takes a 164-page look at overeating. To research his ode to overeating, Hoffman traveled 25,000 miles and consumed 600,000 calories, adding twenty-two pounds to his frame.

Opposite the pot at the end of Hoffman's gastronomical rainbow is the food obsession called bulimia. Also called the binge-purge syndrome, it causes in millions of American women dental enamel erosion, gum disease, cavities, infected salivary glands, ulcers, kidney failure, and loss of menstrual cycles. After consuming as much as fifty thousand calories or sixteen pounds of food at a sitting, bulimics vomit what they've eaten. Others take as many as sixty laxative doses in twenty-fours hours. The addictive compulsion to consume enormous amounts of food and circumvent weight gain by vomiting has reached epidemic proportions in this country.

Dr. William Davis, director of the Center for the Study of Anorexia in New York City, suspects that at least 5 percent of adult females are bulimics. David Herzog, director of the Eating Disorders Clinic at Massachusetts

General Hospital, says 25 percent of college-age women exhibit bulimic behavior.

Although bulimia is related to the starvation syndrome known as anorexia nervosa, there are major differences. An anorectic usually knows she is sick and needs help. A bulimic's weight and health appear normal. Instead of seeing herself as a diseased victim of a severe emotional disorder, the bulimic believes she can have the best of both worlds and eat everything without gaining weight. ("Eat this, eat that—but stay slim" is a message constantly fed to us by the media. Some people begin to believe it is really possible.)

Anorexics go days without eating, or nibble a few small pieces of lettuce. Conversely, bulimics' have an obsessive concentration on food. Parental background of bulimics includes weak mothers concealed behind facades of apparent strength, and fathers who remained physically and emotionally detached. Inadequacy drives bulimics to please their fathers. Bulimics feel approval can be reached only by attaining slenderness and constantly meeting the ideal of a slim society.

With hair pulled back, face poised over a toilet, and the shower running so family members can't hear, a bulimic drinks a glass of water, sticks a finger down her throat, and throws up everything she ate. Occasionally, such women turn to promiscuous sex to further punish themselves with self-disgust.

Translated from ancient Greek, the word bulimic means "ox hunger." That Hellenistic society was not the only culture familiar with binging and purging. Gorging and vomiting was common in classical Rome. During huge feasts, guests frequently retired to the vomitorium so they could return and consume more delectable delights. Hieroglyphics on the walls of Egyptian tombs tell us bulimia was socially acceptable during the reign of Ramses.

Today, bulimia is a private affliction, its tortured victims caught in a web of shame while maintaining a public demeanor of well-being. Outsiders and spouses may not detect their unimaginable horror. They may spend up to one hundred dollars a day supporting their habit by huge purchases of foods and laxatives. Bulimics also battle depression, loss of self-esteem, brain weight abnormalities, potassium deficiency, hernias, epileptic-like seizures, the possibility of paralysis, and punctured esophaguses.

Most bulimic women are middle-class whites, generally in their twenties and thirties. Many are in college, or are college-educated and highly successful in their careers. Health authorities say bulimia epidemics exist on some college campuses. Frequently, bulimics include gymnasts, models, ballerinas, and other professionals to whom physical fitness is imperative. Some children as young as eight are bulimics, and so are some pro football players.[1]

Most bulimics begin this aberrant behavior around age eighteen and suffer for as long as three to fifteen years. They generally grew up in homes where perfection was demanded of them, and purging was a way of pleasing critical parents. Others were compelled by the societal image of slim women who exude self-control.

Many bulimics go through a first stage of anorexia (see following chapter) in which they starve themselves. Later they turn to consuming large quantities of food. The sickness is so severe that counselors say that decreasing the gorge-vomit episodes to once a week signifies progress. Even when the war is won, the bulimic may have difficulty keeping food down. Intestinal muscle tone is so severely affected that constipation becomes a constant threat.

What drives the bulimic? She is thrilled to do something dangerously unique. After throwing up, a state of calm follows, similar to the ecstasy of a drug high. Later, she crashes. Is it worth it? Society conveys a powerful message: if you are thin enough, your relationship with others will be perfect, a fulfilling love will come your way, and all your life will be wonderful. The pressure to maintain that image is incredible. To stop, the bulimic must understand the emotional responses created by this cultural conveyance.

Ironically, psychiatrists point out that bulimia inadvertently saves the lives of its victims. Without it, some would have committed suicide. But the short-term gain is offset by continuing bingeing and purging. The bulimic seeks escape from the rejected ugly person she sees within herself. The battle of bulimia can be won after self-esteem and personal integrity are achieved.

Jackie Barrile, a former bulimic and author of the book *Confessions of a Closet Eater,* says of her former addiction, "Food becomes a baby-sitter, a tension releaser, an emotional painkiller, and keeper of all the responsibilities the bulimic does not want to handle." She continued, "I had to rely on laxatives to wash my sins away. It's one thing to make polite conversation over a steak dinner, but tamping down a chocolate cake with a quart of ice cream, eating until the only thing I feel is physical pain, requires total concentration!"[2]

Jackie won her battle with bulimia. Others can, too, but they must admit as she did, "I am the by-product of a society that, because it grew too fast with too much, insists I grow up at the same awesome pace, absorbing even quicker to catch up. I'm locked in a prison of whose making I cannot discern, even though I am told it is mine. Remember, there is no self-esteem in shoving your head down a toilet!"[3]

RECOMMENDED READING BIBLIOGRAPHY

Barrile, Jackie. *Confessions of a Closet Eater.* Wheaton, Ill.: Tyndale, 1984.

Rowland, Cynthia Joy. *The Monster Within.* Grand Rapids: Baker, 1984.

COUNSELING/INFORMATION SOURCES

Anorexia Nervosa and Related Eating Disorders (ANRED)
Box 1012
Grover City, CA 93033

Anorexia Nervosa and Associated Disorders
Box 271
Island Park, IL 60035
Hotline number: (312) 831-3438

47
Anorexia

The bride at the altar stands radiant in a flowing white gown. As she smiles at the groom, the soloist for the wedding begins to sing, "We've only just begun...."

Those lyrics were first recorded by Karen Carpenter, who made the song "We've Only Just Begun" into a pop classic. With her brother, Richard, Karen sold 80 million records. But on February 4, 1983, her death at age thirty-two brought to public awareness a frightening disease Karen Carpenter had kept in the closet: anorexia nervosa. Anorexia (literally, "nervous eating") refers to a self-destructive starvation diet. Those afflicted with this so-called "good girl's disease" exhibit a compulsive urge to control weight. It is particularly endemic among hyperachievers.

The actual cause of Karen Carpenter's death was heart failure, brought on by an irregular heartbeat resulting from low serum potassium level in the body. (This has happened to many anorexics.) A friend recalls that Karen was self-conscious about her chubby figure, an insecurity that led to her nine-year bout with anorexia. Karen's weight at one time ballooned to 140 pounds. But at one point she weighed a mere 80 pounds.

The years of starvation exacted their price. Hospitalization and intravenous feeding of two thousand calories a day put weight back on her body, but it happened too fast and strained her heart. At her death, Karen Carpenter weighed a normal 110 pounds. If only her fans had known when she sang "rainy days and Mondays always get me down" that something else got her down all those years.

How do anorexics become so painfully thin? Some use diuretics. Twenty-five million Americans take these water-expelling pills to control weight and high blood pressure.[1] Television ads promote diuretic pills that cause loss of five to six pounds overnight. But water and salt are lost by increased urination—fat isn't. When sodium is secreted, so is potassium. This mineral loss killed Karen Carpenter.

Freud called anorexia "melancholia of the sexually immature." Today's psychiatrists recognize the malady as the victim's anxious attempt to sculpt a perfect body. In a further attempt to assure her identity, the anorexic redefines her physical boundaries. Adult female sexuality is offensive, so she reversed the biological clock by starvation. Her body becomes childlike again.

Some researchers believe anorexia may have biological as well as behavioral roots. Vasopressin, a hormone that helps regulate the body's fluid balance, exists in abnormal levels in the anorexic.[2] Medical researchers feel this hormonal imbalance forces ordinary eating habits into dangerous obsessions. Although perfectionism may be the psychological motivation that propels a woman into anorexia, it later triggers biological changes that influence her perceptions of hunger.

Cherry Boone O'Neill, Pat Boone's daughter, fought a prolonged fight with anorexia, as detailed in her book *Starving for Attention.* She writes, "When you start denying yourself food and begin feeling you have control over a life that's been pretty much controlled for you, it's exhilarating. The anorexic feels that, while she may not be able to control anything else, she will control every morsel that goes in her mouth.''[3]

Cherry's diet reduced her weight to eighty pounds; her pale skin was stretched across her bones like a mummy. Her famine in the midst of luxury was a form of self-determination, a kind of control in a world that made unendurable demands of her. After many years of psychiatric help and the love of a concerned husband, Cherry Boone O'Neill conquered anorexia.

Zeal for perfect hour-glass slenderness pervades our society. A recent study at Stanford University shows most teenage girls are unhappy with the normal body fat that accompanies sexual development. A Chicago researcher did a study showing that *Playboy* centerfold models have become progressively thinner year after year since the magazine's inception.[4] It is this obsession with slimness as a sexual ideal that worries psychiatrists treating anorexia. Gymnasts and dancers for whom thinness represents recognition and livelihood are also easily seduced by anorexic appeal.

Parents should watch for danger signals that indicate they have set impossible standards of achievement for their children and exert unreasonable control over their lives. Extreme weight loss is a cry for help as the youth withdraws from adult sexuality and responsibilities.

The anorexic Christian is confronted with hope—and with serious moral questions. Compulsive lying is a common characteristic of the anorexic. She must lie constantly about food consumption, which affects other areas of life and creates emotional patterns of deception. She becomes so preoccupied with self that her spiritual life suffers a worse anemia than her body. The Bible tells us in John 10 that Satan is a thief who comes ''to kill and to destroy.'' The devil will seek one's life any way he can. Anorexia is an effective tool. But the Christian is promised victory over such weapons of Satan. Nothing— not even the self-centeredness that is at the root of anorexia—can separate us from Christ, so long as we are willing to put our lives in his hands and forget about conforming to a society obsessed with thinness.

RECOMMENDED READING BIBLIOGRAPHY

O'Neill, Cherry Boone. *Starving for Attention.* New York: Dell, 1982.

O'Neill, Cherry Boone. *Dear Cherry.* New York: Continuum, 1985.

Vredevelt, Pam, and Joyce Whitman. *Walking a Thin Line.* Portland, Oreg.: Multnomah, 1985.

COUNSELING/INFORMATION SOURCES

Anorexia Nervosa Center
Michael Reese Hospital
Psychosomatic and Psychiatric Institute
2929 S. Ellis Ave.
Chicago, IL 60616

Center for the Study of Anorexia
One West 19th Street
New York, NY 10024

48

Fitness

The location was an Australian television studio. I was a scheduled guest on a nationwide interview program and was waiting in the green room just before walking on the set. Seated across from me was another guest, a corpulent platinum blonde. Then, a producer stepped into the room and spoke to her. He addressed her as Miss Diana Dors.

I was shocked. In the 1950s, British actress Diana Dors was a silver screen sexpot with enviable dimensions of 35-23-35.[1] As England's answer to Marilyn Monroe, she voluptuously filled tight sweaters. Now she filled everything. How had she ballooned into such obesity?

Since I met Diana several years ago, she reverted to the figure of her halcyon days. She shed over fifty pounds and resumed a role in the public spotlight. Of her fat years, she says, "Everyone else was watching my figure, but the last person to watch it was me. I was tired of being described as pleasantly plump, matronly, buxom, and all the other adjectives we use to describe fat."

Diana Dors isn't alone on her fitness kick, a trend that has sold millions of Jane Fonda's books and videotapes.

More than 100 million Americans swim, 75 million bicycle, 75 million do exercises, and 37 million jog. The athletic equipment industry is a $12 billion a year business.[2]

Encouraging physical fitness among Americans, the seed planted by President Kennedy more than two decades ago, has finally blossomed. In 1960, only 24 percent pursued fitness. On any given day in our republic now, almost half the total adult population practices some sort of corporal self-betterment.

On jogging tracks, at diet clinics, and in health restaurants a concerted attempt is being made to transform the body into a thing of beauty. Grueling triathlons attract thousands of men and women who swim, cycle, and run their way to fame. What if it takes forty hours of training per week and eight to ten miles of jogging per day? With so many people pursuing sedentary life-styles, the challenge of pushing one's body to the limit holds an almost mystical appeal.

Prime-time ads promote diet sodas, yogurt, and designer clothes to drape on lithe bodies. At times, it seems as if the whole country is running. Some run from death and old age; others run toward the fountain of youth and well-being. They are backed by an American Public Health Association study that surveyed 2,679 men who jog. The results? Those who run more than three hours a week have half the risk of heart attack as men who do not exercise.[3]

Christians are caught in a conundrum. On one hand, they are reminded of Paul's warning to a sports-crazed society that deified physical fitness: "Bodily exercise is all right, but spiritual exercise is much more important" (1 Tim. 4:8, TLB). What might he say today to Jack LaLanne, who at age sixty-eight sports a forty-seven-inch chest? LaLanne, speaking about television evangelists, recently commented, "These evangelists are for the hereafter, but I stick with the herenow. I know a lot more about the success of my system than they do about theirs."[4]

Undoubtedly, Paul would treat this blasphemous

attitude of body worship with spiritual severity. But he would have equally harsh words for the flabby physiques of many Christians. After all, the apostle did say, "I beat my body and make it my slave" (1 Cor. 9:27, NIV).

Our bodies are temples of the Holy Spirit, so they deserve more than an occasional walk around the block. I have discovered that my mental clarity and spiritual insight are enhanced by physical conditioning. One need not sacrifice proper perspective about the needs of the spirit to concentrate on a slimmer waist.

In 2 Chronicles 29:16 we read of young King Hezekiah going into the house of the Lord to expel accumulated garbage. The Scripture says, "And the priests went into the inner part of the house of the LORD, to cleanse it, and brought out all the uncleanness that they found in the temple." If our bodies are the temple of the Holy Spirit, shouldn't this be the task of every Christian?

Your church doesn't need to buy rowing machines and sign up members for marathons as symbols of noble intention. But a physical fitness program can be part of any church's ministry. Helping husbands and wives to rediscover the bodies they married could go a long way toward healing some homes. The long-term benefit of improved mental outlook and increased stamina can mean much to one's spiritual life. In an age of fast foods, fatness or fitness is a crucial choice for every committed Christian.

RECOMMENDED READING BIBLIOGRAPHY

Chapian, Marie. *Fun to Be Fit.* Old Tappan, N.J.: Revell, 1983.

Coyle, Neva, and Marie Chapian. *There's More to Thin Than Being Thin.* Minneapolis: Bethany House, 1984.

Kuntzleman, Charles, and Daniel Runyon. *The No-Diet Fitness Book.* Wheaton, Ill.: Tyndale, 1985.

49

Nutrition

I have a reputation for craving sweets, especially chocolate chip cookies. Nettie and Norti, two ladies in Phoenix who listen to my nationwide talk show, are worried about me. They write:

If possible, try to eat nothing but those good apples grown in Colorado and drink two gallons of distilled water one day per week. No chocolate please! It coats the colon. Get carob from a good reliable health food store if you must have chocolate-flavored stuff. Cut down on coffee and sugar and manufactured salts. That's a no-no too.

Nettie and Norti are such health food fanatics they cite Proverbs 27:27 as a pretext for drinking goat's milk. ("You will have plenty of goats' milk to feed you" [NIV].) No, thank you! But I do begin each day with an assortment of vitamins selected by my wife. She's the nutrition expert in the family and knows exactly what mineral deficiencies debilitate my body.

Nettie and Norti and my wife aren't the only ones

concerned about nutrition. Almost everyone is, including many Christians. Some Christians claim we compromise our spiritual convictions and lose our war against the powers of darkness by allowing bad nutritional habits to dominate our lives. Though they probably wouldn't judge a visit to Wendy's as sin, they suggest that purifying the temple of the Holy Spirit through proper food consumption is a meritorious grace. Medical research strongly supports their healthful concerns.

Researchers in a California criminal institution studied the eating habits of five thousand inmates. Their findings revealed that a high sugar diet combined with junk food can provoke violent, criminal behavior. In Stanislaus County's Juvenile Hall, sugary snacks, sweetened cereal, soft drinks, and candy bars were replaced with more nutritious fare. The result? A 21 percent drop in assaults, and a 42 percent drop in violent incidents.[1] Apparently, we are what we eat. Though Jesus pointed out evil comes from the intent of man's heart, what goes into the belly seems to affect belligerence.

Today's wheat germ and brown rice enthusiasts will find a friend in Scripture. Drinking water is mentioned over 350 times in the Bible, and eating fruit more than 200 times. Daniel ate vegetables and drank water, thereby winning a contest of health with the Babylonians. Too many believers have succumbed to the fast food franchise system and to the enticing ads for junk food.

Some "gospel of health and wealth" Christians claim that God blesses true believers with financial success and physical health. There are problems with such claims, since some ailments are caused by genetic factors and other causes. Let's face it: All Christians are not healthy. But it is true that God wants us to be both spiritually and physically healthy. The natural, health-giving foods—fruits, vegetables, lean meats—are given out of God's bounty. They are preferable to the artificial junk foods we produce and consume in large quantities.

God is indeed concerned with our physical well-being. When the Hebrews came forth from Egypt, the Scripture tells us, "There was not one feeble person among their tribes" (Ps. 105:37). When God sweetened the waters of Marah (Exod. 15:23-26), he promised divine health to those who would heed his commandments. "I will put none of these diseases upon thee," the Lord declared.

Good health involves more than good nutrition, of course. It encompasses a right attitude of the heart: "Fear the Lord and shun evil. This will bring health to your body and nourishment to your bones" (Prov. 3:7, 8, NIV). David spoke of God as "the health of my countenance" (Ps. 42:11), a sign that sickness can evolve from anxiety and dissatisfaction with life. Good health involves peace in man's soul as well as a properly nourished body.

RECOMMENDED READING BIBLIOGRAPHY

Kuntzleman, Charles. *The Well Family Book.* San Bernardino, Calif.: Here's Life, 1985.

Omartian, Stormie. *Greater Health God's Way.* Canoga Park, Calif.: Sparrow, 1984.

THE FAMILY
AT WORK AND PLAY

50

Working Women

She flirts, and she may even have an affair. The men in
her life are exciting and well-to-do. Some are married,
but that doesn't matter. In fact, that's better. If the man is
tied down, there will be no commitment, no chance for
extended intimacy, and little chance of disrupting their
mutual goal. She is career-oriented, the consummate
businesswoman who intends to stay single and make it to
the top.

According to 1980 U.S. Census statistics, the number of
women between twenty-five and thirty-five who live alone
tripled in the 1970s.[1] In 1981, 52 percent of twenty-four-
year-old women were still unmarried, twice as many as
1980.[2] With 53 percent of adult women working, many
forego marriage and families for the sake of upward
mobility.[3] Barbara Artson, a San Francisco psychologist
who studied the working woman phenomenon, says,
"These women may fear falling in love if they think it
means giving up something they've worked hard for."[4]

An increasing number of women find satisfaction in the
marketplace instead of (or, sometimes, in addition to)
being a housewife and raising children. One out of every

eight wives earns more than her husband. Last year, six million wives brought home the biggest percentage of the bacon. In some cases, they are better educated than their husbands. Others labor because the jobless man adapts poorly to today's employment market.

But women in the workplace claim they have a long way to go. Though more than half of adult stockholders in America's major corporations are women, only 3 percent are corporate directors. That statistic reflects what some feel is a discriminatory attitude of business toward women in the boardroom and in executive suites.

More than half of accounting graduates are women, but only 18 percent of the partners in large accounting firms are women.[5] While 35 percent of law students are female, only 5 percent of the partners in major firms are women.[6] Recently, the Supreme Court ruled in favor of a female lawyer in a much-celebrated antidiscrimination suit. Henceforth, large law firms that exclude female attorneys on the basis of sex will be subject to legal prosecution.

Some women start their own businesses because they feel it's hopeless to battle male chauvinism in the workplace. A study at the University of Illinois shows that while men respect other men with powerful management styles, they dislike women with the same qualities. An advertising agency founder, Jane Trahey, observed, "The only way a woman can get to be president of a corporation is by owning it."[7]

Many evangelicals are disturbed because of the number of women choosing to forego the traditional wife-and-mother role. But some studies of working women indicate the phenomenon may not be the nemesis depicted by some evangelicals. Findings by a UCLA researcher indicate that women who stay home suffer from depression three times more often than women who work. Apparently the career woman has an outlet for her stress. The study also reveals that married women who stay at home often suffer from loneliness, isolation, and low self-esteem. Married women who work, even those in high-pressure, management-level jobs, can express their frustration and release it constructively.[8]

The Christian community has usually viewed women in the workplace as infertile or frustrated, incapable of bearing children or too selfish to be mothers. If she happens to be successful, the working woman is generally considered pushy and bossy, not an example of the femininity reflected in 1 Corinthians 11. Articulate Christian working women remind their detractors that Lydia (Acts 16) was a businesswoman engaged in the selling of dye. Because of her business activity, she was able to open her home for gatherings of Christians to worship. The writer of Acts makes no disparaging remarks about her career.

The church may need to reassess its attitude toward working women in view of their entrepreneurial success. Indeed, women may be uniquely suited for certain work. One female attorney observed, "Women make a tremendous contribution to business because they are willing to ask questions without fear of losing face." Perhaps women's uniqueness in the business world can influence positively the ethics and etiquette of American capitalism. Christian working women can be special witnesses in the male-dominated workplace, demanding the respect of their peers. They can demonstrate that females are gifted by God with managerial capabilities, not just skirts to chase into company storerooms.

The church should reexamine its stereotype of the career woman as a domineering female who competes fiercely with men and cares little for her children. Christian males should reassess their chauvinist attitude that working women are sexually promiscuous on the job and overbearing at home. Christian employers can address the pay equity issue of comparable worth by rewarding women who excel, being careful to remind them (as they would male employees) of commitments at home.

Having said all this, let us also admit that women who choose to be "only housewives" are not necessarily bored or frustrated. Life in Christ means we have the freedom to avoid conforming to society's norms. In a society that increasingly sneers at women who claim they find fulfillment in being wives and mothers, Christian women can show that the role of homemaker can be a rich and fulfilling one. They can demonstrate that one need not have a career to keep up one's self-esteem. And they can keep alive the image of the nurturing mother whose most attractive quality is lack of selfishness.

51

House Husbands

There are fifty-thousand of them in the United States, up twenty-thousand since 1972. Still, they constitute only 3 percent of all nurses. They are men in a traditionally female profession. Like male secretaries, they assume roles usually reserved for those with softer hands and more tender graces.

With women entering the work force in greater numbers, the role of breadwinner is increasingly assigned to the wife. In 1950, more than 60 percent of American households were headed by a male provider with a full-time wife/mother at home. Today, less than 15 percent of households fit this pattern. Now, many men are staying home for good as house husbands.

Traditionally, a husband mowed the lawn, weeded the garden, and painted the house. He changed oil filters, tuned engines, and cut firewood. Today's husband may do all these things—or he may cook, sew, clean the house, and raise the kids. Some think house husbands represent a new attitude of shared domestic responsibilities. With more women in the marketplace (some earning more than males), more men stay home to

simmer the soup and change the diapers. Though some
resent the role reversal, others are happy to escape the
stress of the marketplace.

The work done by men and women has always varied
from society to society. In some cultures, grinding grain
is the man's job, while women work the field. In rural
America today, many woman drive the tractor as often as
their husbands. Such exceptions aside, women have
traditionally fulfilled the role of housekeeper.

A house husband must harden himself against people
saying, "Oh, you took the day off to be with the kids," or
"Did you lose your job?" Discriminated against by male
peers, he's also an outcast with neighborhood women.
He can't join a coffee klatch without suggestion of
indiscretion. A house husband incurs dislike among
some neighbor women who resent their own husbands'
inability to be home.

The poor house husband is painfully aware that no one
seems to know what a "real man" should be like
nowadays. The old images are still around, of course.
Silent strength, suavity, independence, bravado—these
traditional masculine qualities are portrayed on screen by
Harrison Ford, Tom Selleck, Christopher Reeve, and
Richard Gere. Women still like rugged, handsome men—
in fact, many women are becoming as openly lecherous
as men used to be. Men are treated as sex objects, with
baseball player Jim Palmer posing in Jockey briefs and
Olivia Newton-John singing "Let's get physical." Yet, Mr.
Macho Man is faced with feminist demands for more
openness and sensitivity. Men are expected to live up to
the old standards *and* also be sensitive toward women
and their rights. This is a tall order. The house husband
realizes he may be seen as an emasculated wimp who
sacrifices his manhood on the altar of the Equal Rights
Amendment.

The house husband encounters social stereotypes that
include the tough-guy image. He also must fend off
innuendos that he has surrendered his virility. Christians
who believe only women can be keepers at home
wonder what he's doing there. But does God really want

women back at the sink and men back on the job? Too
often our perception of American manhood is influenced
more by Clint Eastwood and Burt Reynolds than
Abraham and Isaac. To engage in defined feminine
responsibilities does not render the house husband a
precursor of an androgynous age. The Bible, in fact, has
nothing negative to say about men who wash and clean
house.

The Titanic syndrome—women and children first off a
sinking ship—unquestionably collides with demands for
equality from the sexier sex. The Christian male must
refuse affiliation with the men's lib movement to enforce
his manhood. More than ever, the biblical role of
manhood must be asserted, perhaps especially by house
husbands.

Manliness has nothing to do with specific chores or
cultural stereotypes. The Bible speaks of the fruits of the
Spirit without sexual distinction. A man is one who loves
his wife as Christ loved the Church. A man leads his
family in the ways of the Lord. Breadwinner or
housekeeper, it makes no difference as long as the
husband is head of the wife, and Christ is the head of the
home.

52

Working Mothers

Raquel Martinez earns $2000 every day she goes to work. She's not wealthy, however, since her job isn't the kind that requires employment five days a week. Still, the occasional Sunday afternoons when she is called upon are frequent enough to provide a substantial salary. Raquel deserves it. Her job is to square off at a half-ton bull with a nasty temper and two sharp horns. Raquel Martinez is a bullfighter, the world's only professional female matador.[1]

Most working mothers engage in professions far less exotic and dangerous. Their biggest apprehension is separation from their child and knowing someone else is mothering him for eight to ten hours a day. Fewer than 15 percent of all Americans live in the traditional setting where the husband is the sole breadwinner and the wife stays home with the children.[2] In fact, 56 percent of all mothers are now part of the labor force, and 54 percent of all married women with school-age children work outside the home.[3] Forty-eight percent of all married women with preschool children are employed.[4]

These statistics represent a fundamental shift in

mothers' attitude toward work. According to a national survey, only 12 percent of working mothers would rather stay home with their children.[5] In another survey, researchers found that 59 percent of all women believe employed mothers do as well with their children as those who do not work outside the home.[6] Some believe they are even better mothers because they work.

Such statements raise more than a few eyebrows in Christian circles. Working mothers often are seen as independent-minded women who threaten the submissive role Paul set forth in Ephesians 5. In Hitler's Germany, a popular slogan was *Kinder, Kuche, Kirche.* It meant *children, kitchen, church,* and it defined women's proper role in Nazi society. Some working mothers today think the evangelical attitude is no improvement over Hitler's. They feel frowned upon for leaving their children in the care of others while they labor nine to five. Christians sometimes stereotype working mothers as closet feminists, driven by ambition, running roughshod over their husbands' wishes, and neglecting their children's needs.

Working Christian mothers believe the divine injunction to fill and till the earth was given equally to women and men. They identify the industrious wife of Proverbs 31 who engaged in a variety of commercial pursuits that ranged beyond her immediate responsibilities of child care. Born-again working women say motherhood and a career can go hand in hand.

Christian working mothers thrust into the marketplace because of divorce or economic necessity should make certain their vocational role is demanded by circumstances, not chosen by preference. Some working mothers brag about bringing home extra goodies with a second paycheck, but this cannot compensate for the lack of early childhood training. When the child in a Christian home knows his parents are committed to each other and the Lord, the working mother has an opportunity to be an exemplary figure of a godly female at work in our culture. Conversely, working mothers must beware of fatigue, coming home worn-out and unable to meet a child's emotional needs after he has waited all day for Mom.

A new study by the American Educational Research Association shows that elementary school students whose mothers work outside the home don't do as well in school as children whose mothers are full-time homemakers. The study found that children of employed mothers spend significantly more time watching TV and less time reading and participating in youth activities. They are more problematic at school and enjoy their classes less.[7] This conclusion should warn working women who claim that quality time spent with their children compensates for not being there when needed most.

Contributing to the life of a child during crucial formative years may be more valuable to America economically and morally than being another cog in the wheels of business. Motherhood is our most demanding profession. While Scriptures may not specifically prohibit working mothers, any vocation beyond the confines of child-rearing should be carefully considered.

53

Day Care

She was a grandmotherly seventy-six and known simply as Miss Virginia. For years she had provided parents in Manhattan Beach, California, with day-care services, and she had been honored for outstanding community service. Then, Virginia McMartin and six of her coworkers were charged with molesting the children entrusted to them for safekeeping.

Once news of this day-care debacle reached national headlines, cases of similar horror began to surface. In New York City, it was revealed that officials of the Puerto Rican Assocation for Community Affairs Day-Care Center had raped, sodomized, and terrorized children.[1] Such publicity forced awareness upon parents that, while they were earning extra income, their children could be subjected to rape.

Absentee motherhood is normal in Amercian family life. This year, 45 percent of mothers with children under one year of age are in the work force, a jump of 30 percent in just five years.[2] Divorce and single parenting leave five million children under the age of ten with no one to look after them when they come home in the afternoon.[3] For significant portions of the day and night, many working parents cannot care for their children. Many have no relatives or friends to help baby-sit.

The day-care industry responded to this deficiency. Almost two million children currently receive formal licensed day care.[4] In addition, uncountable millions of kids are looked after informally by unlicensed baby-sitters.

Consumer advocate Ralph Nader calls day-care centers children's warehouses.[5] Whether or not the epithet is accurate, such facilities are a permanent part of the American landscape. A baby boomlet is taking place, and more middle-class couples work to maintain a standard of living to which they've become accustomed. Baby-sitting has gone professional, with large commercial operations entering the arena, plus the traditional assistance of grandparents and neighbors.

The United States is one of the few industrialized countries without a comprehensive national day-care policy. Many say it is time for Uncle Sam to get in the business of looking after America's youngsters. Others are uncertain.

Dr. Burton White, director of Boston's Center for Parent Education, says, "A child needs large doses of custom-made love. Hired help can't provide that. I see the trend toward increasing use of day care as a disaster."[6]

Some parents worry about infectious ailments that pass on easily in unsanitary day-care institutions. Others cite cases of sexual abuse or physical battering. High fees force parents to wonder where all the extra money goes.

Terri Eurich started the National Academy of Nannies, Inc. Borrowing from English tradition and instilling a distinctive American flare, Terry places qualified graduates of her training academy in homes that provide room, board, and benefits, plus reasonable salaries.[7]

Most parents can't afford such highly personalized child care and must depend upon institutions. Those familiar with the abuses already illustrated say some parents ignore what's going on while their children are gone. Allen Galinsky, a New York educator, says, "The tendency is to find a child care center that is convenient and get out of there fast."[8] Unfortunately, many parents turn deaf ears to apprehensions their children express about being left in the arms of a surrogate parent. Because they don't listen, child abuse continues to occur.

Headlines of child abuse terrify many working parents. One mother using day care said, "I wake up at night wondering if something might have happened to my son during the day. I feel guilty when I leave him. What if something takes place that ruins my child for life?"

Brutalization and sexual abuse don't occur that often, of course. But a more subtle—and destructive—form of abuse is the separation of the child from his real parents. In a recent *Newsweek* column, Deborah Follows wrote of her abandonment of employment in favor of child-rearing: "All women need to understand that a parent's job as a parent is important, that something is lost when a parent is not there. In saying that a parent's duties are largely replaceable, we put them on the same plane of importance as household chores. We are suggesting that working parents can buy a parent substitute as easily as they can buy a frozen dinner. Since I have been home full-time ... I'm able to do more spontaneous things with my children, like building snowmen at the first snowfall, and interpret the small events that taken together define their values and their views of the world."[9]

Deborah's depiction certainly has biblical merit. Day care is too often a service provided not for the child but as a convenience to a selfish mother who doesn't want the hassle. So-called quality time spent with children in the evening is parental tokenism that demeans the child. Poet Robert Frost said, "Home is the place where when you have to go there, they have to take you in." But, for millions of American children, home is a professional substitute for Mom and Dad.

Every working mother should carefully consider whether gainful employment is beneficial for her child's moral future. If working is a necessity rather than choice, the day-care center must be selected with utmost discretion, giving first consideration to church-operated facilities. If none is available, the day-care center should be visited unannounced and its facilities inspected without warning. If the day-care personnel resent that intrusion, suspicion is unavoidable.

Many Christians are suggesting that the church provide day-care centers so children need not be left in a secular institution. Many churches hesitate to provide day care, lest they appear to condone mothers leaving their children unattended most of the day. But, with more than half of working mothers with preschool children relying upon some kind of child care facility, the resultant spiritual effect on the home cannot be ignored. Christian-sponsored day care can remove some of the potential for child abuse. It also provides Christian instruction for youngsters who can't know the security of being at their mother's knee during the day.

Regrettably, most day-care facilities are not run by Christians. Perhaps this situation will change in the future. Until it does, many Christians will find themselves placing their children in secular institutions. These parents should listen closely to what their children tell them about treatment at the center. The youngster who fears being left alone could be communicating a message about unreasonable treatment that he was warned not to reveal. Every Christian parent should pray that God will provide adequate resources to put the child into the caring hands of one who knows what's best for his welfare—the parent.

54

Comic Books

Dr. Strange. Dr. Druid. Baron Mordo. Brother Voodoo. Shaman of Alphaflight. Adam Warlock. Moondark the Magician. Son of Satan. If these strange occult names are foreign to you, it's obvious you are not a comic book connoisseur.

Gone are the days of Bugs Bunny and Daffy Duck. Even Dick Tracy and Archie fight for a dwindling share of the marketplace. The Katzenjammer Kids, Mutt and Jeff, Krazy Kat, Little Orphan Annie, Prince Valiant, and Superman are fading into memory. Begun as an evolution of newspaper strips in the late nineteenth century, comic books now contain contemporary themes of occultism and eroticism.

Today's comic books boast such titles as *Slaughter Man, Return of the New Gods, The Celestials,* and *Heavy Metal.* Characters inside the covers spew profanity and scatological language. Full frontal nudity is common, including preoccupation with oversized women's breasts. Many repeatedly use the name of Christ in vain. Some depict a nauseating variety of sex acts. For those interested in the occult, a series of

Twisted Tales offers information on conjuring, astral projection, and psychokinesis.

The worst of the lot is *Son of Satan,* known as Daimon Hellstrom, a puny religious weakling who is the sworn enemy of Satan. His rightful heritage takes control at night, and he becomes the son of his father, the devil. As the son of Satan, he opposes his father's purposes, but not from righteous motive. Even when the son of Satan does good, he is not acting from humanitarian motives. Instead, he seeks revenge for unexplained harm done to his mother and sister.

Another comic hero, Dr. Strange, possesses the greatest mastery of magic on earth. Expert in mesmerism and thought-casting, Dr. Strange brags that he can communicate simultaneously with a dozen minds. Dr. Druid has a medical degree from Harvard and excels in yogic powers. He can levitate while meditating, and his Celtic sorcery enables him to control people at will. Brother Voodoo, a black former psychiatrist, summons from the dead the spirit of his late brother, a voodoo witch doctor. He sends forth his brother's spirit to possess people.

A Marvel comic entitled *The New Mutants* illustrates a girl meditating, separating from her body, and astral projecting. She attains the ability to travel anywhere on earth and pass through solid objects. The comic book gives this advice: "The best time for casting spells is very early in the morning when everyone is asleep and not likely to notice."

In several Marvel comics something called Uni-Power energy exists and supposedly creates superhuman powers. So-called psionic powers are also mentioned, including precognition, the ability to foresee future events. Some stories speak of characters who derived these powers by visiting spiritual adepts of Tibetan Buddhism in the Himalayan highlands.

Marvel characters use the term *eternity,* the name of a life force appearing as a humanoid configuration. This eternity is accessible by sorcerers of cosmic perception. Characters like Dr. Strange refer to demons as expressions of "extra-dimensional energy" acquired by "invoking entities."

Bizarre characters have even entered into series that have amused kids for years. The Archie comic series features Sabrina, a teenaged witch. In one issue, Sabrina is confronted with Della, the head witch, who is upset because Sabrina wants to celebrate Christmas. Della argues this festive day is "for mortals only." In the end, however, the spirit of Christmas Future shows Della a party during which warlocks drink eggnog and toast Christmas as a time for "peace and joy around the world." Della returns to tell Sabrina she can now celebrate Christmas, since she has learned its true meaning, "love and sharing."

Many of today's comic books are not published for kids. The market aims at teenage and young adult audiences. While researching comic books, I found the following: a vividly illustrated Black Mass showing Satan cohabiting with a female; sadomasochism and various forms of perverted sex; frequent use of profanity; Eastern mystical overtones with characters using yoga and bowing before various pagan deities; a nude heroine possessing a sacred sword in the form of genitalia.

Children may say "It's only a comic book," but they can't read a comic like *Son of Satan* and remain unaffected by its demonic overtones. Children are being tempted to experiment with occult powers after reading these pages of pulp. They dangerously pass beyond fantasy into fact, and the color illustrations become, to a child, reality.

Consider the following example: For three weeks, a sixteen-year-old boy had Fort Lauderdale police convinced his name was Raven Darkholme. He claimed he lived a vagabond existence with an older, mysterious woman who had abandoned him. He said his luggage had been stolen in a bus station when his adoptive mother, Amanda Stewart, left him. Raven said he never attended school and had no living family or friends.[1]

Detectives became suspicious when the strange youth repeatedly asked to buy comic books. They eventually found similarities between his stories and comic books from the *X-Man* series. The Marvel characters were so real to him that he borrowed the name of a blue-skinned villain and concocted a scenario of his own life from the comics he had been reading. Raven was finally committed to a mental health facility.

Most comic book aficionados don't need psychotherapy. But those familiar with the themes of today's comics must question the mental and spiritual stability of any comic book buff.

55

Cartoons

Twenty-five years ago a children's book writer named
Peyo Culliford reached across a Belgian dinner table.
Momentarily forgetting the Flemish word for salt, he
asked for the *schtromps.* The lingual slip gave birth to a
race of four-fingered blue trolls wearing white bonnets, a
creation that led to twenty-five best-selling books.
American audiences know Culliford's concoction as
popular cartoon creatures called Smurfs.[1]

During their Saturday morning time slot on NBC, the
Smurfs pull nearly half of the viewing audience, a
legendary accomplishment for any television program.
Whether they are rescuing their lone female companion,
Smurfette, from the evil wizard, Gargamell, or just
"smurfing around," they attract millions of child viewers.
The same youngsters head straight to toy stores and
gobble up $600 million worth of Smurf figurines, records,
coloring books, dart boards, and other Smurfabilia.

Papa Smurf and his clan resemble genial gnomes, but
there is concern that Smurf potions and magic tricks
precondition children to enter the occult world.

Art Clokey, creator of the 1950s cartoon character

Gumby, was a devout Hindu and a follower of Sai Baba,[2] whose demonic supernaturalism is described in my book *Larson's Book of Cults*. Various Gumby serials were replete with Eastern religious overtones.

Christian parents wonder whether Saturday morning cartoons enhance childhood social development or corrupt prepubescent spiritual values. Are the superhuman powers portrayed by today's cartoon characters an introduction to occultism? Will children who watch cartoons become too comfortable with the idea of occultism? No one is sure, but the potential for harm is there.

Whether or not cartoons familiarize children with the occult, they do familiarize them with violence. Before they reach the age of eighteen, children will have watched an average of twenty thousand hours of television.[3] Dr. Paul J. Fink of Thomas Jefferson University in Philadelphia has studied childhood viewing habits and concludes those obsessed by TV are less creative and more passive. They also purchase 23 percent of all TV-advertised products.[4]

According to the National Coalition on Television Violence, cartoon violence has increased 20 percent over the last year to an average of thirty-six violent acts per hour. Cartoon violence should be taken seriously. Children don't always understand that the characters are make-believe, and that violent, antisocial behavior is unacceptable in reality. Christian parents have additional moral responsibility when purchasing products by General Mills, McDonald's, Kellogg's, General Foods, and Mattel Toys, the prime cartoon advertisers. Since purchasing these products provides revenue for violent cartoons, we must ask whether we want to help finance such questionable entertainment.

Cartoons indulge blatant commercialism. Critics charge that programs like "Dungeons and Dragons," "The Smurfs," and "Strawberry Shortcake" are crass attempts to market products in disguised thirty-minute commercials. Cartoons cleverly blur the distinction between entertainment and product promotion. They exploit gullible children in order to sell dolls, games, and sugary cereals.

Critics are demanding that the Federal Communications Commission require programs like "The Smurfs" to be logged as commercial time, since its purpose seems to be marketing. Such a measure would drive most cartoons off the air, since stations would surpass the FCC's requirements that no more than sixteen minutes of commercials be aired each hour.

Newsweek magazine, not noted for its defense of biblical morality, recently expressed concern over cartoons in an article that eloquently summarizes parental worry regarding Saturday morning kid-vid: "TV's most impressionable constituents have become victims of what can almost be viewed as a form of child abuse: a weekend morning diet that causes severe intellectual malnutrition. Today's cartoons employ mythical super-heroes to impart a lesson—even the most trivial human problems require superhuman intervention. Commercial television is designed primarily as a vehicle for advertisers whose decisions are based on marketing research rather than what is best for the viewers."[5]

Cartoons are certainly not the most evil influences on the lives of children. Most are fairly innocuous entertainment that do little but kill time. Many readers of this book can think back over many hours spent watching the likes of Bugs Bunny and Daffy Duck, whose wacky antics did not turn viewers into violent, antisocial adults. However, our children's minds should be carefully guarded. When apparently innocent entertainment has the potential to familiarize children with occult practices, teach them to accept violence as a way of life, and lead them into lives of crass consumerism, that entertainment should be carefully watched—or turned off. A Saturday morning can be a time for families to play together, rather than a time for relying on the television as an electronic baby-sitter.

56
Television

Recently, I selected a typical weekday evening to survey network television. CBS aired a movie that featured a man who divorced his wife of twenty-one years to take up with a young stewardess. ABC's competition starred Angie Dickinson as a new bride who is introduced to her husband's mistress. On NBC, viewers found two adulterous cops involved in a love triangle and two detectives hiding out with a sexy centerfold girl.

Depending on your moral stance, such programs either titillate or depress. There are other things to view if you have access to cable or religious programming. But the network standbys of sex and violence still dominate television. Most cable programming is as bad, if not worse, than the network fare.

Blatant sexual immorality isn't all that TV has to offer. There's booze, for instance. On TV, alcohol is consumed fifteen times more frequently than water. There's violence, and lots of it. In fact, there's much more on TV than there is in real life. This frequent exposure to violence has its effects. George Gerbner, Dean of the Annenberg School of Communications at the University of Pennsylvania, conducted a study revealing that those who watch TV experience more fear and buy more guns. They also think crime is worse than facts indicate and create what Gerbner calls the "mean world syndrome." Gerbner believes such people will easily "yield to totalitarian control to restore order."[1]

This is unfortunate. Television, basically just entertainment, seems very real to people. Its biggest danger seems to be that it alters reality. People watch a distorted view of the world and come to accept it as true. Viewers watch six hours and forty-eight minutes a day in the average home, so they get quite a lot of distorted reality. David Rintels, former president of the Writers Guild of America, concludes, "The only way to get ratings is to feed viewers what conforms to their biases and what has limited resemblance to reality. From eight to eleven o'clock each night, television is one long lie."[2]

Someone has to create this lie. Who orchestrates the themes of network TV shows and formulates the images that shape our culture? Producers and writers do. The writers are hardly the sort Christians would like to have producing program material. A poll by Public Opinion of the American Enterprise Institute for Public Policy Research in Washington shows that, among television writers, 45 percent profess no religion and only 7 percent attend a religious service once a month. Eighty percent do not regard homosexual relations as wrong, 97 percent favor abortion on demand, 75 percent call themselves political liberals, and only 17 percent condemn adultery.[3]

The average American will spend fifty to seventy-five thousand hours in his lifetime watching what these people create.[4] What's the effect of this obsession? Mental bondage, according to 2 Peter 2:19: "For a man is a slave to whatever controls him" (TLB). Christians who absorb large quantities of TV are captivated by secular thought control instead of "bringing into captivity every thought to the obedience of Christ," as 2 Corinthians 10:5 declares. It is possible to be exposed to hours and hours of immoral entertainment and not have one's own morals affected. But the Bible warns against indulging in a presumptuous possibility (2 Thess. 5:22).

Of course, many families now own videocassette recorders, which means there are numerous alternatives to network and cable programs. Some alternatives are great—classic Hollywood films, for example. Today's video rental stores also feature tapes describing first aid, photography, and even a specialty item entitled *How to Watch Pro Football*. People can learn how to tone their bodies, snap their shutters, and improve their Sunday afternoons in the fall.

But the inclusion of sex on videotape is no surprise. The MCA Company has released a fifty-six minute video equivalent of *The Joy of Sex* entitled *Love Skills.* Costing $39.95, the tape features five young couples demonstrating varieties of sexual experiences. There's frank language, frontal nudity, and intercourse.[5]

To blunt criticism, the producers obtained the backing of Dr. Joshua Golden, director of UCLA's Human Sexuality program. Dr. Golden acted as chief consultant for the production and says, "This film is an excellent attempt to teach people how to be sexual. The opportunity to see how sexual relationships may be sexually accomplished can be learned in the security of one's own home."[6] According to those who have seen the tape, it encourages couples to think about another lover if that enhances erotic appeal. Other suggested fantasies include sex with a stranger, homosexual conduct, being seduced against one's will, and having sex in public.

With X-rated videos flooding the market and sexually suggestive acts being depicted in the flesh, what was left? Director Peter Conn strung together seven thousand photographs of nude women into a video centerfold.[7] For those too lazy to turn the pages of *Playboy*, Conn's porn video is like having your own *Playboy* magazine library on tape.

Sex-on-tape has its defenders. Wardale Pomeroy, a San Francisco psychologist with the Institute for Advanced Study of Human Sexuality and coauthor of the original

Kinsey Report, says, "Most of us have been brought up in
a culture that's inhibited. There has been no way to
actually watch sex until these videos came along."
Pomeroy does not address the issue of whether sex is
something to be watched.

Even so, there are multitudes of buyers and renters of
porn. If most are pleased to see explicit sex in the
comfort of their living rooms, at least a few are aware that
life does not—thankfully—imitate the lustful world of
video porn. One video porn purchaser named Debbie
told a reporter, "I hope my boyfriend knows people
don't do this stuff endlessly in real life. I'd need a
chiropractor to imitate what's on these video cassettes."[8]

Unfortunately, video porn is no joke. It threatens the
moral fiber of America in a way that X-rated art films
never did. It takes sex from the theater and moves it into
the home to make voyeurism convenient for those who
usually avoid flagrant perversion. Traditionally, X-rated
films draw people to theaters. Now, 60 percent of the
profits from X-rated films come from video sales and
rentals, a reversal of the pattern just two years ago when
70 percent came from theater rentals. Since 1983, X-rated
movie houses have closed at the rate of about fifteen per
month. With seven thousand X-rated movies on tape,
video porn is a booming business.

According to an article in the entertainment publication
Billboard, video sales of $2 billion were expected in
1985.[9] An estimated 25 percent to 50 percent of video
cassettes are X-rated. One industry analyst said that
rentals for adult videos outstrip purchases of other videos
twelve to one.

A *People* magazine poll revealed that 40 percent of its
readers watch X-rated tapes on VCRs. One sex video
marketer said, "It's the ideal vehicle. People don't want to
go to sleazy adult theaters." Video rental stores no longer
cater to the trenchcoat crowd. Instead, upscale urbanites
and oversexed suburbanites devour the major market
share of what has become known as "sex vid."

Cable TV operators are worried about video porn.

They fear that hard-core X-rated videos will stimulate people beyond ever wanting to watch the Playboy channel again.

Galatians 5:19-21 describes the "works of the flesh" and classifies the sins of fornication and lasciviousness in the same ranking with witchcraft and murder. Though film fans of X-rated videos may consider themselves morally respectable, God says their sins are the same as those who kill or worship Satan. Christian video addicts should heed the appeal of 1 Thessalonians 4:3: "It is God's will that you should be holy; that you should avoid sexual immorality" (NIV). Paul also warned us with these words: "For God did not call us to be impure, but to live a holy life" (1 Thess. 4:7, NIV).

Most Christians neither buy nor rent porn videos. Those who do, defy Scripture. If porn video were never brought into the home, the dangers of television abound, a threat illustrated by children's endless fascination with the medium. A recent Michigan State University study revealed that when four- and five-year-olds were offered the choice between giving up television or their fathers, a third opted to give up Daddy.[10]

Such results worry Cornell University psychologist Urie Bronfenbrenner, who observes: "The danger of TV lies not so much in the behavior it produces as in the behavior it prevents."[11] What concerns Bronfenbrenner and others is that television hinders communication between parent and child. Evidence indicates that television interferes with the capacity to entertain oneself and stifles the ability to express ideas logically and sensitively.[12] Television is the world's major means of communication, but it actually seems to hinder interpersonal communication and clouds the ability to distinguish between reality and fantasy.

No one would advocate doing away with television, but it behooves the caring parent to recognize its inherent dangers. Limit the time your child spends watching television and monitor the quality of what he does see. Encourage family talk, and spend time walking, reading, and resting the mind from the cacophony of constant TV blather.

RECOMMENDED READING BIBLIOGRAPHY

Bill, J. Brent. *Stay Tuned.* Old Tappan, N.J.: Revell, 1986.

Logan, Ben, and Kate Moody, eds. *Television Awareness Training: The Viewer's Guide for Family and Community.* Nashville: Abingdon, 1980.

Wildmon, Donald. *The Home Invaders.* Wheaton, Ill.: Victor, 1984.

COUNSELING/INFORMATION SOURCES

National Coalition on Television Violence
P. O. Box 2157
Champaign, IL 61820
(217) 384-1920

National Federation for Decency
P. O. Drawer 2440
Tupelo, MS 38803

57

Soap Operas

Joan loves Warren, who will divorce his wife Cindy as soon as she recovers from her mastectomy. But Cindy's doctor is also in love with Joan and plans to keep Cindy hospitalized as long as possible. He's got other worries too, including Nurse Cassandra, who's pregnant with his child following a late-night post-operative liaison. Rudi, Joan's husband, knows all about her affair with Warren and plans to tamper with the brakes on her Mercedes the next time she goes out for the evening.

To make matters worse, Rudi's pain over Joan's affair drove him to commit incest with his thirteen-year-old daughter, who was gang-raped last year after a football game. Will Joan and Warren ever fall into bed? Will Cindy ever make it out of bed? Will Rudi confess his incestuous lechery and give up his murderous schemes? And will Warren feel sorry for Cindy after her disfiguring surgery and dump Joan, leaving her free for the doctor's pursuit? And oh, yes, I almost forgot the pregnant nurse. How about an abortion for her?

Confused? This scenario is tame compared to the

convoluted sexual intrigue played out each day on the soap operas.

And with so many scenes emphasizing sex, you can be sure soaps won't reflect biblical values. Temple University conducted a study revealing that sex acts appear on soap operas with the frequency of 6.58 incidents per hour. A separate study by Dr. Bradley Greenberg of Michigan State University indicates that incidents of intercourse are almost always extramarital or premarital. Forty-nine percent involve lovers, 29 percent involve strangers, and only 6 percent depict married partners. Viewers of soaps must inevitably conclude that married couples hardly ever make love (or love each other), while unmarried people fornicate joyfully and often.

If you think the soaps are as sex-saturated as they're likely to get, think again. Actress Donna Pescow recently broke a last daytime TV taboo by playing a lesbian. But instead of depicting the unhappiness of those the Bible says have unnatural affections, the producers of "All My Children" chose to portray perversion positively. Brian Frons, NBC vice-president for daytime programming, says that soaps will soon feature "regular recurring homosexual characters."

Doug Marland, a writer for the soap "Loving," wants to present a full-blown homosexual romance story. Marland says, "It should be shown not as a problem but as a life situation."[1] The writers and producers of soap operas boast that frontal nudity and homosexual acts will be depicted once the barriers of public resistance collapse.

Perhaps the most dangerous aspect of the sexy soaps is the soap addict's overpowering urge to identify with characters whose make-believe stories seem real. After months of watching unbridled afternoon lust, the most innocent, unsuspecting woman can subconsciously become a willing candidate for adultery. The woman's rather ordinary husband may seem dull and uninteresting compared to the handsome—and sexually proficient— men on the soaps. The woman may conclude that everybody has extramarital flings anyway. Soap addicts would be hard-pressed to name one marriage on TV that has endured without constant threats of unfaithfulness and divorce.

Science fiction subplots, labyrinthine underworld intrigue, exotic dream sequences, and love—lots of love, whether it's romantic, parental, illicit, unrequited, or frustrated—that's what soaps are all about. Daily themes include abortion, frigidity, illegitimacy, and marital mayhem. Women are wicked, men manipulative.

Do you know any family that could sustain five affairs, four abortions, three seductions, two suicides, and one attempted case of incest in just one week? Are real families like this? Few are, but seeing such behavior played out on the screen every day desensitizes viewers. They cease to be shocked at immorality. Soap opera glorification of debauched characters encourages evil to infiltrate our whole society. Psalm 12:8 puts it this way: "The wicked freely strut about when what is vile is honored among men" (NIV).

The viewers who are being desensitized are not just coffee-sipping, apron-clad housewives. Many viewers are younger and better-educated now. College students and professionals watch soap operas. To reflect changes in the audience, the plots feature professional women, minorities, and blue-collar workers. But it's still immorality that sells soaps: illegitimacy, adultery, rape, incest, seduction, blackmail, theft, murder. And sell it does.

An average week's plot is seen in whole or part by fifty million people, mostly females aged eighteen to forty-nine.[2] An audience this large means big business for the networks. ABC earns an estimated 40 percent of its profits from daytime programming.[3] The thirteen soap operas broadcast by the major networks, spanning fifty-five hours a week, earn over $700 million in advertising revenue annually.[4] Just thirty seconds of exposure on a daytime soap brings in $26,000 in revenue.[5]

Can a big business based on immoral stories have any socially redeeming qualities? Gloria Monty, the producer of "General Hospital," says soap operas meet viewers' needs for family and community. But who wants a family consisting of a gang-raped teenage daughter whose father committed incest last year and has three affairs going simultaneously while he plots the murder of a business associate?

No, the soaps do little to promote the moral or mental health of individuals or society at large. David Phillips, associate sociology professor at the University of Southern California at San Diego, studied soaps and discovered that the nation's suicide rate increases about 3 percent after a soap opera character commits suicide. In addition, serious car accidents rise by 14 percent, leaving Phillips to conclude that "violent fictional television stories trigger imitative deaths and near-fatal accidents."[6]

Those who watch soap operas often exhibit depression and anxiety, aimlessness, and apathy. Viewing soaps does nothing for feminine self-esteem. Most viewers aren't as beautiful and elegantly dressed as the sleek screen women. Housewives don't have time for daily dalliances, since their only "afternoon delight" is likely to be changing diapers or wiping the baby's nose.

Soap opera characters are usually wealthy and conveniently free to engage in all kinds of conduct with limitless resources and boundless energy. You seldom see anyone wash dishes, vacuum a rug, or make a bed. Household responsibilities are missing, and so are positive parenting role models. Everybody's busy fornicating so fast they don't have time to look after kids. Soap operas don't show children being nurtured in positive values and raised to become productive citizens of society.

In spite of the blatant immorality in the soaps, Bible-believing housewives (and men) often watch these sin-saturated programs to fill idle time, to smother loneliness, or to escape the routine dullness of housekeeping responsibilities. Others are attracted by the voyeuristic nature of soap operas, checking in on the private lives of others to be tantalizingly titillated. In the process, they find themselves condoning immoral behavior and looking less disdainfully upon reprehensible conduct.

Galatians 5:24 tells us, "Those who belong to Christ Jesus have crucified the sinful nature with its passions and desires" (NIV). And 1 Peter 2:24 says, "We, being dead to sins, should live unto righteousness." It would seem difficult to "live unto righteousness" and honor Christ while watching soaps.

58

Movies

"The cinema is our greatest weapon." Lenin, the architect of Russian communism, wanted those words inscribed on every movie theater in the Soviet Union.[1]

The first master of moving pictures and science fiction cinema was a French stage magician, George Melies, who was also an avid occultist.[2] Both Lenin and Melies recognized that light and dark images flickering on a screen could alter states of consciousness. It could also produce a mild hypnotic trance, making the viewer more susceptible to unconscious manipulation.

In the early days of the Soviet Union, Russian film director Sergei Eisenstein said, "We have discovered how to force the spectator to think in a certain direction. By mounting our films in a way scientifically calculated to create a given impression on our audience, we've developed a powerful weapon for the propagation of ideas upon which our new social system is based."[3]

Swedish director Ingmar Bergman is one of the world's most famous filmmakers. His honors for his many films are too numerous to list. In 1983, his *Fanny and Alexander* won the Academy Award as the best foreign film of the year. Bergman, son of a Lutheran minister, says the secret to his success is a pact with the devil. While shooting scenes for the 1957 movie, *Wild Strawberries,* he waited for the sky to clear. Bergman says, "I tapped the ground and offered my soul to the devil if he would give me sun. Ten minutes later it was glaring sunshine." (Bergman also admits that as a child he used to invoke mental willpower to get revenge on others.)[4]

Successful director Ken Russell reveals his cinematic prejudice by declaring, "Politics is the dirtiest business we know, and religion isn't far behind it."[5] Such comments, as well as Russell's proclivity for salacious moral themes in his films, caused *Newsweek* magazine to note, "Sexual power is precious to him, and he jams it right under our noses."[6]

The picture isn't totally bleak. In 1981, *Chariots of Fire,* a stirring tale about Olympic runners, won the Academy Award for Best Picture and used no sex, violence, or profanity. In 1985, Robert Benton's *Places in the Heart* portrayed Christians in a sympathetic light and told a warm, inspiring story. Australian director Bruce Beresford's *Tender Mercies* gave us the touching tale of a washed-up country singer who becomes a Christian and settles down to a happy home life. These award-winning films were popular with both the public and the critics, but they are not representative of most movies shown in America today. Sex and violence dominate most stories, and movies get away with more explicit sex and graphic violence than television productions.

Cable TV and video rental centers have done nothing to diminish the public's appetite for movies. Multiplex theaters with six and ten auditoriums under one roof satisfy the desire for new flicks, partly because some films look better on the wide screen (e.g., *Star Wars* and *Gone with the Wind*). Another reason is that theaters are convenient places for kids to congregate.

The daily newspaper's movie section proves that more and more films are being produced for teenagers. In fact, 58 percent of moviegoers are under age twenty-five. Because of that youth, today's movies seldom bother with intricate plots and well-developed characters. An MTV generation wants fast visual images saturated with violence and sex. Tragically, most parents don't seem to care. They drop their kids off at the theater while they pursue their own interests. When the little ones are picked up several hours later, Mom and Dad rarely stop to think that their children watched a movie that may have drastically altered their perception of morality.

There is, of course, a rating system to serve as a guide to moviegoing, but it doesn't seem very helpful. The Motion Picture Association of America classifies films according to the following: X = morally obscene—no one under seventeen is admitted (the age limit varies in different places); R = restricted—moviegoers under seventeen (again, the age limit varies in different locales) must be accompanied by a parent or guardian; PG = parental guidance suggested; G = general audience— suitable for persons of all ages. Looking at all the films during a recent film season, these are the categories by percentage: R and X = 56 percent, PG = 40 percent. In other words, 96 percent of all films were unsuitable for family viewing.

Beginning in 1984 there is a new PG-13 rating. A movie labeled PG-13 contains material which, in the opinion of the ratings people, might be unsuitable for children under the age of thirteen. But "Parental Guidance" is strongly lacking, so the whole ratings system is, for the most part, a joke. Stand outside a theater some evening and watch who lines up. In most cases, the queue will consist of adolescents who have come for the thrill of gore and eroticism. No movie has ever been rated X because of its violent content. Producers can show bloodbaths, bashed brains, and pummeled people without fear of sanction. For the producers, the ratings system must be something to laugh at. They know the kids will sit through hours of gore and sex, and the parents don't seem to care.

Jack Valenti, president of the Motion Picture Association, once said, "It's unrealistic to think that once a kid starts driving you can monitor moviegoing."[7] Gene Shalit, the NBC film critic, cynically observes, "Ratings are forged to protect investors. At the heart of the hocum is the permissive R-rating, which is just a violent X-movie that kids can see, thereby increasing the profit potential."[8] One movie censor said it best, "PG should be called pure garbage."

Should Christian teens—or any Christian—attend movies? Many do, of course. Some Christians justify moviegoing because they like the high-tech visual images and special effects of today's Spielberg/Lucas film genre. Sounding like rock music fans rationalizing their unsavory musical tastes, born-again aficionados of film declare, "We don't pay attention to the message." That defense falls short when subjected to God's Word compelling us, "Prove all things; hold fast that which is good. Abstain from all appearance of evil" (1 Thess. 5:21, 22).

"Where does the Bible say I can't go to movies?" more than one Christian film fan has asked. Nowhere. But before you enter the theater again, consider the Scriptures:

All things are lawful for me, but all things are not expedient: all things are lawful for me, but all things edify not. . . . Whatsoever ye do, do all to the glory of God (1 Cor. 10:23, 31).

Let us not love in word, neither in tongue; but in deed and in truth (1 John 3:18).

Set your affection on things above, not on things on the earth (Col. 3:2).

The intent of this chapter is not to issue a blanket edict: "Don't go to movies." As indicated in an earlier paragraph, not all movies are demoralizing. Some are almost inspirational, and many are simply lighthearted, innocuous entertainment that harms no one. However, the great majority seem to glorify a self-centered and immoral lifestyle that can affect audiences, especially children and teens. Perhaps the best word of advice regarding any individual film is "When in doubt, avoid."

COUNSELING/INFORMATION SOURCES
Preview Movie Bulletin
1309 Seminole Dr.
Richardson, TX 75080

59
Science Fiction

In 1945, science fiction writer Arthur C. Clarke published a paper predicting a worldwide radio network via signals beamed from rocket stations. Today we call these stations *satellites* and take for granted a global village of instantaneous international communication.

Without Clarke's encouragement, President Kennedy might not have encouraged landing a man on the moon. Clarke's twenty-seven nonfiction books and twenty-nine novels have sold 20 million copies in twenty languages. Still on the drawing board of his science fiction visions are manned flights to Mars by 2005, space cities by 2010, and manned exploration of the solar system by 2030.[1] But while he has one foot firmly planted on the pillar of scientific research, Clarke's other foot is supported by an occult and metaphysical world view.

Arthur C. Clarke is hostile to biblical Christianity and exalts scientific humanism. He believes, "Any sufficiently advanced technology is indistinguishable from magic." Clarke lives as an expatriate in Sri Lanka and resides in a house he claims is inhabited by "a presence."[2]

There is much to learn from the ingenuity of some

science fiction writers, but Christians must carefully discern the occult theme of futuristic mystery. As in Clarke's case, the writer's pen may be guided by an ideology opposed to biblical thought.

Apparently many readers are not bothered by this. An estimated half-million science fiction fans devour the writings of Clarke, Frank Herbert, and others. Most of these aficionados are dissimilar to the stereotyped science-obsessed, pimply-faced bookworm. Until recently, science fiction fans were 95 percent male between thirteen and twenty. Today the median age is thirty-two to thirty-three, and climbing. Thirty-five percent of all science fiction fans are female.[3] In other words, science fiction is no longer the realm of a cultic minority. It has become mainstream, and has had an enormous effect on other media especially film.

The year 1984 was a high water mark. Nineteen of thirty-five major Hollywood films featured science fiction or fantasy/adventure. (Some science fiction buffs argue such films are ten years behind in terms of scientific accuracy.) *Star Wars, Star Trek, Gremlins, The Search for Spock, Ghostbusters, Dune, Supergirl, Dreamscape, Cocoon, Back to the Future,* and *2010* are just a few science fiction adventures recently attracting the public.

From the days of H. G. Wells and other pioneering authors, science fiction (SF) has been based on the most up-to-date findings of science—and on what scientists could predict (however hesitantly) about future developments. But all that passes for science fiction today is not so concerned with science. Today's film and literature genre is more often metaphysical than scientific, based on romanticized fantasy instead of futuristic theorizing. With its postulation of worlds that might be, science fiction goes too far for some Christians, especially when it passes beyond adventurism to serious consideration of psychic powers.

"Hard" SF is about gadgets, the places they take us, and the trouble they get us into, the old-fashioned stuff dating back to Buck Rogers and still with us in *Star Trek* movies. "Soft" SF is more fanciful. It speculates about the human predicament rather than spaceships. Some suggest this trend results from the decline of actual space exploration. With NASA research degenerating into cargo-ship voyages to ferry people into the ionosphere, those intensely interested in extraterrestrial endeavors probe soft SF novels to read about faraway worlds.

Reading about faraway worlds and unearthly characters is not necessarily bad. Children and adults have been fascinated for centuries by fantasy, and there is no harm in telling tales about strange creatures that everyone knows don't exist. Much good science fiction uses elements of storytelling that have been used for hundreds of years.

The late Frank Herbert, writer of the *Dune* novels, declared that science fiction depends on mythology, which he described as "the wise old man, the prince in search of the Grail, the virgin princess, the witch queen, and the sorcerer."[4] These mythical figures appear in literature throughout the centuries. In fact, they appear to be universal. Science fiction writers take these tried-and-true characters and place them in futuristic settings, or galaxies far from our own. These characters and stories are not harmful in themselves, but many writers introduce demonic forces or psychic powers as elements in the plots.

The growing trend of SF to indulge in occultism is disturbing. Science fiction fairs and conventions promote Clarke and Herbert products next to tarot cards and witchcraft literature. Clairvoyance has become as interesting as spaceships to SF fans.

Clairvoyance is only one of the questionable phenomena one finds in science fiction. Reincarnation and Eastern spirituality are also present in many books and movies.

"*Dr. Who*" has a hundred million television viewers in fifty-four countries. The series produced 602 episodes. Hardly a dashing figure, Who is a klutz constantly falling into danger. He has regenerated his life into as many as seven new entities. George Lucas's Yoda, (in *The Empire*

Strikes Back and *Return of the Jedi*) was unquestionably the personification of a Zen master. Obi-Wan Kenobi in the *Star Wars* trilogy represents a spiritualistic adept who guides humans, including Luke Skywalker, from "the other side." *Star Wars* producer Lucas says that perceiving auras enables us to see the future and the past, and to read minds. He admits his concept of The Force came from Carlos Castaneda's *Tales of Power,* the account of Castaneda's dealings with a Yaqui Indian sorcerer's apprentice. The *Star Wars* epics frequently invoke the mystical influence of telekinetic powers and present themes that are more Brahmanistic than scientific. Such films may entice youngster to explore the realms of demons, wizards, humanoids, and other-worldly creatures, perhaps leading them to take the first step into occult bondage.

This is not to suggest that science fiction is all demonic or that all the people who saw *Star Wars* are godless unbelievers. But the potentially harmful aspects of SF bear watching. We can be sure that SF is here to stay.

An entire generation is fascinated with the possibilities of space travel and encountering extraterrestrial aliens. Thus it is increasingly difficult for science fiction writers to avoid theological implications in their stories. They often explore from a nonbiblical perspective the themes of the origin of life and hope for the human condition. Many science fiction writers, like Clarke, openly oppose biblical Christianity and propose technology as the answer to man's problems.

Sometimes, however, science fiction novels and movies recognize the limits of technology and the inability of man to save himself. The need for a messiah to save humanity from its bondage of self-destruction recurs in movies like *Dune* and *2010.* Apocalyptic themes with a savior remind man of his frightful potential for mismanaging technology. As in the original Frankenstein films, the message seems to be, "Play God, and you end up with a monster." Such messages are not opposed to Christian teaching, since they reflect themes central to the Bible.

There are writers of science fiction and fantasy who have openly declared themselves to be Christian. But some Christians are even concerned about the writings of such Christian authors as J. R. R. Tolkien, G. K. Chesterton, George MacDonald, and C. S. Lewis. Lewis's *Space Trilogy* includes profanity and frequent references to supernaturalism. *The Chronicles of Narnia* features nymphs, dwarves, and satyrs as benevolent beings. In the Narnia series, Aslan, who represents Christ, participates in Dionysian rituals. Christians wonder how to approach books like *The Lord of the Rings* and *The Hobbit*, or *The Chronicles of Narnia* and the *Space Trilogy*, which contain demonic creatures.

Critics say these writers should be given the benefit of the doubt. While these writers may use questionable allegories and symbols, these excellent literary tools can convey truth, much like the parables of Jesus. Christians can use science fiction to convey spiritual truth, but must separate the biblical from the metaphysical.

Fantasy plays an important part in the development of man's intellectual processes. Without it there would be no art and literature to ennoble man's perception of his potential. But when corrupted with indulgent mystical speculation, fantasy entices evil. Chesterton, MacDonald, Lewis, and Tolkien may flirt with the boundaries of biblical propriety, but their fantasies occur in a theistic universe, not the cosmic void of Clarke, Herbert, and Lucas.

THE FUTURE
OF THE FAMILY

60

Sperm Banks

Inside several twenty-liter tanks in a cluttered garage in Escondido, California, lies what some think is the hope of mankind. The tanks are owned by eccentric millionaire Robert Graham, who believes the genetic heritage of children should be engineered by man. Those tanks contain the frozen sperm of men with above-average IQs, including Nobel Prize winners.[1]

Women who wish to bear the children of such illustrious men contact Graham's Repository for Germinal Choice. Supposedly, the applicants are screened carefully, but recently news leaked that one woman injected with sperm from the repository is Victoria Kowalski, a convicted federal felon accused of child abuse.[2] The future of her newborn daughter is questionable.

Women are waiting in line to bear the next superchild. Afton Blake is a forty-year-old unmarried mother of an eight-pound-eleven-ounce baby girl named Doron. The child was conceived by artificial insemination after her mother turned to page 28 in the catalog of the Repository for Germinal Choice. Mrs. Blake saw the picture of the man with whose sperm she would be impregnated. Ms. Blake, who has a Ph.D. in psychology, says, "I used the sperm bank instead of inviting someone to parent with me to leave the option open for a man to come into my life and adopt Doron and me."[3]

This year in the U.S.A., little Doron will be one of twenty thousand babies born through artificial insemination.[4] To some of the 10 million couples troubled by infertility, sperm banks answer their longing for a child. Sixteen American cryobanks accept the sperm of men who may have sold up to five hundred specimens each.[5] One donor who masturbates regularly to sell quantities of sperm says, "You make a trade . . . your life force for their money!"[6]

Unlike blood bank donations, which save lives, ejaculated specimens of seminal heritage portend frightening possibilities of manipulating man's future. (Sperm donations can also be deadly, as the recipient of an AIDS-contaminated specimen recently discovered.) Uniting sperm and egg from unmarried participants should come under the condemnation of the seventh commandment. Surely the mere physical union of sperm and egg is adultery in such cases. God ordained that human reproduction should occur within the bonds of matrimony as the result of an intimate, loving relationship between man and wife.

The case of a thirty-year-old Southern California man who died in an auto accident also raises moral questions. At his parents' request, sperm was taken from his body and is still stored to insure perpetuation of the family line. While such incidents appear emotionally desirable, sperm banks bring us another step closer to making babies consumer market items to purchase off the shelf.[7]

The stage for this moral dilemma was set by America's past promiscuity. According to a study based on a 1982 National Survey of Family Growth, fecundity has reached an all-time low. Only about half of couples of child-bearing age are physically able to conceive.[8]

The most common cause of infertility is a blockage or an abnormality in the fallopian tubes, resulting from

sexually-transmitted pelvic-inflammatory-disease (PID).
Each year a million or more women are afflicted, and at
least 15 percent become infertile as a result.[9] In the
American Medical Association *Journal*, researchers cite
two major reasons for PID: sexual activity at an early age
and intercourse with multiple partners.[10]

A generation that believed the lie "If you can't be with
the one you love, love the one you're with" suddenly
faces the fact that progeny may not bear its name. Hence,
sperm banks and similar means of circumventing
infertility appear attractive. The edict of Genesis 2:24,
"Therefore a man shall leave his father and his mother,
and shall cleave unto his wife: and they shall be one
flesh," fuses marriage and parenthood into a single, God-
ordained institution. Furthermore, the covenant between
Christ and his church is expressed on earth by the union
of man with woman in holy matrimony.

To separate sexuality from this context for narcissistic
motives destroys the meaning of the marriage union.
Becoming "one flesh" is a spiritual mystery not
necessarily fulfilled by the mixing and matching of
biological plumbing and its by-products. Before babies-
for-brew become a stocked shelf item at our local labs,
Christians need to seriously consider God's mandate for
matrimony and his scheme for sexuality.

61

In Vitro Fertilization

It was the time of month for Mrs. Brown's ovulation. Dr. Patrick Steptoe carefully inserted a laparoscope and removed several eggs. They were placed in a petri dish and exposed to her husband's semen. The mixture of eggs and semen was left in an incubator for two days. Then, several fertilized eggs were drawn into a Teflon catheter and inserted into Mrs. Brown's uterus.

Medical history was made with the 1978 birth of Mrs. Brown's daughter, Louise, the world's first test-tube baby. Hundreds of couples flocked to the Cambridgeshire Clinic seeking to duplicate little Louise's birth. Since obstetrician Dr. Patrick Steptoe and reproductive physiologist Robert Edwards combined their skills to pioneer *in vitro* (in glass) fertilization, approximately seven thousand test-tube babies have been born.[1]

In vitro fertilization unites egg and sperm outside the body in a petri dish, and the embryo is implanted in an infertile woman's body. Several variations on his procedure are employed. The standard American procedure is to unite the egg and sperm of husband and wife, implanting the fertilized embryo in the mother. In

Australia, the husband's sperm is often united with a donor egg flushed from the body of an anonymous woman. The fertilized egg is then placed in the wife's uterus. Another technique impregnates a donor by injecting the husband's sperm. The fertilized egg is washed out of the donor's uterus in a procedure called lavage, then placed in the recipient's womb. The child born of this sterile union belongs to the wedded husband and wife.

There are two hundred *in vitro* fertilization clinics worldwide and an estimated seventy in the U.S.A.[2] For the infertile, the hope of a family may rest in a small glass dish. But moral questions can't be ignored. One man who accompanied his wife to England for the procedure said, "You take a jar and walk to a room where there's an old brass bed and a couple of *Playboy* magazines. Everyone knows you are in there to get sperm, and they are waiting for you to finish." What has happened to the process of parenting when life is conceived because a man masturbated with pornographic magazines to supply sperm for *in vitro* fertilization? Because of this concern, some hospitals are setting up human protection committees, ethical committees for establishing guidelines for *in vitro* fertilization.[3]

What are the ethical implications? Since more than one egg is usually fertilized, moral consideration must be given for those not implanted. Some pro-life advocates believe it is murder to flush fertilized eggs down the drain. If they are frozen for later use, what legal right do these embryos have? Many Christian ethicists believe test tube babies circumvent God's natural order by separating sex from conception and the act of love from procreation. In an age when we insist on fast food cooked to order with all the right ingredients, we are in danger of treating eggs and sperm as if they were hamburgers to go with all the trimmings.

The effects of sin through drugs, alcohol, and venereal disease damaged the reproductive processes of an entire generation. Still, couples want babies, even if it means borrowing genes from someone else to assure parenthood. What will happen when thousands of *in vitro* fertilized babies grow into adulthood? Will they be like the genetically engineered droids in the film *Blade Runner,* uncertain of their parentage and responding angrily to establish identities denied them by natural biology? We may reap a generation of children who have lost the reproductive direction of where they've come from and unable to determine morally and spiritually where they are going.

In vitro fertilization isn't just another medical advance to welcome with open arms as the grand dream of the infertile. Its Orwellian implications are sobering. After all, without knowing the source of the egg with whom his sperm unites, a man could end up biologically married to his mother!

In Holland, a baby boy was born from an embryo that was frozen, thawed, and implanted in his mother's womb. His was the second such birth. The first product of a frozen embryo was an Australian girl born in March of 1984. At a cost from five to ten thousand dollars, many are considering cryopreservation, freezing unused embryos in a liquid nitrogen to try again if the first *in vitro* procedure fails. Thus participants avoid the need to undergo retrieval and fertilization all over again.

Other potential problems have to be considered. The British government formed a blue ribbon Committee of Inquiry into Human Fertilization to explore yet another twist in this enigma. Tests were conducted using hamster eggs to investigate male sub-fertility. The basis for this research is that men whose sperm will fertilize a specially treated hamster egg may eventually father a child, whereas those whose sperm will not are probably infertile. If these trans-species fertilization processes produce embryos capable of surviving more than a few days, we would have to deal with the dilemma of new life forms.

This isn't the only potential problem. Dr. Robert Edwards announced a desire to perform experiments on spare human embryos created during the *in vitro* fertilization process.[4] By doing so, Edwards says he'll be able to identify embryonic cells destined to develop into specific organs. Edwards wants to use these cells to correct blood disorders and to investigate diseases. The possibility of such research raises the question of whether a woman about to undergo *in vitro* fertilization should be treated with fertility drugs so doctors can harvest a large quantity of eggs. Theologians and moralists are understandably concerned with the prospect of using fertilized embryos as guinea pigs for genetic research.

In Australia, Dr. Ellen Trounson of Melbourne's Queen Victoria Medical Center has requested that fertilized embryos be allowed to grow beyond the current government-imposed seven-day limit.[5] Dr. Trounson wants to cannibalize embryonic tissue for use in curing people of fatal illnesses. The motives of Edwards and Trounson seem laudable, but can their intent mask the violence caused to life in its embryonic phase?

What might become of future investigation into transspecies fertilization and the possible treatment of impregnated embryos? Not to worry. Dr. Edwards assures us, "All this research is not designed to produce ogres. It is designed to help human life. The losers if it is prevented from happening will be patients. I believe the need for knowledge is greater than the respect accorded an embryo."[6]

Dr. Ian Kennedy, professor of medical law and ethics at King's College in London, eloquently addressed the issue of embryo experimentation in these words: "To prefer the interests of future children or science against those of a minuscule entity just because it is minuscule and immensely vulnerable is to assume what has to be proved, that the embryo's interests, because it is minuscule, are worthless."[7]

Like Sarah seeking to intervene with God's grace and provide a child for Abraham, some scientists infringe dangerously on the territory of God's sovereignty. The animosity that still exists between the descendants of Ishmael and Isaac should caution those who would charge recklessly into the brave new world of bioengineering. It seems even less prudent for modern man to tamper with life's beginnings than it was for Sarah to offer Hagar as a substitute for submission to God's will. We have already allowed the most intimate moments between a husband and wife to become passionless test-tube encounters. Our experimentation with *in vitro* fertilization puts us in the position of reconstructing man in man's image.

62

Surrogate Mothers

"I enjoy being pregnant," says Valerie, a New Jersey mother of two and wife of a truck driver. Valerie's joy of motherhood extends no further than the delivery room. She is a surrogate mother who answered a newspaper ad declaring: "Couple unable to have child. Willing to pay $10,000 fee and expenses to woman to carry husband's child. Conception by artificial insemination." Aaron and Mandy, the parents-to-be, kept Valerie's fee in an escrow account until the child was in their legal custody. In addition, they paid an agency fee of $7,500 and were responsible for up to $4,000 in doctors' fees, lab tests, legal costs, maternity clothes, and other expenses.

Other instances of surrogate mothering have gone less smoothly. The Alexander Malahoff case made headlines after he paid Judy Stiver of Lansing, Michigan, to bear his baby. The child was born mentally retarded. Malahoff said he wouldn't pay for an inadequately manufactured product. A blood test revealed the baby really did belong to Judy Stivers and her husband. Judy, who said she felt no maternal bond with the child, gradually accepted the legitimacy of her motherhood, though she complained she should have been warned to abstain from sex before the insemination.[1]

Several litigious issues surround the phenomenon of surrogate mothering. If the surrogate wants an abortion, should she be permitted to have it in spite of the investment made by the "customer"? What if the surrogate mother becomes emotionally attached to the baby and wants to keep it? Should the bonding between her and the baby be destroyed because of a prior agreement she signed? Could the biological father sue for custody? Suppose during the pregnancy the soliciting couple is divorced, or one of them dies and the remaining spouse doesn't want the baby on the way? Other ethical issues have been raised about one member of a lesbian couple being artificially inseminated, and homosexual couples purchasing babies through female surrogates.

In Kenya, surrogate motherhood is an ancient tribal custom for natives living in the Kissii area.[2] If a woman is infertile, she agrees to marry a younger woman. Her female bride receives a dowry and a traditional wedding. The wife selects a local bachelor to father a child with the bride, the infant becoming the property of the surrogate mother's female husband. Any future children born of this unusual woman-to-woman marriage belong to the female husband. The natural father of the children is ignored, and the natural mother, who serves as a surrogate, has no legal claim to the babies. Enlightened Kenyan citizens are appalled by the practice. As Africa becomes more Christianized, the practice of tribal surrogate motherhood is fading. Ironically, we in the West are seeking ways to produce babies by means that disregard moral considerations.

Dr. Richard Leven of Louisville, Kentucky, the first physician to institutionalize the surrogate system through his Surrogate Parenting Association, uses a computer to match his clients. Potential surrogates must be married with children of their own and undergo extensive physical and psychiatric examination. In addition, they must sign a contract agreeing to surrender the child at birth and abstain from tobacco, alcohol, and drugs during the pregnancy.[3]

Is surrogate mothering a selfish interference with the divine moral mandate to "be fruitful and multiply," or is it a modern means of bringing joy to infertile couples? Advocates argue that adoption is sometimes the end result of promiscuous sexual activity. If an illegitimate adopted child can be accepted by loving parents, proponents say the infant of an artificially inseminated surrogate should be equally welcome.

Childless couples have other alternatives to consider. With artificial embryonation, a couple pays a fee to a fertile woman who agrees to be inseminated with the husband's sperm. Four or five days after fertilization, the doctor harvests the embryo and implants it in the wife.

When the husband and wife are both infertile, embryo adoption can be arranged. A volunteer is inseminated with the sperm of a donor. The embryo is then harvested and implanted in the wife. In this case, the developing child does not bear the genetic identity of either the mother or father. When an infertile woman can carry a baby but cannot get pregnant, an egg may be surgically harvested from a fertile woman and implanted in the infertile woman.

Some consider surrogate motherhood a form of prearranged child abandonment because the mother surrenders the personhood she physically invested in her child. Others believe surrogate motherhood constitutes adultery by proxy, though it might be argued that the absence of lust removes it from any biblical prohibition. The harshest critics say that surrogate mothers are legitimized prostitutes whose services are maternal instead of sexual.

Scientific research reveals that unborn babies perceive emotional messages from their mothers. Even in the womb, fetuses experience the effects of rejection or acceptance from their biological mothers. What kind of torment does a baby by proxy suffer, knowing he is not wanted by the one in whose womb he resides?

The Roman Catholic Church opposes all forms of

artificial insemination, including that between natural parents.[4] The Orthodox Jewish community also views surrogating as immoral.[5] The American College of Obstetricians and Gynecologists expresses "significant reservations" because of the potential physical and psychological risks.[6]

Children should be the result of two people expressing their commitment to one another. High-tech parenthood as a business removes the mystery of life and reduces maternal instincts to a hireable commodity. Brewing a baby by consignment in a hired oven doesn't replenish the earth as God intended. It takes two to make a baby, and the surrogate mother must deny that her identity permeates the being she bears. Having the necessary reproductive plumbing allows our generation to separate the sexual act from the meaning of marriage. Surrogate mothering destroys the covenant of parenthood by simply making parents.

63

Genetic Engineering

Dr. Ronald Ericson has an unusual car license plate. It reads: *X OR Y?* The plate refers to Ericson's role as a self-styled genetic engineer. For a fee of $300, Ericson offers to determine in advance your child's sex. The *X* refers to the chromosome transmitting femaleness, and the *Y* indicates the chromosome resulting in a male baby.[1]

Ericson doesn't guarantee results, but he is 77 percent accurate. He takes male semen and puts it in albumen to separate the faster-swimming Y sperm from X sperm, and then injects the mother-to-be with the appropriate chromosomes. (Japanese scientists have a simpler technique, using electrical currents to segregate the Ys from the Xs.)

Some researchers think that sex selection of future children could occur in the bedroom. Couples could buy a cream or jelly that, used before intercourse, would kill the undesired X or Y chromosomes.[2] Imagine the possibility of buying at your local drugstore a product in pink and blue bottles that promises sex selection of your baby.

How can man presume the right to control the sexual

ratio of God's creation? The whole idea of genetical engineering sounds like something from the Book of Revelation, complete with strangely manufactured organisms and devasting plagues.

The prospect has caused concern among many Christians. An ecumenical coalition of Catholics and evangelicals recently signed a seven-point declaration asking Congress to ban genetic engineering that could alter genetically transmittable human characteristics. Their concern was not with the mass production of insulin for diabetics or the cure for hemophilia. The clergymen were alarmed that genetic scientists might go beyond solving chromosomal abnormalities to eugenically formulate a race of presumably perfect men.[3]

In 1982 a British science journal, *Nature,* reported on the results of researchers to produce a jumbo mouse.[4] Mr. Mighty Mouse looked like a normal squeaker, except he was genetically endowed with a rat growth hormone. What if some scientist were to accidentally create a new immune-resistent virus like AIDS? Dr. Stanley Barban of the Recombinant DNA Activities Office of the National Institute of Health admits that some genetically engineered microbes may have escaped from laboratories.[5] What strange strain lurks under a microscope, waiting for a puff of wind to waft it into someone's bronchial passages and thence lodge in the intestines, taking the first step to becoming a worldwide killer plague?

We would do well to wonder if we can trust scientists. Their methods are hardly foolproof, and their philosophy is suspect. It's impossible to understand today's genetic scientists without first comprehending their philosophy's foundation: evolution. As we consider how some scientists want to genetically alter the makeup of man, we first need to analyze Charles Darwin's theories, which reduced man to merely the highest rung on evolution's ladder.

In 1809, Shrewsbury, England, witnessed the unpretentious birth of a new male citizen, Charles Darwin. Born into a middle-class family, he subsisted on the inheritance left by his father. As a young man, he observed the efforts of cattle breeders to perfect the bovine strain and was fascinated by the results.

Later, on a five-year cruise around the world, he landed on the Galapagos Islands off the coast of South America. From his observations there, Darwin wrote two famous books: *The Origin of Species* in 1859 and *The Descent of Man* in 1871. The first book proposed that because offspring can vary from their parents, and because nature can tolerate only the survival of the fittest, the principle of natural selection can explain the evolution of a species. Natural selection refers to the process that results in the survival of individuals or groups best adjusted to their living conditions. His famous phrases "natural selection" and "survival of the fittest" have been incorporated into our language. Darwin's theories gained the avid admiration of Marx and Engels, the founders of communism, and guided their views of man and nature. They liked his idea that natural processes gradually weed out the weak and undesirable, leaving the strong and desirable to thrive.

As Darwin's theories began dominating his age, living creatures were seen as mere machines, evolutionary products that could experience neither pain nor pleasure. To illustrate this fact, nineteenth-century biologists experimented with animals. They nailed the feet of dogs to boards and cut animals open without anesthetic to watch their internal organs function firsthand.

Not only did Darwinism influence biology, it also influenced scientists' view of the universe's origins. Many scientists not only threw out the idea that man is a special creature made in the image of God but also the idea that the universe has a divine and purposeful origin. Evolution was made to apply not only to animals and man, but to the entire universe.

Psychiatrist Karl Stern of the University of Montreal describes the theory of evolution this way: "At a certain time the temperature of the earth was such that it became most favorable for the aggregation of carbon atoms and oxygen with the nitrogen-hydrogen combination, and that from random occurrences large clusters of molecules occurred which were most favorably structured for the coming about of life. And from that point it went on through vast stretches of time until, through processes of natural selection, a being finally occurred which is capable of choosing love over hate and justice over injustice, of writing poetry like that of Dante and composing music like that of Mozart and making drawings like that of Leonardo. Such a view of cosmo-genesis is crazy . . . psychotic . . . and has much in common with certain aspects of schizophrenic thinking."[6] Even so, such ideas dominate scientific thought and influence geneticists. It apparently has influenced the Supreme Court also.

In 1980 the Supreme Court ruled that when molecular biologists genetically engineer new life forms, such inventions are patentable and can be registered with the U.S. Patent Office.[7] When opposition lawyers argued that a living organism should not be patented, the Court countered by stating life is a "composition of matter." If a living thing is merely a specified composition of matter, does that definition apply to human beings also? The highest Court in our land has legally defined humanness in terms of a congealed quantity of atoms and molecules!

At the turn of the century, America favored eugenics, the systematic elimination of undesirable human characteristics. States passed sterilization laws and the U.S. Congress legislated an immunization law based on eugenics. Thousands of Americans with inferior traits were sterilized. After World War II started and Nazi practices were uncovered, the procedures were terminated.[8]

Few know that eugenics originated with Darwin's cousin, Francis Galton, who believed that curvature of the spine and club feet were evidences of inherited criminal characteristics. Galton suggested that families with this genetic defect should be prevented from breeding.[9] He wanted laws that favored healthy men and women. It is not comforting to realize Darwin's and

Galton's philosophical disciples are today's genetic engineers.

Nobel Prize winner Linus Pauling, a world famous scientist, suggests that carriers of genetic diseases should be tattooed on their foreheads, warning others not to mate with them. Pauling also wants compulsory testing for defective genes so that faulty couples could be legally forbidden to bear children.[10]

A U.S. Court of Appeals ruled that parents of a Tay-Sachs child be held negligent for not having aborted their unborn child.[11] Is genetic engineering setting the stage for the Antichrist? Could the mark of the beast be a tattooed sign indicating who is eugenically fit, as well as who can buy and sell?

Fans of the TV series "Star Trek" recognize the term *beam up*. The starship *Enterprise* contained a transporter room where matter is changed into energy and people can be instantly transported anywhere. Some genetic engineers subscribe to a similar theory, believing man's body merely encases a genetic record of information that could be dematerialized and preserved forever. These scientists view humans as composites of manipulable molecular patterns. Some even speculate about cloning this genetic imprint to make humanoids, robots without personal identity. The need is critical for Christians to beware of such speculation and guard our human family's genetic future.

RECOMMENDED READING BIBLIOGRAPHY

Anderson, Kirby. *Genetic Engineering.* Grand Rapids: Zondervan, 1982.

Rifkin, Jeremy. *Algeny.* New York: Viking, 1983.

64

Abortion

Rebecca is a beautiful two-year-old with curly dark brown hair. Her mother, Helen, loves her, but turns from Rebecca in occasional anguish. "I'll recognize a bit of her father in her, and I just can't take it," Helen sobs. Even though the pain seemed unbearable then, Helen is glad she gave birth to Rebecca.[1]

A victim of rape, Helen chose to keep her baby instead of killing her as do more than 1.5 million mothers each year who choose to have abortions. What makes this figure even more abhorrent is the fact that not all these abortions are performed on nonviable fetuses. Because 1.3 percent of all abortions are performed by hysterotomy, which results in the baby being born alive, more than twenty thousand such victims were murdered by America's physicians.

For the most part, these abortions were *not* requested by victims of rape or incest, which account for a negligible percentage of unwanted pregnancies. Most aborted babies were unwanted by women who were reluctant to interrupt career plans, or feared losing personal freedoms or disclosure of promiscuous affairs.

Abortion has become a form of postcoital birth control.

The 1973 *Roe v. Wade* Supreme Court decision on abortion legalized a form of infanticide. According to the majority opinion of the court, abortions during the first six months of pregnancy have no more significance than minor surgery. The Court stated that, during the first trimester, the decision to abort must be left "to the medical judgment of the woman's attending physician." Individual states are restrained from regulating abortion until after the fetus has developed enough to survive on its own, usually after seven months.

Justice Blackmun, who wrote the majority report, stated that the fetus is not a person under the Constitution and thus "has no legal right to life." Consequently, today's abortion statistics are obituary notices of lives with no record or history. Just as ancient pagans sacrificed their young to bloodthirsty idols, so today we offer our unborn on altars of selfishness, dishonor, and cowardice.

One cannot understand the murderous implications of abortion unless he first grasps the condition of the victims upon which such crimes are perpetrated. A brief chronology of fetal development clearly illuminates the picture.

At conception, a new and totally different being exists with forty-six chromosomes (the same as any human) and the capability of replacing its own dying cells. Within a week, the vertebrae, spine, and nervous system form, and the kidneys, liver, and digestive system begin to grow. By the eighteenth day, a primitive heart pumps its own blood. At thirty days, nubbins of limbs appear. The skeleton is complete at a month and a half, and its first movements are made. At five weeks, the brain divides into its three parts and grows rapidly. The eight-week-old fetus is barely an inch long and most of its internal organs are in place. The baby can grasp objects, swim, hiccup, suck its thumb, wake, and sleep with regularity.

At the eleven-week stage, all body systems are formed and functioning. The fetus now breathes, swallows, and is an independent individual sensitive to pain. Present systems will grow and mature, but nothing new will develop in the body. The sixteen-week-old fetus has grown to five-and-a half inches. Toes and fingers are formed, and facial features are clearly evident. "Quickening" is first felt at eighteen weeks as the fetus, now active and energetic, flexes its muscles, punches, and kicks. By the twentieth week, approximately half of the gestation period, babies are often prematurely born alive.

Considering this progression of fetal development, the question is raised as to when life might rightfully be terminated. It is argued that the definition of life depends upon the fetus's ability to survive outside the womb. This position is relativistic because such viability was at the thirty-week stage thirty years ago. Today, a twenty-week fetus can survive outside the womb.[2] Soon medical science may lower viability to ten or twelve weeks. If it is determined that life starts at conception, all other designations are subjective.

Of course, some will set forth emotional and seemingly plausible defenses for abortion. It has been argued that abortion is preferable to bearing unwanted children. But a recent study shows that nine out of ten women or families involved in child abuse admitted planning the pregnancy of the abused child. Being wanted offers no assurance of being loved. Statistics show that the overwhelming majority of abortions are performed on young, single, middle-class whites who are pregnant for the first time. Indeed, over 30 percent of all legal abortions are performed on teenage girls, the majority of whom are unmarried.[3]

Others contend abortion is justifiable if the mother's life is endangered, an irrelevant argument. Any conscientious doctor will attempt to save the life of both mother and child. If only the mother's life can be saved, the surgical procedure cannot be considered an abortion. A similar circumstance occurs when a multiple of lives is endangered, as in a fire or plane crash. If it is impossible to save everyone, rescuers cannot be accused of killing those who were lost, assuming a reasonable attempt was made to save as many as possible.

Arguments favoring abortion would probably fall silent if more people had a clear understanding of how they are performed. There are four methods of abortion:

Suction: Seventy-five percent of all abortions are performed by suction, which is used prior to the twelfth week of pregnancy. A suction tube is inserted, and pressure tears apart the baby's body. These embryonic pieces are trapped in a jar or tissue paper. The broken and crushed body is recognizable.

D & C: This form of abortion is used between seven and twelve weeks. The physician inserts a sharp, curved knife into the uterus and cuts the tiny body to pieces. The attending nurse has the disgusting duty of reassembling the fetus to ensure no tissue is left in the mother.

Saline injection: This process is normally used in sixteen- to nineteen-week pregnancies and is the second most common form of abortion. An eighteen-inch-long needle is inserted into the mother's stomach, and a toxic solution is injected. The baby breathes in the solution and is poisoned. The outer layer of his skin burns away. The baby dies in about an hour, and the next day the mother delivers the stillborn child.

Hysterotomy: This operation is similar to a caesarean section. Instead of saving both mother and child, however, a hysterotomy terminates the baby's life. The child is always born alive and often fights to survive by breathing, moving, and crying.

Abortion constitutes the premeditated killing of a helpless victim and must be considered an atrocity. No matter now it is done, the process is violent and painful. Even the possibility of birth deformities (sometimes used as a justification) seems less cruel. After all, the Scriptures declare in Exodus 4:11, "Who maketh the dumb, or deaf, or the seeing, or the blind? Have not I the Lord?"

Of course, the evolutionist should have no qualms about abortion. He is only disposing of another animal, an action no different from taking one's aged dog to the veterinarian for euthanasia. But Christians are bound by the Bible, and the Scriptures have much to say about the origin and importance of life.

Exodus 21:22 is a reference pro-abortionists often quote, suggesting this passage approves abortion by defining the phrase "her fruit depart from her" as a reference to a miscarriage. Thus, when the Mosiac Law applies only a fine to the supposed miscarriage and the death penalty is applied in the event of killing the mother, it is assumed that God places a higher priority on the life of the mother than that of the fetus. The interpretation is erroneous, in spite of its wide acceptance.

Bible scholars have analyzed this passage and conclude that, rather than referring to the destruction of a fetus, the phrase "her fruit depart from her" describes the premature birth of a child.[4] When Exodus 21:22 is viewed in this perspective, the fine is seen as being imposed because birth is induced through malicious injury to the mother. Thus, there is no distinction between harm done to the mother and that done to the child. The text only distinguishes between a premature birth that does not harm the mother or the child, and a premature birth in which one or the other is injured or dies.

There are three basic biblical teachings that reflect on the issue of abortion.

GOD IS THE CREATOR OF HUMAN LIFE AND THIS LIFE IS MADE IN HIS OWN IMAGE

Genesis 1:26-27 states that all human life is created by God. Man is only a partner in the procreative process. Genesis 4:1 shows that Eve viewed Cain as a distinct being from the moment of conception. Psalms 119:73 and 127:3, and Job 31:15 affirm the belief that we are fashioned in the womb by the hand of God. Abortion usurps God's authority by assuming that man has the prerogative to intervene with God's mandate of creation, precisely the definition of murder.

GOD KNOWS EACH OF US AS
A DISTINCT PERSON BEFORE BIRTH

There are many in the Scriptures whom God claimed to
know before birth. They include Cain (Genesis 4:1), Isaac
(Genesis 21:1-5), Ruth (Ruth 4:13), and Samuel (1 Samuel
1:19-20). These words are found in God's address to
Jeremiah (Jeremiah 1:5): "Before I formed you in the
womb I knew you, and before you were born I
consecrated you."

Abortion is an act of man that defies God's will and
purpose for every person. One can only speculate how
many of the current adult population resulted from
unplanned pregnancies that might have been aborted
under our current liberal laws. It is frightening to
consider that some of today's great preachers and
missionaries might have ended up as bloody pulps in a
fetal garbage dump.

GOD RELATES TO THE FETUS AS
BEING FULLY HUMAN

In Luke 1:41-44 we are told that John the Baptist as a fetus
"leaped for joy." A mere piece of tissue has no capacity
to experience emotion. Job (Job 3:11) saw himself as a
person *in utero* and Isaiah (Isaiah 49:1, 5) declares that
Christ was called forth from the womb. King David (Psalm
139:13-15) states that he was intricately fashioned by God
in his mother's womb and that his conception was in a
state of sin (Psalm 51:5). He was thus more than a
potential person, for only a redeemable being could
possess the capacity for sinfulness.

Secular arguments for and against abortion usually
concentrate on genetic uniqueness, the development of
the cardiovascular system, or the prescence of brain
waves. Christians have an additional criterion, the
revealed Word of God. Christ as the living Word was by
his incarnation an anti-abortion argument. Christ became
man at the moment of conception by the Holy Spirit. His
divinity was not infused into Mary's fetus at some later

date. The Bible's position on abortion should be clear: Abortion is not a viable option for Christians, except as a last-ditch attempt to save the life of the mother when only the mother can be saved.

RECOMMENDED READING BIBLIOGRAPHY

Garton, Jane Staker. *Who Broke the Baby.* Minneapolis: Bethany, 1979.

Hekman, Randall. *Justice for the Unborn.* Ann Arbor, Mich.: Servant, 1984.

Willke, Dr. and Mrs. J. C. *Abortion Questions and Answers.* Cincinnati: Hayes, 1985.

65

Infanticide

In April 1982, a baby boy afflicted with Down's syndrome was born in Bloomington, Indiana. His attending physician, Dr. Owens, advised the parents not to treat the child but to withhold food and water until he died. The local judge who ruled on the case stated that Dr. Owens described the child as a "blob" that was unlikely to enjoy "even a minimal quality of life." Six days later, Baby Doe was dead.[1]

Baby Doe became a symbol of pro-life concerns about infanticide. When the government sought to post notices in hospitals asking that any withholding of sustenance from infants be reported, many medical officials were outraged. Why? Why should civil authority not intervene to save the life of a helpless infant? Ironically, the government sets workers' safety standards for police, the environment, food and drugs. If Baby Doe's parents had starved their baby because he was dark-complected or ethnically undesirable, nothing would have been said about intruding upon the parents' private rights.

In effect, infanticide has been legally established as the right of parents desiring to qualitatively evaluate the life of their newborn. A report in the *New England Journal of Medicine* states that a survey of one medical unit revealed 14 percent of infant deaths occurred because parents decided their newborn babies did not have lives worth living.[2] Have humans become no better than certain species of monkeys that eat their young to bring the mother into heat so she can sire a new generation?

Dr. Anthony Shaw is a pediatric surgeon and head of the Ethics Commission of the American Academy of Pediatrics. In an age when Down's syndrome and spina bifida children often survive, Dr. Shaw has devised a formula determining a newborn's potential quality of life. His three criteria are: "What is the child born with? What can medical science do for the child? What is the home life of the child going to be like?"[3]

These criteria shock pro-life advocates. Dr. Shaw's formula is merely a rationale for infanticide. Instead of doing everything possible to preserve the life of every newborn child, Dr. Shaw dares suggest that the qualitative social environment in which the child will be reared should help determine its right to life. Presumably, a Park Avenue paraplegic child has more right to survival than a ghetto-born Tay-Sachs diseased infant.

Nobel laureate James Watson stated in May 1873, "If a child were not declared alive until three days after birth, then all parents could be allowed the choice only a few are given under the present system. The doctor could allow the child to die if the parents so choose, and save a lot of misery . . . this view is the only compassionate attitude to have."[4]

Watson's codiscoverer of the DNA double helix, Francis Crick, argues that no newborn infant should be declared human until it has passed certain tests regarding its genetic endowment. (Crick has also proposed compulsory death for everyone at age eighty.[5])

Peter Singer, a biomedical ethicist, had this to say in the July 1983 issue of *Pediatrics* magazine, the journal of the American Academy of Pediatrics: "Once the religious mumble-jumble surrounding the term 'human' has been stripped away . . . we will not regard as sacrosanct the life of each and every member of our species, no matter how limited its capacity for intelligence, or even conscious life may be. If we compare a severely defective human infant with a non-human animal, a dog or a pig for example, we will often find the non-human has superior capacities, both actually and potentially for rationality, self-consciousness, communication, and anything else that can plausibly be considered morally significant. Only the fact that the defective infant is a member of the species homo sapiens leaves it to be treated differently from the dog or pig. Species membership alone, however, is not morally relevant."[6]

Professor Singer also states: "Something is a person if and only if it is a continuing subject of experiences and other mental states that can envisage a future for itself and then can have desires about its own future states." If this seems cruel, consider another statement by Singer: "Mental defectives do not have a right to life and therefore might be killed for food—if we should develop a taste for human flesh—or for the purpose of scientific experimentation."[7]

Alas, Singer is not the only person who holds such views. In England two years ago, a British pediatrician was charged with the attempted murder of a three-day-old born with Down's syndrome. When he was acquitted by unanimous jury verdict, the pubic gallery erupted into applause and cries of "Thank God!"

Pro-life groups view infanticide as the natural result of legalized abortion. Public opinion seems to say, "Why can't I kill my baby *ex utero* when just a few weeks ago I could have terminated the fetus while still in my womb?" Having accepted abortion as a means of birth control, society is in danger of adopting infanticide as a means of death control.

Joseph Fletcher, responsible for developing the theory of situation ethics, once wrote, "Induced death may not be condemned categorically ... it is unreasonable ethically to say that all acts of euthanasia are wrong." Fletcher also said, "If fetuscide is lucid, why not infanticide?"[8]

In the animal kingdom, infanticide may be excused as

a means of survival in a harsh environment where only the strong will be able to perpetuate the species. In modern life, infanticide is becoming a course of convenience for parental consumers who will not accept a product with genetic defects. If cars can be recalled, why not babies?

The words of Christ in Matthew 12:11-12 are particularly applicable to this generation: "And he said unto them, what man shall there be among you, that shall have one sheep, and if it fall into a pit on the sabbath day, will he not lay hold on it, and lift it out? How much then is a man better than a sheep? Wherefore it is lawful to do well on the sabbath days." The Pharisees prized an animal more than an ailing human. Similarly, today's infanticidal ethicists cheapen the dignity of every living creature. In the words of one writer, "Infant Doe died because he had the misfortune to be born into a brutal nation of activist barbarians and passive Christians!"[9]

RECOMMENDED READING BIBLIOGRAPHY

Schaeffer, Franky. *Bad News for Modern Man.* Westchester, Ill.: Crossway, 1984.

66

Euthanasia

Emily Gilbert would disappear into the ladies' restroom while at a restaurant and stay there indefinitely. Her daughter would look for her and find her staring vacantly into a mirror. Occasionally, Emily told family members she hadn't seen them in ten years, when in truth she had conversed with them earlier that day. As Alzheimer's disease exacted its terrible toll, her husband administered enemas and personally cared for her feminine hygiene. Though her pain from a degenerative bone disease was unbearable, she refused painkillers. Half the time, Mrs. Gilbert awakened in the morning and didn't know who her husband was. After fifty-one years of marriage, she wondered why he was sleeping with her.

On March 4, 1983, Roswell Gilbert, age seventy-five, walked up behind his wife Emily, age seventy-three, and shot her once through the temple. He felt her heart. It was still beating. He went back to the bedroom, reloaded, returned, and shot her again, this time fatally.

Ten years of Alzheimer's disease and osteoporosis had reduced Emily Gilbert's life to painful confusion. In court, the defense attorney argued Roswell Gilbert had given his wife the gift of euthanasia. But the pleas of mercy for a mercy killer went unheeded. Gilbert was found guilty of first degree murder and sentenced to twenty-five years in prison.[1]

Euthanasia, commonly referred to as mercy killing, is taken from the Greek word meaning "good death." Passive euthanasia is interpreted as merciful termination of the life of someone who is hopelessly injured or diseased and kept alive with extraordinary medical measures. Active euthanasia is intentional, artificial shortening of life because of unendurable pain or an individual's desire to terminate what he feels is a qualitatively inferior existence.

In 2 Samuel 1:6-16, an Amalekite came to David claiming he had killed Saul, when in fact Saul committed suicide. In verse 10, the Amalekite declared of Saul, "I was sure that he could not live." Believing the man's story, David had him executed, even though the Amalekite's murder of Saul might have been considered mercy killing. Based on what he had been told, David's response was to enforce capital punishment on the one who had hastened Saul's certain death. This seems to indicate that Christians should take a dim view of so-called mercy killings. The fact that Roswell Gilbert was found guilty of murder indicates that many people share the biblical view of euthanasia. But there is much discussion in our society about the possibility of euthanasia.

While society debates whether terminally ill patients have the right to be removed from respirators, a "death enhancement" movement is taking things a step further. ("Death enhancement" is merely a euphemism used to remove the stigma of what is actually taking place—murder.) For months the world watched a Riverside, California, hospital room where Elizabeth Bouvia, a twenty-six-year-old quadriplegic victim of cerebral palsy, demanded the right to end her life. The American Civil Liberties Union took her side, arguing she had the right to terminate her existence. "I want to kill myself because

I'm tired of living," she said. However, the hospital refused her wish to starve, arguing the decision was neither competent nor rational.

After discharge from Riverside Hospital, Bouvia went to Tijuana, Mexico, where she changed her mind, decided to live, and ended her starvation fast. A few days later, Elizabeth reversed that decision. Such capriciousness is common among the terminally ill and handicapped. It causes much concern for those who oppose euthanasia, for they feel that the person who expresses the wish to die may later change his mind. Granting the person's wish may mean granting the wish of a person whose great stress has led to capriciousness.

Surely it is unwise—and potentially cruel—to grant such person's request to die. But not everyone agrees. Derek Humphrey, author, journalist, and executive director of the Hemlock Society, which advocates the right to suicide, has written, "Mercy killing is a desperate act of love . . . dignified self-deliverance." Humphrey freely admits assisting his cancer-stricken wife to die and calls her death a "rational suicide."[2] Like other advocates of "death enhancement," he sees such actions as "enhancing" an impending death.

It is one thing to turn off life-support machines for comatose or brain-dead patients in agreement with family and physicians. Granting a depressed patient's wish for a lethal drug injection or removing unheroic life-sustaining measures is another matter. Active euthanasia advocates argue that anyone should be permitted to die without invading his right of privacy and self-determination. They reason that everyone should be able to request death and expect hospital officials to cooperate, administering the lethality to terminate life.

William Bartling lay dying of emphysema and a combination of five fatal illnesses. He asked doctors at the Glendale Adventist Medical Center to turn off his respirator. The doctors refused, insisting they would not be executioners. While both sides squabbled in court, Bartling finally died. A California appeals court declared later that competent adult patients have a Constitutional right to refuse medical treatment, even though it means death.

Ellis Mehling, executive director of the Society for the Right to Die, commented, "We want self-determination for the patient, whether that means continuing treatment or dying with dignity."[3]

But the assistant director of public relations for Glendale Adventist Medical Center responded, "Is a depressed patient to be terminated because he requests it on a Blue Monday, even if he changes his mind on Tuesday?"

There is concern that the right to die movement wants to take from the individual and his physician the responsibility for health care and transfer these decisions to a committee. Some worry this could lead to government-mandated deaths because some bureaucrat will determine money can be saved by allowing select patients to die. Those concerned with Medicare costs point out that 11 percent of all Medicare expenditures are incurred in the last forty days of life.[4] If a society becomes convinced that mercy killings are legitimate, what is to stop committees in hospitals, nursing homes, and other facilities from deciding to let patients die in order to save money? Our society allows for quick—and legal—disposal of unwanted infants through abortion. Is it not possible—even likely—that the same society will, for similar reasons of convenience, give its consent to the deaths of extremely ill or handicapped persons?

Opponents of the right to die movement claim the movement has a hidden agenda: removing undesirables—the elderly, the terminally ill, the severely handicapped—from society. The right to die movement would say that such terminations would, of course, be done in the name of mercy and compassion, just as pro-abortion groups proclaim their compassion for the mother and, yes, even for the unborn child.

Christians also claim to be motivated by love and compassion. If we act in accordance with the Scriptures, we must affirm life and the prerogative of God to terminate it. We cannot always be sure when so-called heroic medical procedures have gone too far by prolonging the functioning of bodily organs in a person who is comatose and almost certainly unable to recover. Hospitals are able to prolong biological life for long, long periods. But should they? Certainly they should—if the person is likely to recover consciousness, or if he is still aware of the presence of other persons.

Usually it is more humane to allow the person to live and to let death occur naturally. On rare occasions it may actually be more cruel to prolong biological life simply because the medical resources are available. The Catholic Hospital Association deals with this dilemma in its document called a Christian Affirmation of Life. It states that a person is "bound to use ordinary means to preserve my life, but I am free to refuse extraordinary means to prolong my life. No means shall be used with the intention of shortening my life." The last three words constitute a firm stance against those who advocate granting a person's wish to die. It is also a slap at those who would put such decisions in the hands of a committee or government agency.

Regrettably, some members of the medical community side with the right to die movement. Dr. Joanne Lind, a geriatrician and ethicist at George Washington University, says, "Death may be preferable to life that is brief, painful, or lacking awareness. Long-term nutrition should not be used if it only causes death and pain without compensating benefit."

Such thinking worries Father Richard McCormick of Loyola University's School of Theology. McCormick says, "Once you pass judgment that certain kinds of life are not worth living, the possible sequence is horrifying. In Nazi Germany, they went from mental defectives to political enemies to whole races of people."[8]

It seems the American public as a whole does not share Father McCormick's fears. A recent survey indicates that 60 percent of American citizens believe a terminally ill person has the right to die. But a closer look at that statistic reveals that 75 percent of those between eighteen to twenty-four support the right to die, while only 54 percent of those sixty-five and older support the practice.[6] Obviously, those nearer the reality of euthanasia have less enthusiasm for it. Young people who favor euthanasia perhaps have difficulty thinking of themselves as being "terminated" in the future by a hospital committee that decides who is or is not enjoying a "quality" life.

Malcolm Muggeridge, the noted social critic and Christian commentator, has this to say about mercy killing: "What we think and do about birth and death determines what we think and do about life. No government in the history of the world has ever put a euthanasia bill on the statute books except the Nazi government of the Third Reich."[7]

Notes

CHAPTER 1. SINGLES

1. *Eternity,* March 1983, 23.
2. *USA Today,* 10 Nov. 1983, 3D.
3. *USA Today,* 21 May 1984, 1A.
4. *USA Today,* 10 Nov. 1983, 3D.
5. Ibid.

CHAPTER 2. LIVE-INS

1. *Newsweek,* 17 Jan. 1983, 27.
2. *People,* 14 March 1983, 46-47.

CHAPTER 3. DATING

1. *People,* 16 April 1984.
2. *USA Today,* 29 Feb. 1984, 4D.
3. *USA Today,* 4 April 1984, 3D.

CHAPTER 4. MATE SELECTION

1. *USA Today,* 7 April 1983.
2. Ibid.
3. *USA Today,* 5 April 1983.

CHAPTER 5. MARITAL SEX

1. *USA Today,* 13 March 1984, 1D.

2. *USA Today,* 15 July 1983.
3. *USA Today,* 23 June 1983, 1D.
4. *East/West Journal,* July 1983, 8.
5. *USA Today,* 8 Nov. 1983, 1D.
6. *Christianity Today,* 21 Oct. 1983, 15.
7. *Time,* 4 April 1983, 80.
8. *USA Today,* 14 Aug. 1984, 2D.

CHAPTER 6. BIRTH CONTROL

1. John T. Noonan, Jr., *Contraception* (Cambridge, Mass.: Harvard University Press, 1965), 9.
2. *USA Today,* 23 Nov. 1983, 10A.
3. *USA Today.*
4. *Us,* 3 June 1985, 58.
5. *Newsweek,* 10 Oct. 1983, 37.
6. *Newsweek,* 11 March 1985, 48.
7. *Dallas Times Herald,* 4 March 1984.
8. *USA Today,* 23 Nov. 1983.
9. *USA Today.*
10. *Us,* 3 June 1985, 58.

11. *Fort Worth Star-Telegram*, 6 Feb. 1985.
12. *USA Today*, 3 April 1985, 5D.
13. Ibid.
14. Ibid.
15. *USA Today*, 12 July 1985, 1D.
16. *People*, 14 Jan. 1985.
17. *Time*, 10 Dec. 1984.
18. *Time*, 3 Dec. 1984, 66.
19. *USA Today*, 15 Feb. 1985, 1D.

CHAPTER 7. INFERTILITY

1. *USA Today*, 11 Feb. 1985, 1D.
2. *USA Today*, 18 May 1984, 6D.
3. *USA Today*, 11 May 1983, 3D.
4. Ibid.
5. Ibid.
6. Ibid.

CHAPTER 9. ADOPTION

1. *Newsweek*, 18 Feb. 1984, 80.
2. Ibid.
3. *USA Today*, 1 Sept. 1983.

CHAPTER 10. CHILDBEARING

1. *USA Today*, 7 Sept. 1983.
2. *USA Today*, 11 Jan. 1984, 4D.
3. Ibid.
4. *USA Today*.
5. *USA Today*.
6. *USA Today*.
7. *USA Today*, 9 Sept. 1983.
8. *East/West Journal*, Feb. 1985.
9. *Money*, Dec. 1983, 205.
10. *USA Today*, 7 Sept. 1983.

CHAPTER 11. BABIES

1. *USA Today*, 11 Jan. 1984, 1D.
2. *USA Today*, 26 April 1984, 1A.
3. *USA Today*, 15 May 1985, 96.
4. *USA Today*, 30 August 1984, 1D.
5. *East/West Journal*, April 1984, 11.
6. Donald Joy, *Bonding: Relationships in the Image of God* (Waco, Tex.: Word Books, 1985).
7. Ibid.
8. *USA Today*, 20 July 1983, 3D.
9. *USA Today*, 11 June 1984, 1D.
10. *Forbes*, 25 Feb. 1985, 138-139.

11. *Good Housekeeping*, April 1985, 84ff.
12. *Science*, 221: 1290.
13. *Time*, 15 Aug. 1983, 59.
14. *USA Today*, 2 Dec. 1983, 6D.
15. *Time*, 15 Aug. 1983, 59.

CHAPTER 12. MOTHERHOOD

1. *Newsweek*, 16 March 1981, 86.
2. Ibid.
3. *Psychology Today*, Aug. 1982, 10ff.
4. *Newsweek*, 19 May 1980, 72.
5. *USA Today*, 17 March 1984, 4D.

CHAPTER 13. PUBLIC EDUCATION

1. *Time*, 9 May 1983, 62.
2. *USA Today*, 29 April 1983, 10A.
3. *Fort Worth Star-Telegram*, 23 Nov. 1983, 12A.
4. *USA Today*, 31 May 1984, 2A.
5. *USA Today*, 14 Dec. 1983, 10A.
6. *Time*, 23 Jan. 1984, 57.
7. *USA Today*, 26 June 1984, 3A.
8. *Time*, 18 July 1983, 46.
9. *USA Today*, 28 June 1984, 10.

CHAPTER 14. CHRISTIAN SCHOOLS

1. *Cornerstone*, Vol. 12, No. 69: 16.
2. *Liberty*, May/June 1984, 12.
3. Ibid., 9.
4. Ibid., 12.

CHAPTER 15. HOME SCHOOLING

1. Raymond and Dorothy Moore, *Homespun Schools* (Waco, Tex.: Word Books, 1982).
2. Ibid.
3. *USA Today*, 2 Dec. 1983, 10A.
4. *Reader's Digest*.

CHAPTER 16. MISSING CHILDREN

1. *USA Today*, 14 Oct. 1983, 10A.
2. *USA Today*, 1 June 1983, 10A.
3. Ibid.

CHAPTER 17. SPANKING

1. *USA Today*, 21 May 1984.

2. *Fort Worth Star-Telegram,* 25 June 1985, 4E.
3. Ibid.
4. Ibid.
5. Ibid.
6. Ibid.
7. Ibid.
8. *USA Today,* 11 July 1984, 8A.
9. *USA Today,* 23 Oct. 1984, 8A.

CHAPTER 18. CHILD ABUSE

1. *Rocky Mountain News,* 7 Jan. 1985, 30.
2. *Rocky Mountain News,* 13 April 1983.
3. Naomi Feigelson Chase, *A Child Is Being Beaten* (New York: McGraw-Hill, 1976), 106.
4. *USA Today,* 6 April 1983, 10A.
5. *Time,* 5 Sept. 1983, 22.

CHAPTER 19. CHILD MOLESTATION

1. Linda Tschirhart Sanford, *The Silent Children* (New York: McGraw-Hill, 1980).
2. *Newsweek,* 9 Aug. 1982, 45.
3. *Sign of the Times,* Sept. 1982, 4.
4. *Newsweek,* 9 Aug. 1982, 45.
5. *Society's League Against Molestation,* self-published pamphlet.
6. *Newsweek,* 9 Aug. 1982, 45.
7. *Time,* 17 Jan. 1983, 47.
8. Ibid.
9. *Newsweek,* 14 May 1983, 36.

CHAPTER 20. TEENAGE SEX

1. *Associated Press,* 17 Dec. 1983.
2. *Us,* 31 Aug. 1982, 83.
3. *People,* 6 Jan. 1983, 59.
4. *Us,* 31 Aug. 1982, 83.
5. *Time,* 9 Nov. 1981, 67.
6. *People,* 6 Jan. 1983, 59.
7. *People,* 5 May 1980, 108.

CHAPTER 21. TEENAGE PREGNANCY

1. *People,* 15 Oct. 1984, 72.
2. *Christianity Today.*
3. *USA Today,* 5 Nov. 1984, 1D.

4. *Rocky Mountain News,* 22 Jan. 1984, 48.
5. *Rocky Mountain News,* 5 Sept. 1984, 2.
6. *USA Today,* 21 Feb. 1984, 3D.
7. *Time,* 12 March 1984, 31.
8. *People.*
9. *USA Today,* 21 Feb. 1984, 3D.

CHAPTER 22. TEENAGE RUNAWAYS

1. *The Daily Jeffersonian,* 10 May 1983.
2. *USA Today,* 24 May 1983, 4D.
3. *Newsweek,* 18 Oct. 1982.
4. *The Daily Jeffersonian,* 10 May 1983.
5. "Monitor," NBC-TV, 10 July 1983.
6. *Newsweek,* 18 Oct. 1982, 98.
7. Ibid., 97.
8. Ibid.

CHAPTER 23. THROWAWAY CHILDREN

1. *Us,* 5 Dec. 1983, 66ff.
2. Ibid.
3. *U.S. News and World Report,* 9 June 1980, 66.
4. *Reader's Digest,* Jan. 1984, 63.
5. *U.S. News and World Report,* 9 June 1980, 66.
6. *Reader's Digest,* Jan. 1984, 63.
7. Ibid.

CHAPTER 24. TEENAGE SUICIDE

1. *Dallas Times Herald,* 19 Jan. 1985.
2. *USA Today,* 30 Oct. 1984, 10A.
3. *USA Today,* 29 March 1985, 10A.
4. *Newsweek,* 15 Aug. 1983, 72.
5. *USA Today,* 9 Jan. 1985, 7A.
6. *USA Today,* 30 Oct. 1984, 10A.
7. *Associated Press,* 27 Oct. 1984.
8. *Rocky Mountain News,* 19 Oct. 1983, 58.

CHAPTER 25. EMPTY NEST

1. *Vogue,* April 1985, 228.
2. *USA Today,* 23 Jan. 1985, 1D.
3. *Rocky Mountain News,* 14 Nov. 1985, 69.

4. *U.S. News and World Report,* 25 Oct. 1982, 72.

CHAPTER 26. MID-LIFE CRISIS

1. *Redbook,* Feb. 1984, 88, 89, 147.
2. Ibid.

CHAPTER 27. ADULTERY

1. *Dallas Times Herald,* 3 Nov. 1983, 10B.
2. *USA Today,* 6 May 1983.
3. Ibid.
4. Ibid.
5. *Time,* 20 Dec. 1982, 85.
6. *USA Today,* 30 Jan. 1984, 4D.
7. Ibid.
8. *Us,* 13 Feb. 1984, 29.
9. *USA Today,* 2 Nov. 1983.
10. *USA Today,* 6 April 1984, 2D.
11. *USA Today,* 8 June 1984, 1D.

CHAPTER 28. INCEST

1. *Time,* 7 Sept. 1981, 69.
2. Ibid.
3. Ibid.
4. Jean Renvoize, *Incest: A Family Pattern* (London: Routledge and Kegan Paul, 1982).
5. Katherine Brady, *Father's Days* (New York: Dell, 1979).
6. *USA Today,* 10 Jan. 1984, 4D.
7. *USA Today,* 7 Aug. 1984, 1D.
8. *USA Today,* 10 Jan. 1984, 5D.
9. *Us,* 27 April 1982, 38.
10. Ibid.
11. *People,* 9 April 1977, 50.
12. *Fundamentalist Journal,* July/August 1984.
13. *People,* 9 April 1977, 50.

CHAPTER 29. BATTERED WIVES

1. *People,* 10 Oct. 1983, 41.
2. *People,* 8 Oct. 1984, 100.
3. *USA Today,* 11 Feb. 1983.
4. *Rocky Mountain News,* 21 Aug. 1984.
5. *USA Today,* 12 Dec. 1983, 10A.
6. *USA Today,* 25 Sept. 1984, 10A.
7. *Time,* 15 Sept. 1983, 23.

8. Ibid.
9. Ibid.
10. Ibid., 24.
11. Ibid., 23.
12. *USA Today,* 23 May 1983.
13. Ibid.
14. Ibid.
15. *Rocky Mountain News,* 23 April 1984, 4.
16. *Rocky Mountain News,* 13 June 1983, 59.
17. *The Plain Truth,* April 1984, 28.
18. *Time,* 15 Sept. 1983, 23.
19. *USA Today,* 18 June 1984, 10A.
20. *USA Today,* 8 Nov. 1983, 11A.

CHAPTER 30. ABUSED MEN

1. *Us,* 2 Nov. 1982, 68.
2. Ibid.
3. *USA Today,* 2 Nov. 1984, 1A.

CHAPTER 31. IMPOTENCE

1. *Denver Post,* 24 April 1983, Magazine Section, 26ff.
2. Ibid.
3. *Philadelphia Inquirer,* 1 Aug. 1982, Magazine Section, 14.
4. Ibid., 15.

CHAPTER 32. DIVORCE

1. *Time,* 13 May 1985, 54.
2. *Dallas Times Herald,* 1 March 1985.
3. Ibid.
4. *USA Today,* 5 Sept. 1983.
5. *USA Today,* 16 Jan. 1984, 3D.
6. *Rocky Mountain News,* 9 Sept. 1983.
7. *USA Today,* 12 Oct. 1984, 1D.
8. *People,* 20 Aug. 1984, 91.
9. *USA Today,* 3 Oct. 1985, 1A.
10. *Dallas Morning News,* 3 Jan. 1984.
11. Robert Plekker, *Divorce and the Christian* (Wheaton, Ill.: Tyndale House, 1983), 67.
12. Ibid., 39.

CHAPTER 33. CHILDREN OF DIVORCE

1. *Newsweek,* 10 Jan. 1983, 42.
2. *Newsweek,* 11 Feb. 1980, 59.

3. *Newsweek,* 10 Jan. 1983, 42.
4. Ibid.
5. *Newsweek,* 11 Feb. 1980, 62.
6. *USA Today,* 21 March 1984, 4D.
7. *USA Today,* 5 Dec. 1983, 1D.
8. *Christianity Today,* 12 Nov. 1982, 84.

CHAPTER 34. STEPPARENTING

1. *Rocky Mountain News,* 20 July 1984, 87.
2. Ibid., 86.
3. *USA Today,* 13 June 1984, 4D.
4. Ibid.
5. Ibid.

CHAPTER 35. CHILD CUSTODY

1. Committee on the Family Group for the Advancement of Psychiatry, *Divorce, Child Custody, and the Family* (San Francisco: Jossey-Bass, 1981).
2. Robert Hanley Woody, *Getting Custody* (New York: Macmillan, 1978).
3. *USA Today,* 15 Oct. 1985, 2D.

CHAPTER 36. CHILD SUPPORT

1. *People,* 7 May 1984, 138.
2. *USA Today,* 26 July 1984, 8A.
3. Ibid.
4. *Rocky Mountain News,* 30 Aug. 1984, 65.
5. Ibid.
6. Ibid.
7. *USA Today,* 12 July 1983, 8A.
8. *Rocky Mountain News,* 15 July 1983.
9. *Newsweek,* 5 March 1984, 11.
10. *People,* 7 May 1984, 145.
11. *USA Today,* 26 July 1984, 8A.
12. *People,* 7 May 1984, 141.
13. *USA Today,* 14 June 1985, 12A.

CHAPTER 37. ALIMONY

1. *Time,* 16 Jan. 1984, 51.
2. *People,* 25 July 1983, 35ff.
3. *USA Today,* 13 April 1983.
4. *Glamour,* Dec. 1983, 29.

CHAPTER 38. SINGLE PARENTING

1. *Newsweek,* 15 July 1985, 42.
2. *Christianity Today.*
3. *Christianity Today,* 22 Oct. 1982, 89.
4. *Christianity Today,* 18 July 1975, 12.

CHAPTER 39. LATCHKEY CHILDREN

1. *USA Today,* 10 Aug. 1983, 9A.

CHAPTER 40. STRESS

1. *Time,* 6 June 1983, 48.
2. Ibid.
3. *USA Today,* 14 June 1983, 1A.
4. *Time,* 6 June 1983, 48.
5. *USA Today,* 2 June 1983, 3A.
6. *USA Today,* 20 June 1983, 3A.
7. *Rocky Mountain News,* 1 Sept. 1983, 54.
8. *Time,* 6 June 1983, 50.

CHAPTER 42. BURNOUT

1. *USA Today,* 10 Feb. 1984, 5D.
2. Ibid.

CHAPTER 43. DEPRESSION

1. *Time,* 12 Dec. 1983, 98.
2. *Time,* 28 Nov. 1983, 128.
3. *Newsweek,* 27 Sept. 1982, 63.
4. *USA Today,* 6 Sept. 1983.
5. *USA Today,* 26 Oct. 1983, 4D.
6. *Christianity Today,* 11 Nov. 1983, 39.

CHAPTER 44. GLUTTONY

1. *USA Today,* 5 July 1983.
2. *USA Today,* 29 March 1983.
3. *USA Today,* 2 March 1983, 2D.

CHAPTER 45. DIETING

1. *East/West Journal,* March 1979, 20.
2. *USA Today,* 8 March 1983, 4D.
3. *Newsweek,* 13 Dec. 1982, 90.
4. *People,* 10 Dec. 1983.
5. *USA Today,* 17 Jan. 1984, 1D.

CHAPTER 46. BULIMIA

1. *Newsweek,* 2 Nov. 1984, 60.

2. Jackie Barrile, *Confessions of a Closet Eater* (Wheaton, Ill.: Tyndale House, 1984).
3. Ibid.

CHAPTER 47. ANOREXIA

1. *USA Today,* 5 Sept. 1983.
2. *Newsweek,* 23 May 1983, 69.
3. Cherry Boone O'Neill, *Starving for Attention* (New York: Dell, 1982).
4. *Newsweek,* 7 March 1983, 59.

CHAPTER 48. FITNESS

1. *People,* 12 April 1983, 143.
2. *USA Today,* 10 Aug. 1983.
3. *USA Today,* 17 Nov. 1983.
4. *Us,* 26 Oct. 1982, 10.

CHAPTER 49. NUTRITION

1. *East/West Journal,* Feb. 1984, 9.

CHAPTER 50. WORKING WOMEN

1. *USA Today,* 12 Sept. 1984, 5D.
2. Ibid.
3. Ibid.
4. Ibid.
5. *USA Today,* 29 May 1984, 10A.
6. Ibid.
7. Ibid.
8. *USA Today,* 10 Dec. 1984, 1D.

CHAPTER 52. WORKING MOTHERS

1. *Us,* 9 April 1984, 10.
2. *Eternity,* May 1984, 16.
3. *Time,* 19 Sept. 1977, 118.
4. *Dallas Morning News,* 17 Dec. 1983.
5. *Rocky Mountain News,* 11 July 1983.
6. *Fort Worth Star-Telegram,* 4 Dec. 1983, 5A.
7. *USA Today,* 26 April 1984, 3D.

CHAPTER 53. DAY CARE

1. *Newsweek,* 20 Aug. 1984, 44.
2. *USA Today,* 29 Nov. 1984, 10A.
3. *Newsweek,* 10 Sept. 1984, 14.
4. Ibid.

5. Ibid.
6. Ibid., 16.
7. *Newsweek,* 21 May 1984, 63.
8. *USA Today,* 6 April 1984, 10A.
9. *Newsweek,* 10 Jan. 1983, 8.

CHAPTER 54. COMIC BOOKS

1. *Rocky Mountain News,* 19 Aug. 1983.

CHAPTER 55. CARTOONS

1. *People,* 27 Sept. 1982, 45.
2. *The Des Moines Register,* 28 July 83, 11D.
3. *USA Today,* 18 April 1983.
4. Ibid.
5. *Newsweek,* 17 Oct. 1983, 81.

CHAPTER 56. TELEVISION

1. *Newsweek,* 6 Dec. 1982, 138.
2. Ibid., 140.
3. *Christianity Today,* 1984.
4. *Christianity Today,* 7 May 1982, 21.
5. *St. Petersburg Times,* 14 Jan. 1985, 1D.
6. Ibid.
7. *USA Today,* 27 Aug. 1984, 5D.
8. *USA Today,* 25 Sept. 1984, 2D.
9. *Billboard,* 22 Dec. 1984, 5.
10. *Time,* 11 Oct. 1982, 99.
11. Ibid.
12. Ibid.

CHAPTER 57. SOAP OPERAS

1. *USA Today,* 3 Jan. 1984, 20.
2. *USA Today,* 3 Jan. 1984, 2D.
3. *Time,* 13 Aug. 1984, 96.
4. *Newsweek,* 28 Sept. 1981, 60.
5. Ibid.
6. *Us,* 28 Sept. 1982, 23.

CHAPTER 58. MOVIES

1. *The Bergamun Fifth Column,* 1980, 19.
2. Ibid.
3. Ibid., 16.
4. *The Pretoria News,* 6 Nov. 1984, 7.
5. *Newsweek,* 29 Oct. 1984, 135.

6. Ibid.
7. *USA Today,* 14 Nov. 1983, 10A.
8. Ibid.

CHAPTER 59. SCIENCE FICTION

1. *USA Today,* 7 Dec. 1984, 1D.
2. *People,* 20 Dec. 1982.
3. *USA Today,* 30 Aug. 1984, 2D.
4. *USA Today,* 4 Dec. 1984, 9A.

CHAPTER 60. SPERM BANKS

1. *People,* 18 Oct. 1982, 63.
2. *Newsweek,* 26 July 1982, 24.
3. *People,* 18 Oct. 1982, 64.
4. *USA Today,* 4 April 1983, 1D.
5. Ibid.
6. Ibid.
7. Ibid.
8. *USA Today,* 11 Feb. 1985, 1D.
9. *USA Today,* 18 May 1984, 6D.
10. Ibid.

CHAPTER 61. *IN VITRO* FERTILIZATION

1. *Newsweek,* 6 Dec. 1982, 105.
2. *USA Today,* 20 June 1984, 2A.
3. Ibid.
4. *New York Times Service,* Grand Rapids Press, 16 Oct. 1984.
5. *People,* 22 March 1982, 49.
6. *New York Times Service,* Grand Rapids Press, 16 Oct. 1984.
7. Ibid.

CHAPTER 62. SURROGATE MOTHERS

1. *Rocky Mountain News,* 3 Feb. 1983, 38.
2. *USA Today,* 3 June 1983.
3. *Newsweek,* 7 July 1980, 72.
4. *Eternity,* July/August 1983, 44.
5. Ibid.
6. *USA Today,* 11 May 1983.

CHAPTER 63. GENETIC ENGINEERING

1. *Newsweek,* 30 May 1983, 102.
2. *Vancouver Sun,* 27 Aug. 1982, 1B.
3. *Time,* 20 June 1983, 67.
4. *Newsweek,* 7 Dec. 1982, 67.

5. Associated Press, 1983 report.
6. Jeremy Rifkin, *Algeny* (New York: Viking Press, 1983).
7. *Rocky Mountain News,* 2 May 1983, 53.
8. Rifkin, *Algeny.*
9. Ibid.
10. J. Kirby Anderson, *Genetic Engineering* (Grand Rapids: Zondervan, 1983), 119.
11. Ibid.

CHAPTER 64. ABORTION

1. *People,* 25 March 1985, 30.
2. *Time,* 6 April 1981, 23.
3. *Newsweek,* 5 June 1978, 39.
4. *Christianity Today,* 16 March 1973, 6-9.

CHAPTER 65. INFANTICIDE

1. *Human Events,* 3 Dec. 1983, 1.
2. *Pentecostal Evangel,* 15 March 1981, 12.
3. CNN TV report, 24 Feb. 1984.
4. *Issues at a Glance,* 3 Feb. 1984, 9.
5. *Christianity Today,* 18 Feb. 1983, 53.
6. *Journal of the American Academy of Pediatrics,* Vol. 72, No. 1 (July 1983), 38.
7. Ibid.
8. Franky Schaeffer, *Bad News for Modern Man* (Westchester, Ill.: Crossway Books, 1984), 30.
9. Ibid., 27.

CHAPTER 66. EUTHANASIA

1. *USA Today,* 10 May 1985, 3A.
2. *USA Today,* 2 March 1983, 10A.
3. *Newsweek,* 7 Jan. 1985, 18.
4. *USA Today,* 10 April 1984, 6A.
5. *Time,* 16 July 1973, 37.
6. *Fort Worth Star-Telegram,* 2 April 1985.
7. *The Pentecostal Testimony,* March 1978, 19.

Index